Organising Entrepreneurship and MSMEs Across India

ASIA-PACIFIC BUSINESS SERIES **(ISSN: 1793-3137)**

Series Editor
Léo-Paul Dana
Professor
Dalhousie University, Canada

Published

Vol. 11 *Organising Entrepreneurship and MSMEs Across India*
edited by Léo-Paul Dana, Naman Sharma & Satya Ranjan Acharya

Vol. 10 *Guanxi and Business (Third Edition)*
by Yadong Luo

Vol. 9 *Asian Models of Entrepreneurship: From the Indian Union and Nepal to the Japanese Archipelago: Context, Policy and Practice (Second Edition)*
by Léo-Paul Dana

Vol. 8 *Catalyst for Change: Chinese Business in Asia*
edited by Thomas Menkhoff, Hans-Dieter Evers, Chay Yue Wah & Hoon Chang Yau

Vol. 7 *From Adam Smith to Michael Porter: Evolution of Competitiveness Theory (Extended Edition)*
by Dong-Sung Cho & Hwy-Chang Moon

Vol. 6 *Islamic Banking and Finance in South-East Asia: Its Development and Future (Third Edition)*
by Angelo M. Venardos

Vol. 5 *Guanxi and Business (Second Edition)*
by Yadong Luo

Vol. 4 *Asian Models of Entrepreneurship — From the Indian Union and the Kingdom of Nepal to the Japanese Archipelago: Context, Policy and Practice*
by Léo-Paul Dana

Vol. 3 *Islamic Banking and Finance in South-East Asia: Its Development and Future (Second Edition)*
by Angelo M. Venardos

Vol. 2 *From Adam Smith to Michael Porter: Evolution of Competitiveness Theory*
by Dong-Sung Cho & Hewy-Chang Moon

Vol. 1 *Guanxi and Business*
by Yadong Luo

Asia-Pacific Business Series – Vol. 11

Organising Entrepreneurship and MSMEs Across India

Editors

Léo-Paul Dana
Dalhousie University, Canada

Naman Sharma
Indian Institute of Foreign Trade, Kolkata, India

Satya Ranjan Acharya
Entrepreneurship Development Institute of India, India

World Scientific

NEW JERSEY • LONDON • SINGAPORE • BEIJING • SHANGHAI • HONG KONG • TAIPEI • CHENNAI • TOKYO

Published by

World Scientific Publishing Co. Pte. Ltd.
5 Toh Tuck Link, Singapore 596224
USA office: 27 Warren Street, Suite 401-402, Hackensack, NJ 07601
UK office: 57 Shelton Street, Covent Garden, London WC2H 9HE

Library of Congress Cataloging-in-Publication Data
Names: Dana, Leo Paul, editor. | Sharma, Naman, 1986- editor. | Acharya, Satya Ranjan, editor.
Title: Organising entrepreneurship and MSMEs across India / edited by Léo-Paul Dana, Dalhousie University, Canada, Naman Sharma, Indian Institute of Foreign Trade, Kolkata, India, Satya Ranjan Acharya, Entrepreneurship Development Institute of India, India.
Description: Hackensack : World Scientific, 2020. | Series: Asia-pacific business series, 1793-3137 ; volume 11 | Includes bibliographical references and index.
Identifiers: LCCN 2020013500 | ISBN 9789811212734 (hardcover) | ISBN 9789811212741 (ebook) | ISBN 9789811212758 (ebook other)
Subjects: LCSH: Entrepreneurship--India. | Small business--India. | Entrepreneurship--Government policy--India. | Business enterprises--Finance.
Classification: LCC HB615 .O6764 2020 | DDC 338/.040954--dc23
LC record available at https://lccn.loc.gov/2020013500

British Library Cataloguing-in-Publication Data
A catalogue record for this book is available from the British Library.

For any available supplementary material, please visit
https://www.worldscientific.com/worldscibooks/10.1142/11622#t=suppl

Typeset by Stallion Press
Email: enquiries@stallionpress.com

This book is dedicated to the memory of a great entrepreneur and kind person,

Mr. Eyvin Brandstrup Iversen of Vejle.

https://doi.org/10.1142/9789811212741_fmatter

Contents

https://doi.org/10.1142/9789811212741_fmatter

About the Editors

Satya Ranjan Acharya is with the Entrepreneurship Development Institute of India (EDII). He is a business management professional with over 20 years of teaching and consultancy experience in the areas of Financial Management, Idea Generation and Business Plan Formulation. Trained in teaching entrepreneurship and start-up growth at Stanford Technology Venture Programmes and the Indian School of Business, Hyderabad, and Start-up Accelerators in the Entrepreneurial Ecosystem at MASHAV, Israel's Agency for International Development Cooperation. He has experience as a Research Fellow with the Centre for Innovation, Incubation and Entrepreneurship at IIM Ahmedabad, and is trained in the Application of Simulation for Entrepreneurship Teaching from the University of Tennessee, USA.

Léo-Paul Dana is Professor at Dalhousie University. He is also a member of the Entrepreneurship and Innovation Chair, which is part of LabEx Entreprendre at the Université de Montpellier. A graduate of McGill University and HEC-Montreal, he has served as Marie Curie Fellow at Princeton University and Visiting Professor at INSEAD. He has published extensively in a variety of journals including *Entrepreneurship & Regional Development, Entrepreneurship: Theory & Practice, International Business Review, International Small Business Journal, Journal of Business Research, Journal of Small Business Management, Journal of World Business, Small Business Economics,* and *Technological Forecasting & Social Change.*

Naman Sharma is currently affiliated with the Indian Institute of Foreign Trade, Kolkata (India) as an Assistant Professor, and has nearly five years of academic experience. Dr. Sharma also has substantial research experience and his research has been published in ABDC ranked/Scopus Indexed journals and other reputable publishers such as the Emerald Publishing Group. He has also authored four books with publishers of international repute such as IGI-Global and is a serving guest editor for various journals.

https://doi.org/10.1142/9789811212741_fmatter

List of Contributors

Maumita Choudhury is currently working as an Assistant Professor at the Department of Commerce, University of Science and Technology, Meghalaya. She has submitted her PhD thesis on the topic "An Evaluative Study on Bank Financing of MSMEs in Assam" under the supervision of Prof. Chandana Goswami at the Department of Business Administration, Tezpur University as a full time JRF scholar during 2014–2019. She completed M.Com. from Shri Ram College of Commerce, Delhi University in 2012 and has worked as an Assistant Professor at Guwahati Commerce College for more than a year till 2014. Her research interests include MSMEs, banks, financial market, money market and development finance.

Gaurav Dawar is an Assistant Professor at Institute of Management Studies Ghaziabad. He teaches courses on financial management, financial modelling and financial statement analysis. He holds a Master of Business Administration from Kurukshetra University and Bachelor in Hotel Administration from Institute of Hotel Management, Gurdaspur. His work is published in *Global Business Review* and *International Journal of Higher Education and Sustainability.* His interests are in the area of financial strategy and corporate social responsibility.

Gaurav Joshi is an engineering graduate with a postgraduate degree in Business Administration, specialising in Marketing and Human Resource Management. He has 11 years of work experience and has served various organisations including Maruti Suzuki India, Uttarakhand Grameen Bank and Uttarakhand Road Transport Corporation. He is currently working as an Assistant Professor at the Government Degree College, Pithoragarh (Uttarakhand, India). He has also contributed book chapters for Uttarakhand Open University.

Mihir Joshi, Btech MBA, PhD is an Assistant Professor at Faculty of Management Studies Gurukula Kangri Vishwavidyalaya, India. He has publications on entrepreneurship, IOT, employee engagement with reputed publishers. His wide area of interest includes emotional intelligence, mindfulness, workforce diversity and entrepreneurial education. Besides academia he has several years of industrial experience.

T. Kadalarasane is an engineering graduate and has completed a PhD in Management. His areas of specialisation include green finance, behavioural finance, banking technology management, international trade and finance and international banking. He has been a faculty member of the MSc Quantitative Finance program in Pondicherry University for the past five years. He has published 14 papers in edited books, and national and international journals. Currently, he is working on sustainable development goals where he has published papers on carbon emissions, gender equality, ICT, and women entrepreneurs.

Jugal Kishor is an Assistant Professor of Marketing at the Central University of Rajasthan, India. He has over five years of academic experience and has substantial publications in various reputable journals.

Prashant Kumar is an Assistant Professor (Marketing) at IMT Dubai. His work has been published in a number of international journals, including *Asia Pacific Journal of Marketing and Logistics*, *Industrial Marketing Management*, *International Journal of Retail and Distribution Management*, and *Marketing Intelligence and Planning*. He has also presented papers at a number of international conferences in Asia and Europe. He owns Outstanding Reviewer Award for the *International Journal of Retail and Distribution Management* in Emerald Literati Awards 2017. His research interests are in the areas of green marketing and key account management.

Bhawna Mehra has over 15 years' experience in corporates and academia and has published a book entitled *Marketing Management* and several research papers published in national and international journals. She has also won Best Paper Award for her research work on cold storage. Her association with various journals and newsletters on the Board of Editors, Managing Editor and Editor has benefited students and the related organisations. Currently,

Mrs. Mehra is a research scholar, working on sustainable management of water resources and also writing a book on international management.

Anupama Panghal is Assistant Professor in the Department of Food Business Management and Entrepreneurship Development (FBM&ED) at the National Institute of Food Technology Entrepreneurship and Management (NIFTEM). Her areas of research interest include agribusiness management, food supply chain and agri-entrepreneurship. She has more than thirteen years of experience, in both corporates and academia.

Kumar Shalender is a postdoctoral researcher and Associate Professor at Chitkara Business School, Chitkara University (Punjab). He has over 10 years of experience in the field of strategy, social mobility, acceptance of technology, and business model development. He has more than 50 research papers to his credit including presentations at international conferences, summits, symposiums, and seminars. He has contributed significantly to the field of sustainable mobility with a special focus on the creation of an e-mobility ecosystem in India.

Priyanka Sharma is a PhD student at the Faculty of Business Studies, Department of Commerce, Punjabi University, Patiala, Punjab, India. She completed her master's and bachelor's degrees (Economics Honours) in Commerce at Punjab University. She is a member of the Indian Commerce Association. Her areas of interest are spiritual intelligence, emotional intelligence, organisational commitment, personality, task performance, entrepreneurship, development of the MSME sector, human resource management, and psychological issues in different sectors.

Swati Sharma is an Assistant Professor at Amity Business School, Amity University Rajasthan, Jaipur, India. She teaches to undergraduate and post graduate management students. Her research interest includes e-banking and financial inclusion.

Geetika Shukla is an Associate Professor in the Department of Management Studies at Dewan Institute of Management Studies, Meerut. She possesses an MBA (Finance) and M.Com.

Shilpa Sindhu is an Assistant Professor in the area of marketing and entrepreneurship in the School of Management at The NorthCap University.

She has more than 12 years of corporate and academic experience and holds a PhD in Business Administration.

Harwinder Singh holds a bachelor's in Mechanical Engineering, Master's degree in Production Engineering, a master's in Business Administration, and a PhD in Mechanical Engineering. Dr Singh has published 110 papers in reputable international and national journals. He is an editorial board member of two international journals by Inderscience Publishers and published seven books and two book chapters at international level. Dr Singh has teaching experience in mechanical, industrial and production engineering. His research interests include industrial engineering and operations management.

Jagdeep Singh holds a bachelor's in Mechanical Engineering, Master's degree in Production Engineering, and PhD in Mechanical Engineering. He has published 50 papers in international and national journals of high repute. He is also on the editorial board and member of three international journals by Inderscience Publishers and published five books at international level. The author has experience in teaching different subjects of mechanical, industrial and production engineering. His research interests include management production system, decision making and operations management.

Jagmeet Singh holds a bachelor's degree in Mechanical Engineering from Guru Nanak Dev Engineering College, Ludhiana, a master's degree in Production Engineering from Guru Nanak Dev Engineering College, Ludhiana, and is pursuing a PhD in Mechanical Engineering from Punjabi University, Patiala. He has four years' industry experience as a R&D Engineer. His areas of interest are operations management, industrial engineering, and the Internet of Things.

Priya Singh is an Assistant Professor in the Institute of Business Studies, Chaudhary Charan Singh University Campus, Meerut, U.P. India. She is qualified UGC-NET and is an ICSSR Doctoral fellow.

Sandeep Singh is acting Assistant Professor at the Punjabi University Regional Centre for IT and Management, Mohali, Punjab, India. He is qualified in diverse areas including LLB, MBA (HR) and a PhD in Management and has more than seven years' experience in teaching and research. He is a member of a number of professional and academic bodies. He has published 13 research articles, including conference proceedings and contributed book chapters in ABDC, SCOPUS and UGC listed journals. His key areas of research are related to procrastination behaviour, basic marketing and psychological issues in different sectors.

Seema Singh is Professor of Economics at the Delhi Technological University since 2008. Largely, interested in the issues related to Gender, Higher Education, Employment and Labour Market, she has presented, published several papers and conducted successfully several research projects. She received AICTE Career Award for Young Teachers in 2000. Now, she has been elected Vice President (Education and Research) and Board Member (South Asia) of International Network of Women Engineers and Scientists (INWES) for 2018–2020. She is a member of the editorial team of many journals.

Vikas Singh is a Research Associate in the Department of Food Business Management and Entrepreneurship Development at the National Institute of Food Technology Entrepreneurship and Management (NIFTEM), Haryana (India), where he works on an ICSSR funded project and is a recipient of 'Bharat Ratan Mother Teresa Gold Medal Award' for his contribution in the field of micro-finance and rural development. He has over five years of experience in corporate, teaching and research. Dr Singh's research interests focus on micro-finance, entrepreneurship, and environmental management. He is also a member of the European Association of Environmental and Resource Economists.

Tripura Sundari C.U. has a PhD in International Economics. As a faculty member of the MSc Quantitative Finance program in Pondicherry University, her areas of specialisation are managerial/quantitative economics, econometrics, time series analysis & forecasting and optimisation techniques. She is well versed in software including STATA, E-views, SPSS, Gretl, Minitab, R language, Basics of Python and databases including CMIE PROWESS and BLOOMBERG. She has published 35 papers in edited books, and national and international journals. She is currently working on the sustainable development goals and has published papers on carbon emissions, gender equality, ICT, and women entrepreneurs.

Robin Thomas is a faculty of Management at the Sant Gahira Guru University, Ambikapur, Surguja, Chhattisgarh. He has designed and developed courses on Creativity, Innovation and Entrepreneurship at the constituent engineering college of the university. He is known for implementation of innovative pedagogical tools in teaching and learning. He is an alumnus of Devi Ahilya University, Indore, and holds a doctorate in Strategic Bank Management. He holds master's degrees in Finance and Electronic Media from Institute of Management Studies, DAVV Indore and Educational Multimedia Research Centre, Devi Ahilya University, Indore. He is also a CFA (ICFAI) charter holder.

Navneesh Tyagi is an Assistant Professor in the Department of Business and Management Studies, Meerut Institute of Engineering and Technology, Meerut, India. She is pursuing a PhD and is UGC NET (IR) 2013, UGC NET (Management) 2012 qualified, possessing M. Com and MBA degrees.

Priyanka Vern is a Research Fellow in the Department of Food Business Management at the National Institute of Food Technology Entrepreneurship and Management (NIFTEM). She has a master's in Food Plant Operations Management and has worked on entrepreneurship related projects. Her areas of research include food & agri entrepreneurship, social entrepreneurship, and operations management.

https://doi.org/10.1142/9789811212741_0001

Chapter 1

India*

Léo-Paul Dana and Naman Sharma

1.1 Introduction

Situated in Southern Asia, the Indian subcontinent has over 7,000 kilometres of coastline along the Arabian Sea and the Bay of Bengal. The Republic of India is the world's fastest growing free market economy; it is a vibrant country, covering an area of 3,165,596 square kilometres. The federation shares borders with Bangladesh (formerly East Pakistan), Bhutan, China, Myanmar (formerly Burma), Nepal and Pakistan. As noted by Johnson, "*India's middle class is bigger than the entire 300 million population of the US*".[1] India is very tolerant of minorities and its multicultural society includes Hindus and Muslims living peacefully with people from many different religions.

Dana[2] observed that a combination of historical factors, including the caste system, British occupation, cultural values and government regulations,

---

*This chapter was updated by Léo-Paul Dana and Naman Sharma from Dana, L.-P. (2014). *Asian Models of Entrepreneurship — From the Indian Union and Nepal to the Japanese Archipelago: Context, Policy and Practice,* Second Edition, Singapore & London: World Scientific.

[1]Johnson, J. (2006). "Surging with Self-confidence and Ambition," *Special Report on the World's Fastest Growing Democracy,* London: Financial Times, January 26.

[2]Dana, L.-P. (2000). "Creating Entrepreneurs in India," *Journal of Small Business Management,* 38 (1), 86–91. For discussions of the caste system, see Gadgil, D.R. (1959). *Origins of the Modern Indian Business Class*, New York: Institute of Pacific Relations; Medhora, P.B. (1965). "Entrepreneurship in India," *Political Science Quarterly*, 80 (4), 558–559; and Weber, M. (1958). *The Religion of India — The Sociology of Hinduism &*

Image 1: Entrepreneurial spirit

Source: © Léo-Paul Dana.

limited innovative entrepreneurship in India. Kanitkar and Contractor[3] wrote, "*handicaps to entry into business ownership have been far too many given the traditional, conservative, orthodox Indian society*". In recent years, however, efforts have focused on changing the mindset and creating entrepreneurs by giving youngsters the self-confidence to become high achievers. Raghavendra and Subrahmanya[4] found that inter-firm co-operation increased collective efficiency in India, with a significant influence on capability.

Buddhism, New York: The Free Press. Hazlehurst (1966) focused on merchant castes. See Hazlehurst, L.W. (1966). *Entrepreneurship and the Merchant Castes in a Punjabi City*, Durham, North Carolina: Duke University Commonwealth Studies Center.

[3]Kanitkar, A. & Contractor, N. (1992). "In Search of Identity: The Women Entrepreneurs of India," *Ahmedabad: Entrepreneurship Development Institute of India.*

[4]Raghavendra, N.V. & Balasubrahmanya, M.H. (2005). "Collective Efficiency and Technological Capacity on Small Firms: Evidence from Two Foundry Clusters in South India," *International Journal of Management and Enterprise Development*, 2 (3–4), 325–348.

1.2 Historical Overview[5]

The early history of India stretches back to Mohenjodaro and Harappan times with well laid-out cities, script, and possible evidence of trade. During Vedic times — with flourishing philosophical treaties on life, and intricate writings about astronomy, mathematics, and medicine — the caste system classified individuals based on their birth. The four castes were: (i) the Brahmins or priestly class; (ii) the Kshatriyas or warrior class; (iii) the Vaishyas or merchant class; and (iv) the Shudras or those at the bottom rung of this social hierarchy, who did menial tasks. The untouchables, or Harijans, fell out of this system. The Shudras and untouchables were those who would do work such as the burying of animal carcasses and the cleaning of waste, or in today's terminology 'waste management'. The caste system resulted in occupational specialisations, with the Vaishya class becoming merchants, overland traders, maritime investors for waterborne trade, and intermediaries between the European powers; today their scions form the top management and owners of many of the large industrial organisations and conglomerates in India.

During the Buddhist period in ancient India, travelling monks were accompanied by merchants, whose wealth allowed the for the construction of caves for residences on the trade routes between various villages and cities. Such caves were often lavishly decorated, along with the carved images of deities and donors, and can still be viewed in states such as Maharashtra. The caves were the dwelling places for monks during the monsoon season and served as five-star hotels for the merchants. The Buddhist period also saw the development of major universities such as Nalanda and Taxila, resulting in a wave of Chinese monks who came to India to study and take their learning and relics back to China. Merchants also used the Silk Road of the 1st century, which served as a significant boost to trade with many countries. It was the traders and merchants who were the early entrepreneurs in India, and the *Vaishya* class became, and still is, highly specialised in scanning the environment and setting up

[5]This section benefited greatly from the personal assistance of Edwina Pio incorporating material from Pio, E. (2010). "Religious Merchants? Entrepreneurship in India," in Léo-Paul Dana, ed. *Entrepreneurship and Religion*, Cheltenham, United Kingdom: Edward Elgar, pp. 27–42.

businesses. The early entrepreneurs developed intricate systems for credit and prospective trading to further their entrepreneurial activities such as buying ships, goods, and investing in cargo and land. The Vaishya class was largely the source for sub-castes such as the Marwaris or Banias in northern, eastern and western India and in southern India the merchants were primarily the Nattukottai Chettiars.[6]

In 1700, the East India Company established a formal system of government in Bengal as at the time, India's share of world income was about 23 percent, approximately the same as Europe's.[7] In 1784, the British government took control of the East India Company. Entrepreneurs from various lands saw commercial opportunities in India. In 1790, Shalom ben Ovadiah HaCohen — a well-known Mizrahi[8] Jew — moved from Aleppo (Halab), in Syria, to Bombay. He was followed by other Jewish entrepreneurs from Baghdad and from Basra; Jewish entrepreneurs also came to India from Persia and from Yemen.

In 1832, David Sassoon moved to Bombay where he became a magistrate of the cotton industry. His son Abdullah Sassoon revolutionised the weaving industry in Bombay, helping Bombay become an important manufacturing centre. In 1903, the Sassoon family built the Sir Jacob Sassoon School, next to the Magen David Synagogue, in a predominantly Jewish neighbourhood of Bombay.

Until the late 20th century, the Jewish Club, on V. P. Ghandi Road in Mumbai (formerly Forbes Street, Bombay), served as a meeting place for Jewish entrepreneurs. In 1985, GianiZail Singh, President of India, graced the festivities celebrating the centennial anniversary of the Knesset Eliyahoo Synagogue, on V. P. Ghandi Road, and the Post Office issued a stamp for the occasion.

The Marwaris are a community who specialise in domestic trade. Their enterprises complemented those of English entrepreneurs, who allowed the Marwaris to become prominent in a diversified industrial economy. In contrast, other groups of Indian entrepreneurs had different

---

[6]ibid.

[7]Singh, M. (2006). "India's Economic Challenge," in George Skaria, ed., *India 2006: Taking India to the World*, London: World Link, pp. 12–14.

[8]Dana (2010). op. cit. discusses this ethno-cultural group.

Image 2: The Jewish club

Source: © Léo-Paul Dana.

experiences. During the 1800s, the British discriminated against communities who competed with English entrepreneurs in international commerce. Many Indian entrepreneurs were thus pushed out of the business realm. During the 1880s, local firms with established reputations were defrauded by British partners, an action which led to more withdrawals from the business sector. Consequently, Nafziger[9] concluded that "*the lack of indigenous entrepreneurship... stems in part from the discrimination and duplicity of the British in the 19th century*". Nevertheless, until the turn of the century, Indian entrepreneurs were central to the geographic

[9]Nafziger, E.W. (1971). "Indian Entrepreneurship: A Survey," in Peter Kilby, *Entrepreneurship and Economic Development*, New York: The Free Press, pp. 287–316.

expansion of manufacturing industries.[10] Dilke[11] gave a detailed account of India during the late 19th century. Between 1912 and 1945, industrial production, in India, doubled.[12] During the 1920s and 1930s, the Jains (especially the Marwari Jains) shifted their activity from trading to manufacturing.

Williams[13] provided a war-time account of the British colony. "*Tryst with destiny*" were the words of India's first Prime Minister, Jawaharlal Nehru, to describe independence on August 15, 1947. India became a republic in 1950 and its constitution indicated specifically that the state — not entrepreneurs from the private sector — would play the decisive role in building up the national economy. The Small-Scale Industry Organisation was established in 1954, for the purpose of planning the growth of small businesses as supplements to the efforts of large industries. Also, in 1954, formerly French-owned Pondicherry was transferred to India and the decimal system coinage was introduced in 1957. Goa, under Portuguese rule since 1510, was incorporated into India in December 1961.

Patel[14] gave an historical account of entrepreneurship development in India. "*The first programme to convert potential entrepreneurs into actual owner-managers of manufacturing businesses was held at Ahmedabad in April 1970* (Sebastian and Thakur, 1994, p. v)."[15]

In 1975, unemployment in Rajasthan led to urbanisation and Barefoot College, which encourages people to take risks, innovate, improvise and experiment, began promoting rural handicrafts, providing artisans with access to credit and marketing outlets.

---

[10]Medhora. op. cit.

[11]Dilke, C.W. (1894). *Greater Britain: A Record of Travel in English-speaking Countries*, London: Macmillan and Co.

[12]Balakrishna, R. (1961). *Review of Economic Growth in India*, Bangalore: Bangalore Press.

[13]Williams, M.O. (1942). "New Delhi Goes Full Time," *National Geographic*, 82 (4), 465–494.

[14]Patel, V.G. (1987). "Entrepreneurship Development Programme in India and Its Relevance to Developing Countries," *Ahmedabad: Entrepreneurship Development Institute of India.*

[15]Sebastian, J. & Thakur, S. (1994). "Not Born — The Created Entrepreneurs," Ahmedabad: *Entrepreneurship Development Institute of India.*

Image 3: British colonial architecture

Source: © Léo-Paul Dana.

Economic liberalisation took effect in 1991. The official exchange rate was abolished in 1993 and the government focused on technological development. Wani, Garg, and Sharma[16] suggested that "*to develop and transfer technology for SMEs in India, effective interaction of academic institutions with this sector will be the first step*." Wani, Garg, and Sharma[17] emphasised developing technology-based entrepreneurship, and at the 2006 World Economic Forum in Davos, India was a star player. In 2012, India's rice exports exceeded 9.5 million tons.

---

[16]Wani, V.P., Garg, T.K., & Sharma, S.K. (2003). "The Role of Technical Institutions in Developing a Techno-entrepreneurial Workforce for Sustainable Development of SMEs in India," *International Journal of Management and Enterprise Development,* 1 (1), 71–88.

[17]Wani, V.P., Garg, T.K., & Sharma, S.K. (2005). "Engineer as Entrepreneur: A Necessity for Successful Product Innovation in the Small-scale Industry Sector in India," in John R. McIntyre and Ilan Alon, eds., *Business and Management Education in Transitioning and Developing Countries: A Handbook*, Armonk, New York: M. E. Sharpe, pp. 39–57.

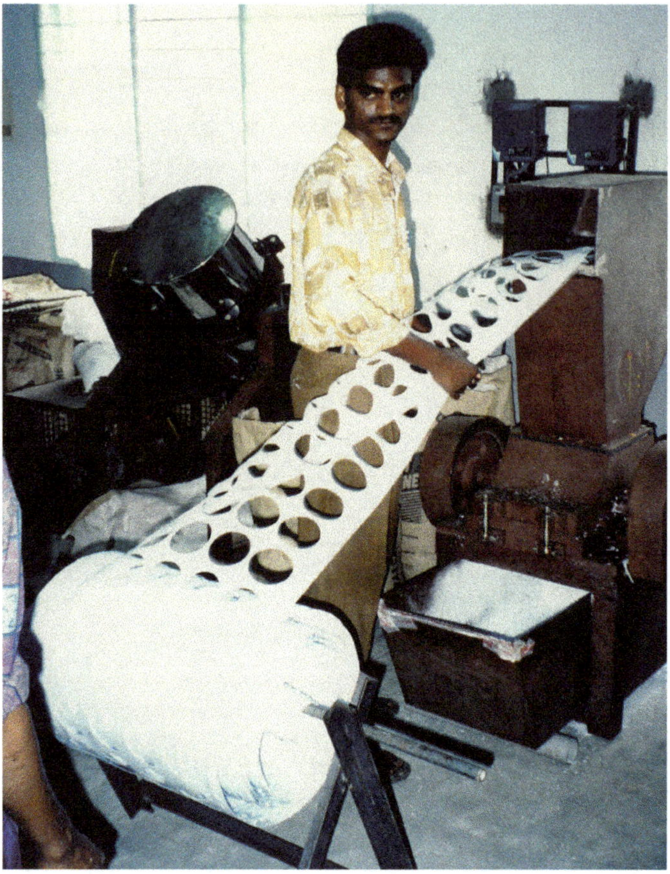

Image 4: Small firm supplements efforts of large industries

Source: © Léo-Paul Dana.

Troubles that were rooted in the past continue to have consequences. Singha[18] showed that good infrastructure in Manipur has had a positive impact on entrepreneurship but the state is still lagging behind the national average in terms of trade and commerce. Thomas and Prasain[19]

[18] Singha, K. (2013). "Infrastructure for Entrepreneurship in India's Trouble-Torn State of Manipur," *Journal of Economic Philosophy*, 1 (1), 12–16.

[19] Thomas, C.M. & Prasain, G.P. (2013). "Problems of Entrepreneurship Development in Hill Districts of Manipur — A Case Study of Ukhrul District," *Research Analysis and Evaluation*, 4 (41), 16–18.

Image 5: Rice has long been important

Source: © Léo-Paul Dana.

wrote about Manipur, "*It is endowed with rich bio-diversity and natural resources with potential for entrepreneurship to thrive. Yet, Manipur continues to be the most industrially backward state with hardly any industrial base.*"

1.3 The Impact of Culture and Social Structure[20]

Pio[21] examined everyday 'Indianness' of work culture and the future dreams of an Indian export hub; it appears that culture continues to be an important force entrepreneurship. Indeed, culture is central in explaining the social acceptability and perceived utility of entrepreneurship. Ever since McClelland's investigation[22] of the need for achievement illustrates how

[20]This section benefited greatly from the personal assistance of Edwina Pio.
[21]Pio, E. (2005b). "A Time to Sew: Work, Culture and Organic Cotton at Knitex India," *Management Case Study Journal*, 5 (2), 69–82.
[22]McClelland, D.C. (1961). *The Achieving Society*, Princeton, New Jersey: D. Van Nostrand.

entrepreneurs have been viewed in the West as those with a high need to achieve. In contrast, India's economy has traditionally reflected Indian culture and social structure. Pio[23] explained how religious and philosophical concepts have practical applications in India; she argued that Indian culture does not segment the spiritual from the secular, and that spirituality is intrinsic to being Indian. She also explained that a person's dharma is interpreted through his/her role in life, and every role has certain expectations of dharma to be fulfilled.[24]

The Jains — ascetic religious group — became traders, not because of an entrepreneurial spirit based on materialism, but due to ritualistic reasons; trading was an occupation free from conflict with religious requirements. Observant Jains have become famous entrepreneurs dealing with textiles and diamonds in western India and abroad — even in Africa. Another group of Indians who have thrived on their business acumen are the Sindhis (from Sindh). Both the Jains and Sindhis are closely aligned to Hinduism in their beliefs. Other early entrepreneurs were merchants from the Islamic religion such as the Bohras from Gujarat, the followers of Zoroastrianism (religion of the Parsees), and Mizrahi Jews who settled in India. Under colonial rule, Marwari enterprises complemented those of English entrepreneurs who permitted them to have an important role in a diversified industrial economy. Today, Marwaris have the reputation of having business acumen and are a very enterprising group. Likewise, Banias are thrifty with an eye on business opportunities.

As noted by Mishra,[25] "*In India there are many castes that are categorised as business castes...Most of the business castes (the erstwhile Vaishya) are now classified under 'Other Backward Castes' for purposes of government regulations.*" While the caste system reinforced the practice of following a family occupation, this impeded class mobility.[26] In fact,

[23]Pio, E. (2005a). "A Change Process Imbued with an Eastern Ethos Revitalizes an Indian Business," *Journal of Organizational Excellence,* 24 (3), 3–10.

[24]ibid.

[25]Mishra, A. (2005). "Entrepreneurial Motivations in Start-up and Survival of Micro- and Small Enterprises in the Rural Non-Farm Economy," *Journal of Small Business and Entrepreneurship*, 18 (3), 289–326.

[26]Dana, L.-P. (2000). "Creating Entrepreneurs in India," *Journal of Small Business Management*, 38 (1), 86–91.

Image 6: Working with spouse

Source: © Léo-Paul Dana.

Nafziger[27] noted that leading entrepreneurs often belonged to communities in which caste divisions were not rigidly observed.

In India, according to Kakar,[28] people are more sensitive to emotional affinity in the workplace than to work and productivity. According to

[27]Nafziger. op. cit.

[28]Kakar, S. (1978). *The Inner World: A Psycho-Analytic Study of Hindu Childhood and Society*, Oxford University Press, London.

Sinha,[29] work — as an end in itself — is not valued in India. Sinha[30] later explained that work is done with enthusiasm only when done for a nurturing superior. This supported McClelland's[31] suggestion that people in India generally performed their work as a favour to their employer.

"*In India, the Planning Commission, central and state governments recognize that women should be in the mainstream of economic development. In particular, the development of microenterprise for women is seen as an appropriate way to attack poverty…*"[32] Yet, Porter and Nagarajan[33] suggested that there "*may be a bias in Indian culture against women who engage in entrepreneurial activities outside the home.*" — the practice of *purdah* keeps women at home.

1.4 A Holistic Approach to Entrepreneurship

Across India, there are countless advocates of holistic management. This is a philosophy which attempts to synergise basic elements, in order to get optimal results. The holistic approach, for instance, encourages an all-encompassing integration of the intellectual with the physical and the spiritual — mental, material and moral aspects are involved.

Although schools teach facts, educational institutions are often lacking when it comes to personality development. It is the belief of many that an entrepreneurial personality can be taught, and that this should be done at a young age as this could lead to more effective members in society.

---

[29] Sinha, J.B.P. (1978). "Superior Subordinate Relationship and Alienation," *National Labour Institute Bulletin*, 4, 209–223.

[30] Sinha, J.B.P. (1984). "A Model of Effective Leadership Style in India," *International Studies of Management and Organization*, 14, 86–98.

[31] McClelland, D.C. (1975). *Power*, New York: Free Press.

[32] Ghosh, R., Gupta, M. & Nina Dhar, S. (1998). "Women and Entrepreneurship in India," in Rabindra N. Kanungo, ed., *Entrepreneurship & Innovation: Models for Development*, New Delhi: Sage, 156–175.

[33] Porter, E.G. & Nagarajan, K.V. (2005). "Successful Women Entrepreneurs as Pioneers: Results from a Study Conducted in Karaikudi, Tamil Nadu, India," *Journal of Small Business and Entrepreneurship*, 18 (1), 39–52.

Various agencies participate in holistic entrepreneurship development. To coordinate and oversee their activities, the Ministry of Industry established the National Institute for Entrepreneurship and Small Business Development (NIESBUD). Among the many programmes of this institute is one entitled, "*Training Trainers for Barefoot Managers*."

In line with the observation that over-population greatly nullifies the effect of overall development, it has been deemed in the national interest to promote birth control. For this reason, a non-governmental organisation,

Image 7: Attention to detail

Source: © Léo-Paul Dana.

Image 8: Work as a favour

Source: © Léo-Paul Dana.

the Progress Harmony Development (PHD) Chamber of Commerce and Industry has become involved in propagating the message of population control. Its Rural Development Foundation has been organised to act with a holistic approach. Likewise, the Entrepreneurship Development Institute of India (EDII) takes a holistic perspective with very impressive results. Located near Ahmedabad, in Gujarat, the EDII promotes independent thinking, creativity, and a spirit of innovation. Its Rural Entrepreneurship Development division promotes micro-enterprise and provides micro-credit. The EDII sponsors research, provides education and training — including its own educational video series — and publishes an academic journal on entrepreneurship. Perhaps the most unique contribution of the EDII is its summer camp, an entrepreneurial adventure for youth to learn achievement, a concern for excellence, creativity, innovation, leadership, problem solving, and systemic planning.

1.5 Towards the Future

Today's merchant princes include the Ambanis, Birlas and Tatas, the Premjis and Narayanamurthys, as well as the Indians of Silicon Valley, such as KanwalRekhi, many of whom are returning to India to invest and manage start-up as well as top performing IT companies. "*Indian family-run businesses have been developing rapidly from firms with limited goals that valued loyalty more than ability into dynamic professionally-managed corporates capable of taking on global competition.*"[34]

While India continues to be a patriarchal society, today there are several Indian women entrepreneurs many of whom are highly educated and run their own businesses, as well as the larger segment of Indian women

Image 9: Rural enterprise

Source: © Léo-Paul Dana.

[34] Skaria, G., ed. (2006). *India 2006: Taking India to the World,* London: World Link.

who are starting their own micro-enterprises through micro-financing schemes. To be top performing is quite a change from the past where women in the early history of entrepreneurship were hard to find.

Traditionally, merchants would marry among their own caste, and even today one finds that arranged marriages, often to keep the wealth in the family, as well as to keep the "purity" of the caste, continue. Nevertheless, there is a change in the air. Torri and Martinez[35] explored the

Image 10: Neighbourhood fruitmongers

Source: © Léo-Paul Dana.

[35]Torri, M.C. & Martinez, A. (2014). "Women's Empowerment and Micro-entrepreneurship in India: Constructing A New Development Paradigm?" *Progress in Developmental Studies,* 14 (1), 31–48.

Image 11: Micro-enterprises

Source: © Léo-Paul Dana.

case of the Gram Mooligai Company, the first female community enterprise in India, formed and managed entirely by "untouchables" and active in the herbal sector.

With Manmohan Singh, the Prime Minister, calling for the 21st century to be the '*Indian Century*,' the geopolitical ramifications of the country's rise are attracting attention."[36] Challenges facing India, however, include the liberalisation of government regulation; this was discussed by James F. Hoge at the World Economic Forum, in Davos.[37] At the same Forum, Bhagwati[38] cautioned not to assume that India's rapid growth was sustainable.

While some people run micro-enterprises, Internet entrepreneurs in Bangalore are preparing taxes for people in faraway places, reading X-rays for doctors around the world and tracing lost luggage. The national

[36]Johnson. op. cit.

[37]Hoge, J.F. (2006). "The Emergence of India," *Statement at the World Economic Forum, Davos*, January 25.

[38]Bhagwati, J. (2006). "The Big Debate: Setting the Business Agenda," *Statement at the World Economic Forum, Davos*, January 25.

economy is growing. Jain[39] reported, "*organised retail is expanding at a rate of 40 to 45 per cent each year.*" In the long run, this will have an impact on small neighbourhood shops. Despite constraints and restrictions, new generation entrepreneurs are emerging as leaders of the future. As suggested by Koster and Rai,[40] a focus of future policy should be increasing the quality of entrepreneurship.

Meanwhile, with a budget exceeding $1 billion, India is planning to put an astronaut in space, and already, in 2013 India's first Mars orbiter was successfully launched.

In 2016, India launched its flagship initiative, named Startup India, to create a strong entrepreneurial ecosystem in the country. The focus of this initiative is to tap young potential and encourage youths to pursue their own start-ups. Besides funding support and other incentives to pursue a start-up, the central government also pledges handholding services, industry-academia partnership, and other incubation facilities.

Following in the footsteps of the central government, various state governments also launched initiatives to support entrepreneurship. For instance, the Student Startup and Innovation Policy (SSIP) of Gujarat aims to foster a culture of innovation among higher education institutions located in the state. It also provides boot camps, and training programmes to students who are pursuing an innovative idea and trying to convert it into a start-up. Various academic incentives, and awards, are also provided to students who have initiated a venture. Similarly, the success of the Kerela Startup Mission has benefitted thousands of entrepreneurs. In 2018, to intensify competition between states, the central government launched State Startup Ranking — during which 30 Indian states and union territories participated and demonstrated the growth of entrepreneurs in their respective regions. Indian industries and experts found these schemes and initiative very effective and predict that India has much entrepreneurial growth to witness in coming years.

---

[39] Jain, A. (2006). "A Dramatic Change in Shopping," *Financial Times*, Wednesday, June 28, p. 4.

[40] Koster, S. & Rai, S.K. (2008). "Entrepreneurship and Economic Development in a Developing Country: A Case Study of India," *Journal of Entrepreneurship,* 17 (2), 117–137.

Image 12: Nirula's

Source: © Léo-Paul Dana.

Case Study: Nirula's

There are literally countless restaurants in India with 20,000 in Delhi alone. Most fast food, in India, comes from dhabas, which are roadside stands. The food is good, but it may be covered with flies, and utensils may be crusty.

India's first fast-food chain, Nirula's was started by Mr. L.C. Nirula and his brother, Mr. M. Nirula, both originally from Lahore, when the city was still in India, prior to the creation of Pakistan. The brothers moved to New Delhi, and in 1934 established a restaurant with a twelve-room hotel. Later, they expanded with a cabaret. During the 1950s, Nirula's introduced fast-food burgers and chips (fries).

Lalit and Deepak Nirula, the sons of the founders, left India to study at the Cornell University School of Hotel Administration, and upon their return, they elaborated Nirula's menu, adding Indian food and 21 flavours of ice cream. They trademarked a logo with pink and white — almost identical to that of Baskin Robbins. A favourite ice cream flavour is *zafranibadaampista*, a pungent blend of almonds, pistachio and saffron.

Nirula's grew to include numerous locations in New Delhi, feeding tens of thousands of people daily. The chain internationalised by opening outlets in Nepal. As huge international chains penetrated the Indian market, Nirula's began promoting itself heavily; it even embarked on joint-marketing campaigns with Lee (jeans). In contrast to foreign companies that paid a corporate tax rate of 48 percent, Nirula's benefitted when the corporate tax rate for local firms fell from 43 percent to 35 percent.

Today, Nirula's caters to an eclectic crowd; sari-clad women eat the vegetarian dishes, side-by-side with their children eating "*Western*" meals. Uniformed employees prepare curries, pizza, tandoori chicken, mutton-burgers and sandwiches. Other popular dishes include *dal* (a lentil dish) and *matar paneer* (a mixture of cheese with peas). Half the meals on the menu are meat-free, reflecting the fact that 80 percent of the population in India practice Hinduism, a religion for which the cow is sacred. A branch of this religion, he Jain sect, is opposed to killing all living beings.

With close to 300 outlets in India and battling for supremacy, in 2012 McDonald's announced it would launch all-vegetarian restaurants. In response, Indian firms were considering measures to compensate for lost market share and in 2014, an alternative idea for Nirula's was to diversify and considered producing its own beverages to add to the menu.

1.6 Culture, Religion & Diet

Mohandas (Mahatma) K. Gandhi (1869–1948), the father of India, once said that much can be known about a society by observing how people treat their animals. Indeed, cultural values are very much reflected in the role of animals. Entrepreneurs in Vietnam prosper exporting dogs to butchers and to restaurants in China. Meanwhile, in the district of Chennai, in India, a hundred stray dogs are rounded up each day to be electrocuted with unreliable antique equipment. People are hungry, but it is not considered proper to eat dogs in this country. A sandwich of roasted almonds is more culturally appropriate than meat.

Eating has long been central to the culture of India, as diet is linked to notions of purity and self-control. The Jains (an ascetic religious sect) in India practice *ahimsa*, the absolute prohibition of killing. As such, they are vegetarians. Among high castes, meat is regarded as impure, as it could lead to undesirable lust. In Hindu society, meat is often shunned, especially among unmarried women and elders. Muslims in India eat meat, provided it has been slaughtered according to religious ritual, facing Mecca; however, pork is not allowed in the Muslim diet. Jews, in India, also refrain from pork and all other meats, which are specified as prohibited according to the Bible. A variety of religions, including Bahai, Christianity, Islam, and Judaism, are represented in India, but the Hindu faith is predominant and consequently, the slaughtering of cattle can be perceived as sacrilege.

According to Christianity, Mary is the mother of Jesus and likewise, the cow in India is venerated as the mother of life. The cow provides transportation, power, milk and calves. Oxen are very important in agriculture as they plough fields. They also provide 350 million tons of fertiliser each year. In addition, the amount of dung used for cooking, in India, provides heating equivalent to 35 million tons of coal or 68 million tons of wood.

The regulatory environment reinforces cultural values through government intervention. A bill of rights for cows was written alongside the national constitution. In Chennai, the police searches for sick cattle and encourages these to graze in fields near the police station. Not only are prayers said for cattle that are ill, but government agencies in India even maintain state-funded old age homes for senior cows.

1.7 The Environment

In 1977, 90 percent of India's villages had no safe drinking water, while Coca-Cola had reached every town. Then, distrust of foreign investment led to the departure of major American firms, including Coca-Cola from India with others, including IBM, being expelled. Consequently, during the early 1980s, there were few multinationals in India.

In 1986, after an absence of several years, PepsiCo applied to return to India. Eventually, foreign products could return, if they had "*Indianised*" brand names, e.g., Hero Honda, Modi Olivetti, Maruti Suzuki. In July 1990, PepsiCo began operations in India, under the name Lehar Pepsi.

Up to the 1990s, India had been greatly influenced by parochial conflicts of caste, religion and region. Cloth was sold by the yard, tea leaves by the kilo, and soap was cut into chunks to be sold by weight. Class mobility was limited, and poverty was widespread. Technological and regulatory changes, however, transformed society. Significant economic reforms raised GDP growth, while the spread of electricity and technology contributed to industrial output.

Major reform came in 1991, when India opened up. Shortly thereafter, Rajan Pillai — a Singapore-based industrialist (of Indian origin) — announced that he would bring Coca-Cola back to India. When Coca-Cola resumed operations in India, it was among the first firms which was not required to use an "*Indianised*" name.

After years of restrictive policies, liberalisation opened India, to imports and to foreign investments. In many industries, foreign technology agreements were granted automatic approval, and no permission was required for hiring foreign technicians. As a member of the Multilateral Investments Guarantee Agency, India would have no restriction on the repatriation of dividends and profits. Across a wide range of industries, India opted to permit up to 51 percent foreign equity participation, regardless of whether foreign technology was in question and the Foreign Investment Promotion Board was given authority to approve investment beyond 51 percent. In the case of small-scale units, the ceiling for foreign equity participation was 24 percent. Also helping new entrants was the reduction of duty on the import of capital goods, from 35 percent to 25 percent.

Industrial policy in India was liberalised such that location of an enterprise did not need approval except in the case of highly populated areas. There were further relaxations of policy regulating non-polluting industries, and firms could generate their own power. Also, India removed its requirement of having a phased manufacturing program. Finally, the controller of capital issues would no longer have control over capital market operations, which instead became guided by an autonomous Securities and Exchange Board of India.

Fiscal policy was also modified. The maximum personal income tax rate (for revenues exceeding 120,000 rupees) had been fixed at 40 percent. After the tax structure was rationalised and simplified, personal tax rates fell to between 10 and 30 percent; the corporate tax rate was reduced to 35 percent for Indian companies and 48 percent for foreign companies.

India became the world's largest producer of groundnuts and of tea, the world's second largest producer of fruit, milk, rice, sugar, vegetables, wheat and woven cotton fabrics. Rising literacy along with surging incomes increased the demand for quality. The spread of electricity also created the demand for electric gadgets; among these was the television, a medium used to persuade people to spend whatever money they have. The buying power of the rising middle class, along with the relaxation of government regulations, made the Indian market very attractive for foreign enterprises. Kellogg's was quick to introduce its new product, Basmati Rice Flakes, and has been advertising Kellogg's Frosties (frosted flakes) as a good source of energy.

With liberalisation, Cadbury-Schweppes launched its beverage line in India. The arrival of such giants was a threat to existing bottling plants in India. PepsiCo India Holdings Pvt. Ltd., in Mumbai (formerly Bombay), was allowed to take over Duke's. Maximum retail prices (MRPs) continued to be government regulated, but not all retailers respected them. MRP for a 300 ml bottle of Duke's Soda was six rupees, and for a 200 ml bottle of Duke's Mangola eight rupees, inclusive of taxes, but excluding the glass bottle.

1.8 Kentucky Fried Chicken, Formerly Owned by PepsiCo

PepsiCo entered India with beverages but soon brought fast food as well. The rise of a new middle class, including 250 million consumers, encouraged PepsiCo to open India's first Kentucky Fried Chicken (KFC), in Bangalore, on June 1, 1995. It was expected that McDonald's would follow. Other American firms expressing interest in India included: AT & T, Black & Decker Corp., Levi Strauss & Co., Mattel Inc., Morgan Stanley & Co., Motorola Inc., Raytheon Co., Sara Lee Corp., Timex Corp., and Walt Disney Co. Even IBM, which had been expelled from India during the 1970s, decided to return to India. The opening of India's first KFC franchise in June 1995 angered thousands of people. The corporation had planned to spend US$40 million in India, opening sixty restaurants there, with an average of fifty employees at each location. However, other issues were considered as having a greater impact than that of job creation.

KFC fattened its chickens on maize, the highest-protein cereal that is also the cheapest source of nutrition for the poor and it was these people whose maize was being taken for the chickens who could not afford KFC meals.

In 1993, the Karnataka Farmers Association accused multinationals of harming local entrepreneurs, and therefore destroyed the Bangalore offices of the corporate giant, Cargill Seeds. In 1995, the same association claimed that KFC would force small-scale chicken farmers out of business. With 10 million members, this group gained political clout; the association could easily round up 200,000 participants to show solidarity at a single protest. Should American fast food restaurants have been concerned?

Indeed, it was argued that KFC would buy chickens from large-scale hatcheries, to the detriment of small-scale farmers. Furthermore, KFC's demand for chicken could affect the demand for chicken feed; grain would be diverted to feed chicken, while the poor would be hungry.

To protect its interests, the Karnataka Farmers Association distributed a leaflet warning of "*chemically poisoned meat*" which it deemed carcinogenic. Accusations, against KFCs franchise in Bangalore, resulted in government intervention. The Health Ministry announced that KFC chicken contained excessive quantities of monosodium glutamate (MSG) so the KFC outlet lost its permit.

Despite problems with its Bangalore store, PepsiCo Restaurants International proceeded to open another KFC, this one in Delhi. Here, health inspectors found flies in the kitchen, and the municipal health commissioner ordered that the outlet's license be revoked on the grounds of unsanitary conditions.

1.9 McDonald's

In 1937, Richard and Maurice McDonald opened a tiny drive-in restaurant east of Pasadena, in California. This was the first McDonald's, and from this new, small business, the two brothers developed food-processing and assembly-line techniques. In 1954, Ray Kroc, a salesman of milkshake mixers at the time, identified an opportunity in this small business; he then negotiated a franchise deal, granting him exclusive rights to franchise McDonald's across the United States. At a time when other franchising companies sold restaurant and ice cream franchises for up to $50,000 for large geographic areas, Mr. Kroc offered franchisees a McDonald's franchise for $950, and a token service fee equal to 1.4 percent of sales for himself plus a royalty of 0.5 percent of sales which went to Richard and Maurice McDonald. In 1956, Harry Sonneborn, a partner in Ray Kroc's enterprise, introduced a formula for leasing stores, to be sub-leased to franchisees at a 40 percent premium. Eventually, McDonald's purchased land for franchisees. Preferring a calmer life, in 1961, Richard and Maurice McDonald sold their shares of this business for $2.7 million.

McDonald's first international venture was in Canada, during 1967. It soon became the country's fast-food industry leader. McDonald's learned that despite the cost savings inherent in standardisation, success is often a function of being able to adapt to an environment. Product lines were constantly evolving, reflecting taste preferences, and potential profitability. In 1980, McDonald's outlets in New York City sold steak sandwiches; however, the product did not prove to be as profitable as others, and it was discontinued. McDonald's introduced lobster sandwiches in New Hampshire, and bagels in Vermont. Some outlets in Canada made available a Quebec specialty called *poutine*, consisting of potatoes covered with gravy and topped with cheese curds.

By the mid-1990s, Cara Operations (the owner of Harvey's and Swiss Chalet) was approaching annual sales of CAN$1 billion, while McDonald's Canada surpassed CAN$1.6 billion in sales during 1994. By 1997, McDonald's Canada operated almost 1,000 restaurants in Canada, and had become involved in McDonald's in Russia.

By the late 1990s, there were about 12,000 McDonald's restaurants across the United States, and this was the single most advertised brand in the nation. About 85 percent of the McDonald's outlets in the United States were franchises, with the McDonald's Corporation receiving a royalty fee based not on profit, but gross sales. Annual advertising and promotion expenditures were $1 billion, and for every three hamburgers prepared in the United States, one was made by McDonald's.

A concern, however, was that domestic growth was on the decline. During the 1970s, the average annual growth rate for the American fast-food industry exceeded seven percent. By the 1980s, the annual growth rate of domestic sales had dropped to below five percent; in 1989, for example, McDonald's reported that its sales in the United States grew just four percent. As the American market approached saturation, marketing efforts were shifted toward foreign markets. Soon, McDonald's lost domestic share to competitors such as Burger King (a unit of Grand Metropolitan PLC) and Wendy's International Inc.

McDonald's first Asian investment was a restaurant in Japan opened during 1971. At the time, fast food in this country was either a bowl of noodles or miso soup. The location selected for this new venture was the Ginza, a swinging neighbourhood of Tokyo. McDonald's Co. (Japan) Ltd. introduced a gratin croquet sandwich with a deep-fried patty of macaroni, shrimp and potatoes, but this product failed, and was withdrawn from the Japanese market. Nevertheless, the brand was a success in Japan, and this led to increased competition. The Japanese candy manufacturer Lotte entered the burger business with its Lotteria outlets, serving deep fried salmon burgers with onion sauce. Suntory, Japan's largest distiller of whisky, penetrated with First Kitchen. Morinaga & Co., Japan's leading caramel enterprise, launched its own fast food business, Morinaga Love, featuring a rice burger with grilled rice patties instead of hamburgers. This product is filled with grilled squid, seaweed and spicy red cod roe.

Despite success in many key markets, McDonald's also encountered difficulties marketing abroad. In October 1991, a poster illustrating the French celebrity Paul Bocuse was displayed in 66 outlets across the Netherlands; the problem was that it showed him with four other French chefs, examining a batch of dressed chickens, while the caption indicated that the chefs were dreaming of Big Macs. This was interpreted as an insult to French haute cuisine. Then, McDonald's aggravated the situation with a letter of apology, in which it was claimed that the internationally reputed chef was not well known in the Netherlands.

McDonald's Co. (Japan) Ltd. introduced Chicken Tatsuta, Teriyaki Chicken, and the Teriyaki McBurger. With its first mover advantage, McDonald's Co. (Japan) Ltd. kept its lead in Japan. By 1997, it had over 1,000 outlets across the nation, and these sold more food in Japan than any other restaurant company. Burgers were garnished with a fried egg. Beverages included iced coffee and corn soup. Several adaptations were particularly successful overseas. In tropical markets, guava juice was added to the McDonald's product line. In Puerto Rico, McJustas del Sabor became a favourite. In Germany, McDonald's did well selling beer as well as McCroissants. Banana fruit pies became popular in Latin America and McSpaghetti noodles became a favourite in the Philippines. In Thailand, McDonald's introduced the Samurai Pork Burger with sweet sauce. Meanwhile, McDonald's in New Zealand launched the Kiwiburger served with beetroot sauce and optional apricot pie. In Malaysia, McDonald's had success with the McRendang and sugar cane juice. In Singapore, where fries came to be served with chili sauce, the Kiasuburger chicken breakfast became a best seller. In Norway, McLaks salmon was introduced. McDonald's also experimented with vegetarian needs. Its first meatless burger was the "*Hula Burger*," consisting of grilled pineapple with cheese on a bun. This product was a failure, but in the Netherlands, during 1992, McDonald's tried to launch another vegetarian item, the Dutch veggie burger, made of spiced potatoes, peas, carrots and onions. Singapore was among the first markets in which McDonald's introduced delivery service and delivery eventually became popular in a variety of other markets, including Egypt.

While KFC had about 10,000 outlets in approximately 80 countries, McDonald's expanded to about 20,000 restaurants, in over 100 countries. The McDonald's outlet in Delhi, the first in India, was a partnership with local entrepreneur Mr. Vikram Bakshi. It opened in late October 1996, substituting the Big Mac with the Maharaja Mac, made from mutton, and offered vegetarian rice-patties flavoured with vegetables and spices.

1.10 The Beverage Sector

India is the world's largest producer of tea, and the second largest producer of milk. It is also the second largest producer of fruit and the second largest producer of sugar, giving India the potential to become a major producer of juice and/or fruit drinks.

Among the most popular drinks in India is freshly squeezed sugar cane juice. Also, almost everyone enjoys coconut water. Mangoes grow in abundance, and mango juice is common with several bottling companies preparing mango-flavoured drinks, including Mangola and Slice.

Duke & Sons Pvt. Ltd. developed Duke's Mangola, containing water, mango, pulp, sugar, citric acids, permitted class II preservatives and colour, as well as Duke's prepared soda, simply mixing treated water and carbon dioxide. West Bengal became the most popular market for India's own brand-name cola, Thums Up, the generic description of which is "*sweetened carbonated beverage*". The S. David Soda Water Factory was one of numerous local producers of soft drinks, and for years business was going well.

Liberalisation of the late 20th century brought major changes. PepsiCo India Holdings Pvt. Ltd., in Mumbai (formerly Bombay), was allowed to take over Duke's. Maximum retail prices (MRPs) continued to be government regulated, but not all retailers respected them. MRP for a 300 ml bottle of Duke's soda was six rupees, and for a 200 ml bottle of Duke's Mangola eight rupees, inclusive of taxes, but excluding the glass container. Coca-Cola's Limca was more expensive than Thums Up, bottled by Prabha Beverages, Pvt. Ltd., in Marthandam.

While Mangola dominated the mango beverage sector in Mumbai, Slice had more extensive distribution channels in Delhi and better brand recognition. Therefore, PepsiCo acquired not only Duke's but also Slice. PepsiCo also launched Pepsi-Cola, the generic description of which was "*sweetened carbonated water*".

The Coca-Cola Company's growing interest in India led to the acquisition of Thums Up, with very well-developed distribution channels and excellent brand recognition, especially in the northeast of India. The Coca-Cola Company also launched Coke. In Calcutta, Black Diamond Beverage Ltd. became a Coca-Cola bottler. Near Mumbai, Britco Foods Co. Ltd. bottled Coca-Cola products in Pune, an industrial town in Maharashtra state.

The Coca-Cola Company benefited from the Thums Up distribution channels, and PepsiCo from those of Duke's and Slice. Cadbury-Schweppes meanwhile benefited from its own reputation and from the established distribution channels of its confectionery line. There was already strong brand recognition for Cadbury chocolates, as Hindustan Cocoa Products Limited used to make Cadbury chocolates, in what was then Bombay. After liberalisation, Cadbury India Limited produced chocolates in its own three factories. One was in Pune and another in Thane, both in Maharashtra state. Cadbury also had a factory in the village of Gurikha (MP state).

Cadbury Schweppes brought orange-flavoured Crush to India and ginger ale under the name Canada Dry. Where there was already strong brand loyalty to Cadbury chocolate, Canada Dry and Crush both did well. In Mumbai, a special promotion was held at the Regal movie theatre, where people were eager to have a Cadbury drink with a Cadbury chocolate, during intermission. In Mumbai, Coca-Cola was dwarfed by Cadbury's shadow.

Another player in the soft drinks industry was Rogers & Co. Pvt. Ltd. (64 Mirza Ghalib Marg, Mumbai 400 008). This firm bottled drinks under license from Kickapoo Joy Juice Limited, in Toronto, Canada.

Table 1: Mango drinks in India

Brand	Producer	Ingredients
Aavin (marketed by Tamil Nadu Co-op Milk Producers' Federation Limited, Chennai)	The Salem District Co-operative Milk producers Union Ltd., Salem	Water, mango pulp, sugar, citric acid, ascorbic acid, colour, flavour
Frooti	Licensee of ParleAgro Ltd., Mumbai	Mango juice drink
Fruitnik	Sivas Beverages, 5/160A Kunathur High Road, Porur, Chennai 600116	Water, mango pulp, sugar, citric acid, permitted colour, added flavour, permitted class II preservatives
Lehar Slice	PepsiCo India Holdings Ltd.	Water, mango pulp, sugar, citric acid, permitted colour, class II preservative, added flavour
Maaza	Chennai Bottling Co. Ltd., 423 Poonamalle High Road, Arumbakkam, Chennai 600106	Water, mango pulp, sugar, citric acid, added flavour, permitted class II preservative
Mango Time	Sree Mahalakshimi Food Industries Limited, Kalamassery	Water, mango pulp, sugar, citric acid, permitted class II preservatives, colour, added flavour

Source: Compiled by Authors.

In summary, Cadbury Schweppes brought Canada Dry and Crush to India, and benefited from the fact that Cadbury's was already a well-known brand, as its chocolates were being made by Hindustan Cocoa Products Limited. Also taking advantage of existing distribution channels, the Coca-Cola Company acquired India's own famous cola, Thums Up; PepsiCo India Holdings Pvt. Ltd. took over Duke's Mangola (a popular mango drink) from Duke & Sons Pvt. Ltd. Later, Coca Cola acquired the soft drink business of Cadbury Schweppes.

https://doi.org/10.1142/9789811212741_0002

Chapter 2

Entrepreneurship in India

Priyanka Vern and Shilpa Sindhu

2.1 Introduction

With the introduction of rapid technological advances and globalisation, the current economic environment has become a global village, defined by intense developments in business. As part of the world economy, the manufacturing and service sectors face major difficulties. Their survival is tough, having to keep pace with the speed of development, and prosper in the challenging environment but at the same time, this introduces numerous fresh possibilities. Entrepreneurship, one of humanity's strongest business forces, empowers people to search for opportunities. The key source of change in any community is entrepreneurship. Entrepreneurship is something that must be promoted by society, governments and organisations. Whether to create new business or breathe life into old, create new goods or find new methods of marketing, or find new ways of doing old things, entrepreneurial management has become an extremely valued skill to be practiced, nurtured, created and supported. Entrepreneurship is likely to be one of the main challenges that business schools in the 21st century will face in all aspects of their learning. Entrepreneurs are finally being acknowledged as an important element in generating economic wealth. They are considered catalysts for financial and social change, forecasting opportunity, marketing it, and making a profit. Entrepreneurship requires dealing with two things risk and uncertainty.

2.2 Entrepreneurship Scenario in India

In human development, world history, and international relations, India and Indian civilisation have played a significant role.[1] According to the Ministry of Statistics and Programme Implementation, India's current population is approximately 1.37 billion which makes India the biggest democracy in the world, and by population the second biggest nation. Entrepreneurship is one of the key drivers of economic growth and India is on the fast track to overcoming its initial struggles as the entrepreneurship structure remains very stable. For years, the share of registered firms has stabilised at a low level of 13 percent. There would be less innovation, less productivity and a higher unemployment rate without enterprises and entrepreneurs. There is no entrepreneurial success in a vacuum. The Global Entrepreneurship and Development Institute (GEDI) defines the entrepreneurship "ecosystem" as "*The combination of attitudes, resources and infrastructure*."[2]

India is becoming a start-up hub. There is tremendous opportunity for development. According to the National Association of software and Services Companies (NASSCOM) – Zinnvo report titled as "*Indian Start-up Ecosystem 2018: Approaching Escape Velocity*",[3] India ranks as the third-largest start-up hub in world. This has been realised by a nation that, through development of an entrepreneurial spirit and motivation among individuals, has created a society that can achieve self-reliance and development.[4] It is now becoming progressively apparent that India's start-up ecosystem has become dynamic and mainstream in many aspects — in terms of work development, customer problem solving, and product development. The Statista Research Department defines India's

---

[1]Koster, S. & Rai, S.K. (2008). "Entrepreneurship and Economic Development in a Developing Country." *The Journal of Entrepreneurship*, 17(2), 117–137.

[2]Ács, Z.J., Szerb, L., Lafuente, E. & Lloyd, A. (2018). *Global Entrepreneurship and Development Index 2018*. Switzerland: Springer Nature.

[3]National Association of Software and Services Companies (NASSCOM) – Zinnvo Report. (2018). *Indian Start-up Ecosystem 2018: Approaching Escape Velocity*. https://www.nasscom.in/system/files/secure-pdf/Indian_Start-up_Ecosystem_2018-Final_Report.pdf. [Accessed 2018].

[4]Dana, L.-P. (2000). "Creating Entrepreneurs in India". *Journal of Small Business Management*, 38 (1), 86–91.

start-ups as "*An entity less than seven years young with an annual turnover of fewer than 250 million rupees and headquartered in India.*"[5]

The Start-up India initiative, led by the Industrial Policy and Promotion Department of India, aims to provide a supportive and efficient ecosystem for emerging entrepreneurs in India. 21 states and union territories have implemented government-led start-up policies. Bangalore, India's biggest start-up hub, followed by Delhi, Mumbai and Hyderabad, which is the biggest root of that tree. With a keen eye on identifying gaps in the market and with correct funding, many businesses have achieved success. One of the fundamental requirements for entrepreneurial success is that they should focus on the characteristics of the place where they want to do business.[6] As per Inc42 DataLab's latest annual Indian Tech Start-up Funding Report, 10 start-ups, namely Billdesk, BYJU'S, Freshwork, OYO, Paytm Mall, Pine Labs, PolicyBazaar, Swiggy, Udaan, Zomato were registered as 'unicorns' (a term used when a start-up is worth more than a billion U.S. dollars) in 2018. Indians and Pakistanis exhibit a fair rate of entrepreneurship due to comparatively better access to markets, skill sets and other resources.[7,8]

In India, start-up funding has drawn large investors from all around the world. Flipkart is one of the most successful start-ups in India. Other companies that have emerged successfully in India are SnapDeal (a Delhi based online platform), Ola (India's largest mobility platform and ride-hailing leader), and Paytm (a digital wallet and e-commerce payment system company). Existing Indian start-ups continue to collaborate with

---

[5]Statista (2019). *Start-ups in India Statistics & Facts.* https://www.statista.com/topics/4839/startups-in-india/. [Accessed 17 January 2019].

[6]Jafari Sadeghi, V., Nkongolo-Bakenda, J.-M., Anderson, R.B., & Dana, L.-P. (2019). "An Institution-Based View of International Entrepreneurship: A Comparison of Context-Based and Universal Determinants in Developing and Economically Advanced Countries". *International Business Review*, 101588.

[7]Reeves, F. & Ward, R. (1984). "West Indian Business in Britain" in Robin Ward & Richard Jenkins (eds.). *Ethnic Communities in Business: Strategies for Economic Survival.* (pp.125–148). Cambridge, U.K: Cambridge University Press.

[8]Dana, L.-P. (1997). "The Origins of Self-Employment in Ethno-cultural Communities: Distinguishing between Orthodox Entrepreneurship and Reactionary Enterprise". *Canadian Journal of Administrative Sciences/Revue Canadienne des Sciences de l' Administration,* 14 (1), 52–68.

large conglomerates to expand and grow market share. Entrepreneurship is the key factor in addressing unemployment, poverty and gearing up for globalisation to achieve overall economic progress in India.

2.3 Agri-Food Entrepreneurship in India

Agriculture is essential to the socio-economic growth of India and is the immediate source of income for more than 55 percent of its population. Agriculture and related businesses are regarded as the cornerstone of the Indian economy, as they provide significant raw materials for industries. In India, 52 percent of the soil is arable as opposed to 11 percent globally. India's large population depends on agriculture for its primary source of income. Small and medium enterprises are emerging in rural areas, which provide supplementary income to rural people and create employment options for them. According to a NASSCOM report "*Agri-tech in India: Emerging trends in 2019*", India hosted more than 450 agri-tech start-ups in the first six months of 2019.[9] The agri-tech industry in India has experienced some of the worldwide and sector-focused funding directly in agri-tech start-ups over the past few years, receiving more than US$248 million as of June 2019, representing a 300 per cent increase over the previous year.

Interestingly, every ninth agri-tech start-up in the world comes from India. Average farmer income has increased 1.7 times over the last decade, allowing farmers to seek innovative technology alternatives. More than 50 percent of agri-tech start-ups give services like supply chain management, market connections, better access to inputs, etc.

There is a huge potential for entrepreneurial activity in agriculture, and efficient management can harness that potential to be utilised by young 'agripreneurs'. Agriculture can contribute to national income while offering employment and revenue to society at large and its deprived segments.[10]

---

[9]National Association of Software and Services Companies (NASSCOM) (2019). *Agritech in India: Emerging Trends in India.* https://www.nasscom.in/system/files/secure-pdf/agritech-in-india-emerging-trends-in-2019.pdf. [Accessed July 2019].

[10]Uplaonkar, S.S. & Biradar, S.S. (2015). "Development of Agriculture in India through Agripreneurs". *International Journal of Applied Research*, 1(9), 1063–1066.

2.4 Emergence of Sustainable Entrepreneurship in India

The main aim of a sustainable entrepreneur is to contribute towards solving many environmental and/or social problems and lead to a country's sustainable development.[11] The health of the environment has become a significant problem given the growing population and urbanisation, and it is rapidly deteriorating. Due to lack of attention and heedless behaviour of people, mother nature bleeds due to pollution and contamination, losing its greenery and natural resources.

Traditionally entrepreneurs prefer present gains rather than present losses or future gains and therefore ignore environmental damage.[12] Presently, this landscape appears to be transforming as many young entrepreneurs are emerging with creative thoughts and ideas to recover/sustain Earth's natural resources. These entrepreneurs have discovered alternatives to protect nature through their skills and converting these opportunities into income; from the recycling of floral waste, the production of herbal clothes, to the provision of solar energy in their homes. Sustainability needs fresh thinking, not just among researchers and technologists but across the wider spectrum of human effort.[13] Technological innovations need to maintain pace with economic, social and institutional developments. Sustainable development involves the growth of a nation in the fields of science and technology, R&D, finance, IT, health services, politics etc. The reality of today is changing as many young and budding entrepreneurs have launched start-ups which work on managing the supply chain of agriculture produce.

Mystic Aromatics is a start-up which utilises recycled paper for manufacturing air fresheners and in agricultural product developments. The start-up provides alternative ways of utilising farmers' produce apart

---

[11] Schalteggar, S. & Wagner, M. (2011). "Sustainable Entrepreneurship and Sustainability Innovation: Categories and Interactions". *Business Strategy and the Environment*, 20(4), 222–237.

[12] Gurău, C. & Dana, L.-P. (2018). "Environmentally-driven Community Entrepreneurship: Mapping the Link Between Natural Environment, Local Community and Entrepreneurship". *Technological Forecasting and Social Change*, 129, 221–231.

[13] Ahmed, A. & McQuaid, R.W. (2005). "Entrepreneurship, Management, and Sustainable Development". *World Review of Entrepreneurship, Management and Sustainable Development*, 1(1), 6.

from the conventional so that they can earn better livelihoods and waste can be reduced. Entrepreneurs need to unlearn the traditional ways of marketing and keep pace with innovative marketing models.[14] India is the second-largest producer of fruit and vegetables, but 13,300 crores are wasted because of inadequate cold storage facilities, lack of transportation facilities and poor weather conditions. These young Agri-food start-ups collaborate with farmers and provide them with proper facilities and digital solutions like precision farming, artificial intelligence, geo-tagging, and providing an E-trading platform. Ultimately these solutions help in sustaining earth's natural resources. Two such start-ups: **M/s Dhaanika** and **M/s Rural Roots** are worth mentioning in this context.

2.4.1 *M/s Dhaanika*[15]

Dhaanika is a fusion of three words — dhaan, dhaani and dhaanika — meaning grain, goodness, and prosperity, because they are trying to make farming thrive for both farmers and customers alike. The start-up is based in Kanpur, Uttar Pradesh (UP), India. Their mission is to generate a different Agri-value chain by introducing '*zero budget nature agriculture*' among females led by '*farmer groups*', which involves food processing and market space provisions in which they can thrive and trade chemical-free nourishment. Dhaanika is a revolution that begins with traditional seeds planted in the organic soil belonging to 1,200 female farmers and provided all the goodness of India's culture, separating flavour and traditions. In addition to PGS Organic certification, Dhaanika by Aikya Organics has the guarantee from women farmers that it has been cultivated free of chemicals with traditional seeds. Their goods come from a location where their wealthy legacy is respected, and for Dhaanika, their mantra is "*To eat the right food, in the right season, grown the right way*".

Their journey started with an NGO partner Shramik Bharti who promotes sustainable and ecologically conscious nature farming in Kanpur

[14] Sadiku-Dushi, N., Dana, L.-P., & Ramadani, V. (2019). "Entrepreneurial Marketing Dimensions and SMEs Performance". *Journal of Business Research*, 100, 86–99.
[15] Dhaanika Organics. https://www.dhaanika.com/

Image 1: Dhaanika farmers

Source: Dhaanika Organics direct to Authors.

Nagar, Kanpur Dehat, Chandauli, Bhadohi, Fatepur and Barabanki, UP. The training has developed into a collective of female farmers who are now farmer-producer organisations that provide organic products direct from their fields. The strategy of directly procuring products from the fields enables a strong and nutritious connection with customers as they want to make the authenticity of their product their key selling proposition.

Their major activities include training farmers about organic methods of farming, the formation of Self-Help Groups and installing seed and tool banks, forming them into farmer-producer organisations (FPOs).

Further, they install processing and packaging units under the FPO, owned and handled by women farmers. Finally, they provide a market platform to a wide range of over 30 packaged organic products under the brand name "*Dhaanika*" via a B2C model and for bulk buying. Their farming specialists train farmers to use local resources to create agri-inputs. They also help farmers to plan their crops based on seasonality, local environment, availability of land and demand in the market. Under

FPOs additional storage, manufacturing, processing and packaging units are established. Through entrepreneurship and job opportunities within these units, 100 percent of the value achieved by farmers is returned to them. They have successfully introduced 1,200 female farmers to organic farming with their current NGO partner Shramik Bharti and installed more than 50 seed banks in 97 villages from six districts of UP. These women farmers are farming, processing and packaging the products of Dhaanika through their two registered FPOs. With a turnover of Rs. 3350 Cr in 2016, it is expected that the market for organic products in India will triple by 2020. They have seen over 500 per cent development in B2B and B2C revenues over the past six months and they are targeting Rs 50 Cr revenues in the next five years.

2.4.2 *M/s Rural Roots*

In 2017, Rural Roots started with their first product category of niche pickles from Deoria region, Uttar Pradesh. Keshav Parthasarathy is one of the co-founders of Rural Roots who procure raw materials directly from farms and mandis, according to the produce available.

They have trained about 50 marginalised women in production of eight different types of niche pickles, and currently, employ 20–25 women with a salary of approximately Rs 2,500 per month (an increase of 150 percent from their previous salary levels). They also provide skills development training and educate these women about health, hygiene, sanitation and child education. They not only want to give these women salaries but also monitor how these salaries are used to be most effective for the development of their families. They have sold over 10,000 bottles of pickles since 2018 through informal retail networks and exhibitions and received excellent feedback from their customers on the quality, uniqueness, and taste of their pickles (especially the stuffed red chilli, green chilli, garlic and jackfruit pickles).

Their aim is for significantly more progress in the future as they are planning to scale-up their sales activities, as well as introduce more innovation in their products (e.g., developing organic and healthy products for the environmentally and health-conscious consumers). Their mission is to create employment for 500 women in remotest part of India by 2022

Image 2: Rural roots employees & products

Source: Rural Roots direct to Authors.

through a sustainable food enterprise. Rural Roots aims to solve the two main challenges through their start-up: (i) lack of available employment opportunities (especially for women, with only 10 percent in the work-force); and (ii) absence of value-added industries with agriculture driving most of the local economy.

Rural Roots aims to generate sustainable employment for at least 500 women who live in extreme poverty by five years and raise their families above the poverty line by training them and employing them in food-processing activities. They plan to do all this through an enterprise-led model, i.e., ensuring sustainability over time through revenue generation.

2.5 Growing Emphasis of Technology Entrepreneurship

India is often defined as a youthful, innovative, aspiring, and opportunity-filled entrepreneurial ecosystem. According to a report "*Tech Start-up in India: A bright future*",[16] India has evolved into the fourth largest technology start-up base in the world and the home of a new generation of young start-ups. The number of new start-ups in India has increased significantly with 3,100 start-ups in 2010 and more than 800 new start-ups in 2014. If the current scenario remains the same, it is projected that more than 11,500 start-ups are expected to emerge, generating 250,000 employment opportunities for youth by 2020. Many start-ups are integrating emerging technologies into their solutions, constructing digital solutions and digital platforms for India.

India's agriculture industry also continues to progress towards its digital transformation, with the start-up ecosystem playing a key role and bringing innovation to much-needed fields. Adopting agriculture technology has always required a structured organisational focus and technology companies are striving to break into agriculture through new company models such as adopting deep technology like artificial intelligence, machine learning, big data, and the internet of things to become more efficient and effective to gain more trust and faith of customers and distinguish them from competition in the market. Krishihub is one

[16] National Association of Software and Services Companies (NASSCOM). *Tech Start-up in India: A Bright Future Report*. https://www.nasscom.in/system/files/secure-pdf/Start-ups_Landscape_Report14_0.pdf

example using an Artificial Intelligence (AI) powered supply chain which enables them to do farm-to-doorstep delivery in less than 12 hours, reducing fresh produce wastage by up to 25 percent.

Two case studies of technology entrepreneurs **M/s Green Agrevolution Pvt Ltd and M/s Instabring** are discussed further.

2.5.1 *M/s Green Agrevolution Pvt Ltd (DeHaat)*[17]

M/S Green Agrevolution Pvt Ltd is adopting technology interventions as a core to their business. Owned by Green AgRevolution, **DeHaat** is a technology-led platform that connects small farmers to their broad network of qualified micro-entrepreneurs to assist them by providing seeds, fertilisers, machinery, crop advisory and market connections. Registered farmers have direct access from competitive sources to a broad spectrum of agricultural inputs (seed, fertiliser and crop protection). They then receive customised crop reminder calls in the local language, as well as support for crop surveillance from the same micro-entrepreneur DeHaat. Finally, they sell the products direct to institutional buyers. Farmers position their unique, demand-related agri-input, field visit or agri-output through either the toll-free number or mobile application and receive last-mile services through the assigned micro-entrepreneur.

DeHaat is a tech-based platform founded by Mr Shashank Kumar, an Indian Institute of Technology Delhi, alumnus, the company is presently working with about 10,000 farmers mainly in northern and eastern India — including Bihar, Uttar Pradesh and Odisha. Through their dual delivery model of technology platform and service delivery centre, they provide farmers with 360° alternatives under one roof. They connect farmers at an inexpensive cost throughout the season to the latest technology, data, market quality input, and technical support. Dehaat offers Agri Input, Agri Output and Crop Advisory. Farmers are often misguided about the correct variety, solution, and dosage of different agri-inputs leading to uncertain productivity and elevated cultivation costs. DeHaat is a one-stop solution for farmers as they have access to a wide range of genuine crop

[17]Green Agrevolution Private Limited. http://agrevolution.in/home

Image 3: Green Agrevolution farms & farmers

Source: Green Agrevolution direct to Authors.

protection, nutrition for crops, seeds and fertilisers, and it enables them per season to decrease their cultivation expenses by 10–15 percent.

DeHaat also assists Agri-input players in proper product placement, immediate access to farmers, feedback from farmers, and avoids the black market. Previously, multiple intermediaries have been engaged between farmers and institutional buyers, leading to an absence of price transparency for farmers, and price increases at both ends owing to excessive handling, as well as losses after harvest. DeHaat has full control over the quality and amount of the product associated with the right of farmers from sowing to plant growth. They firmly believe in offering farmers with full end-to-end agri-services from "Seed to Market." To guarantee maximum output cost-effectively, the role of efficient agri-extension and crop advisory for farmers is highly crucial. DeHaat provides an extremely cost-effective crop scheduling services module for farmers, local language crop reminder calls, crop tracking, and other appropriate weather and market data.

2.5.2 *M/s Instabring*[18]

M/s Instabring was established in 2017, founded by Mr Prateek Katiyar. Currently, they are a team of seven running this start-up based in Kanpur, Uttar Pradesh. Their start-up follows five principles: reducing waste by faster and planned route network to ensure better & timely deliveries; better efficiency by implementing demand-driven management system for precise evaluation; quality mapping; end-to-end traceability of farm produce; mitigating risks via proactive and transparent ICT enabled networks. They have over 30 B2B clients, over 500 deliveries, zero customer acquisition costs, and 233 percent month-on-month growth. They have also won an Entrepreneurial Spark Award (UK Business Accelerator).

Image 4: Instabring farms

Source: Instabring direct to Authors.

[18]Instabring. http://instabring.in/http://agrevolution.in/home

They deal directly with farmers, providing them better market linkages and transparent pricing policy and they are currently dealing with around 150 villages.

2.6 Major Challenges and Road Ahead

The business climate has become increasingly complicated, unstable, ambiguous and unpredictable. Large enterprises aim to establish their innovation research centres, establish alliances with other clients and other innovation agencies, and develop alliances with incubation centres. The big business groups are always strongly related to innovation and the driving force for economic development. Currently, companies look for alternatives in the market due to the high cost of innovation, prolonged deadlines for solution growth and the search for diversity to respond to fresh market requirements. Financial inability is one of the major challenges faced by budding Indian entrepreneurial start-ups. For start-ups to survive, cashflow is vital. Small companies face one of the main difficulties in financial terms today. As revenues rise, spending also rises, and start-ups are highly dependent on investors who provide powerful economic assistance to them.

India is at a crossroads. Most industries have struggled to achieve the growth levels attained in the past, and a dynamic business environment needs to be fostered to ensure that India maintains the 10 per cent development that is necessary to fulfil its collective ambitions. The Government has designed a range of programs to encourage entrepreneurship. Entrepreneurship Development programs are sometimes not enough to create entrepreneurial abilities. Emerging entrepreneurs are not aware of the existence of such programs and the desired results cannot be produced if policies created for entrepreneurs are not implemented fairly. Major challenges that may hinder entrepreneurship are corruption, excessive taxation and legislation, and factors that may promote entrepreneurship are quality education, reduction of entry barriers, reduction of excessive regulation, corruption & bureaucracy, and freedom to compete.[19] Two

[19]Dana, L.-P. (2014). *Asian Models of Entrepreneurship — From the Indian Union and Nepal to the Japanese Archipelago: Context, Policy and Practice*, Second Edition, Singapore: World Scientific.

years ago, Prime Minister Narendra Modi's initiative "*Start-Up India Stand Up India*" gave a tremendous boost to the entrepreneurial movement in this nation. The advent of start-up incubators across the nation helped increase the ecosystem's visibility. However, with the right strategy and a focused approach to products and markets, existing entrepreneurial companies can add scope and scale to their operations and new, growing companies can succeed and raise the level of their ambitions.

2.7 Conclusion

Entrepreneurship plays a very major role in growth of a developing nation. Entrepreneurship gives the capability to youth to contribute to a wide scope of social and economic development categories such as income generation, employment generation, improving basic livelihoods, and reducing poverty. Agribusiness is an emerging field with large scope for entrepreneurs in India because of growing research and industrial development in this sector. The Government of India (GOI) has many entrepreneurship development schemes for development in the agricultural sector and other emerging areas like technology and sustainability. Government schemes and policies in India need more focus on attracting youth to the emerging area of entrepreneurship.

https://doi.org/10.1142/9789811212741_0003

Chapter 3

Entrepreneurship Policy and Support Framework in India

Vikas Singh, Shilpa Sindhu and Anupama Panghal

3.1 Introduction

Entrepreneurship creates value by organising efforts of individuals and groups to meet demand through innovation and uniqueness in a state of limited resources.[1] Entrepreneurship helps to give direction of modern economics and constitutes one of the four mainstream economic factors: land, labour, capital and entrepreneurship. India is the fastest emerging economy and has the potential to become the first global power by 2050.[2] Its increasing population offers it a competitive advantage in terms of labour. The current population of India is 1,370,339,445, which contributes to 17.74 percent of the total world population[3], with the rural population share at 65.97 percent of India's total population.[4] Indeed, a huge population gives a competitive advantage to the country, but at the same time, it can be a hinderance in terms of unemployment. India's unemployment

[1]Coulter, M.K. (2001). *Entrepreneurship in Action*. Prentice Hall.
[2]India's Culture. "India, A Fast-Emerging Economy". http://www.iccrindia.net/culture/ [19 September 2019].
[3]Worldometersinfo. https://www.worldometers.info/world-population/india-population/. [19 September 2019].
[4]World Bank. "Rural Population (% of Total Population)". https://data.worldbank.org/indicator/SP.RUR.TOTL.ZS. [19 September 2019].

rate is currently hovering around 8.0 percent[5] and the unemployment rate is observed more in rural areas as compared to urban areas. The majority of the rural population is dependent on agriculture or agricultural-related services which only contributes 15.87 percent of total Gross Value Added (GVA) at current prices. The different sectors of the economy show varied changes in the Gross Value Added (GVA) at basic prices. The service sector has the highest percentage of GVA at current prices and has shown increasing trends since the financial year 2011–2012 to 2018–2019. The service sector of India covers water, sanitation, health, trade, financial, real estate and software services.

Agriculture is a primary source of livelihood for 58 per cent of India's population for whom Rs 140,763.97 crore as per Union Budget 2019–20 were sanctioned. The agriculture sector of the economy shows comparatively less growth in the last eight financial years. Despite this, India's horticulture production shows a Compound Annual Growth Rate (CAGR) of 3.69 percent between FY2008–2019. The updated agricultural policy was introduced by the Government of India on December 2018, which aims to increase the country's agricultural exports with a stable trade policy regime. Along with this for marketing and financial assistance, the government of India came out with Transport and Marketing Assistance (TMA) which helps in boosting agriculture products' exports.[6]

Also, India stood at sixth in the global food and grocery market with food processing industries contributing 32 percent, representing 13 percent of total exports and six percent of industrial investment.[7] Furthermore, the dairy sector has also made a significant contribution to revenue collection. To enable the continued growth of the food processing sector, India needs better support for infrastructure. In line with this, in 2017, 42 mega

---

[5]CMIE. "Unemployment Rate in India". unemploymentinindia.cmie.com/kommon/bin/sr.php?kall=wshowtab&dtype=rural%20https://www.cmie.com/ [19 September 2019].

[6]Press Information Bureau, Government of India, Ministry of Commerce & Industry. "Transport and Marketing Assistance (TMA) for Specified Agriculture Products Notified". https://pib.gov.in/newsite/PrintRelease.aspx?relid=189200 [19 September 2019].

[7]Branson, A., Mani, R., & Anthony, R. (2018). "India's Food Processign Sector Poised for Growth:Global Agriculture Information Network". *USDA Foreign Agriculture Service,* Report No.IN8302, pp. 1–11.

food parks were sanctioned by the Government of India, out of which 25 mega food parks were operational by year end 2018.[8] Foreign direct investment (FDI) in the food processing sector is expected to cross US$28b in 2019 which was corroborated by the increase in sales of processed food in the domestic market. The packaged food industry in India is also expected to develop at a significant pace.

Notwithstanding this, recent trends favour the growth and open new opportunities for entrepreneurship. Furthermore, the expansion of international companies corroborates this sector's promise. Consumers from abroad prefer Indian products. Indian consumers are also shifting their preferences towards packaged food and fruits and vegetables.

Such promising facts support India in providing an encouraging and supportive base for entrepreneurs. The shift in consumer preferences is motivating entrepreneurs to come up with innovative business models. As per the existing literature base, it has been observed that the entrepreneurial ecosystem in developing Asian nations focuses more on relationships and long-established networks, while developed nations focus more on firm-based entrepreneurship.[9–15]

Historically in India, innovative entrepreneurship has been limited due to the prevailing caste system, cultural norms and government

---

[8]Ministry of Finance, Government of India (2017). "Economic Survey".

[9]Dana, L.-P. (2000a). "Creating Entrepreneurs in India". *Journal of Small Business Management,* 38 (1), 86.

[10]Dana, L.-P. (1995). "Small Business in a Non-entrepreneurial Society: The Case of the Lao People's Democratic Republic (Laos)". *Journal of Small Business Management,* 33 (3), 95.

[11]Dana, L.-P. (1997). "The Origins of Self-employment in Ethno-cultural Communities: Distinguishing Between Orthodox Entrepreneurship and Reactionary Enterprise". *Canadian Journal of Administrative Sciences/Revue Canadienne des Sciences de l'Administration,* 14 (1), 52–68.

[12]Dana, L.-P. (1998). "Small Business in Xinjiang". *Asian Journal of Business and Information Systems*, 3 (1), 123–36.

[13]Dana, L.-P. (1999). "Entrepreneurship as a Supplement in the People's Republic of China". *Journal of Small Business Management,* 37 (3), 76–80.

[14]Dana, L.-P. (1999). *Entrepreneurship in Pacific Asia: Past, Present and Future.* World Scientific Publishing Company.

[15]Dana, L.-P. (2000b). "Change and Circumstance in Kyrgyz Markets". *Qualitative Market Research: An International Journal,* 3 (2), 62–73.

regulations, but now the emphasis is given on changing mindsets and promoting entrepreneurship.[16] This chapter discusses the policy structure and infrastructural framework for entrepreneurs in India.

3.2 Policy Framework for Entrepreneurs

Any entrepreneurship policy in general, aims at the whole entrepreneurial process from its initial phase of inception until the early post-start-up phase to frame the way of delivering motivating perception, skills, and opportunities.[17] The objective of policy should not only be to maximise a certain indicator of entrepreneurship; rather, it must be focused on creating a context, a system, in which productive entrepreneurship can flourish.[18] Furthermore, entrepreneurship must foster opportunities in terms of enhancing value-addition by manifesting innovation and increasing marginal labour productivity.[19] Collectively, adopting innovation and improving marginal labour productivity results in employment growth and diversifying the market which consequently impacts positively on the social and economic development of a nation.[20]

Edoho[21] suggests that entrepreneurship is a central part of economic growth and social development, and for policymakers in search of a sustainable and competitive entrepreneurial economy, a policy can be defined in various ways.[22] The policy is a guiding tool for individuals or groups of

---

[16]Dana (2000a). op. cit.

[17]Dana, L.-P., Etemad H., & Wright R.W. (2008). "Toward a Paradigm of Symbiotic Entrepreneurship". *International Journal of Entrepreneurship and Small Business,* 5 (2), 109–126.

[18]Lundström, A & Stevenson, L.A. (2005). *Entrepreneurship Policy: Theory and Practice.* Springer, New York, NY.

[19]Acs, Z.J. & Szerb, L. (2007). "Entrepreneurship, Economic Growth and Public Policy". *Small Business Economics,* 28 (2–3), 109–122.

[20]Stam, E. (2015). "Entrepreneurial Ecosystems and Regional Policy: A Sympathetic Critique". *European Planning Studies*, 23 (9), 1759–1769.

[21]Edoho, F.M. (2016). "Entrepreneurship Paradigm in the New Millennium: A Critique of Public Policy On Entrepreneurship". *Journal of Entrepreneurship in Emerging Economies,* 8 (2), 279–294.

[22]Akbaba, A. (2012). "Business Performance of Small Tourism Enterprises: A Comparison Among Three Sub-sectors of the Industry". *Anatolia,* 23 (2), 177–195.

individuals to achieve the solution for a common concern.[23] An entrepreneurship policy's objective is to instil a sense of entrepreneurship among social agents and promote productive businesses activities.[24] Anderson[25] suggests that entrepreneurship policy in a developing nation must focus on individual and small businesses rather than large corporations. Rigby and Ramlogan[26] found that earlier, entrepreneurship policy only targeted improving the operational environment of small businesses without considering the issue of creating new companies. Typically, an entrepreneurial economy is a knowledge-based economy that targets small and new businesses rather than an industrial economy.[27] It must render the innovation and quality of offering which results in self-employment and empowerment of individuals and groups.[28]

Henrekson & Stenkula[29] state that a well-designed entrepreneurship policy can help reduce poverty. The policy must be well-designed for a better entrepreneurial environment.[30] Thus, to create a conducive environment, the entrepreneurial policy should encompass every dimension of growth and policy. Entrepreneurship policy when designed and implemented will need to eventually increase motivation amongst individuals to attempt entrepreneurship, create a conducive environment where motivated individuals will find potential opportunities for exploitation and/or exploration, and they will have the required support in terms of education,

---

[23]Tsai, W.H. & Kuo, H.C. (2011). "Entrepreneurship Policy Evaluation and Decision Analysis for SMEs". *Expert Systems with Applications,* 38 (7), 8343–8351.

[24]Stevenson, L. & Lundström, A. (2001). "Entrepreneurship Policy for the Future: Best Practice Components". *Keynote Speech for the ICSB Conference, Taipei.*

[25]Anderson, J.E. (2014). *Public Policymaking*. Cengage Learning.

[26]Rigby, J. & Ramlogan, R. (2013). "The Impact and Effectiveness of Entrepreneurship Policy". *Nesta Working Paper 13/01.*

[27]Norbäck, P.J, Persson, L., & Douhan, R. (2014). "Entrepreneurship Policy and Globalisation". *Journal of Development Economics*, 110, 22–38.

[28]Stevenson, L. & Lundström, A. (2007). "Dressing the Emperor: The Fabric of Entrepreneurship Policy". *Handbook of Research on Entrepreneurship Policy*, 94–129.

[29]Henrekson, M. & Stenkula, M. (2010). "Entrepreneurship and Public Policy". In Acs Z., Audretsch D. (Eds.) *Handbook of Entrepreneurship Research*, pp. 595–637. Springer, New York, NY.

[30]Acs, Z.J. & Virgill, N. (2010). "Entrepreneurship in Developing Countries". In: Acs Z., Audretsch D. (Eds) *Handbook of Entrepreneurship Research*, pp. 485–515. Springer, New York, NY.

skill development, resources, and support services to create and capture value from these opportunities. In addition to this, the ultimate nature of an *Entrepreneurship Policy Framework* must be inclusive, and it should help nations achieve sustainable development.

3.3 Policy Framework in India

The Indian government is introducing and promoting various policies to foster entrepreneurship in India and examples of these are as follows.

3.3.1 *Policy/Scheme Initiatives for Entrepreneurship Development in Indian Agriculture Sector*

- Agriculture Export Policy 2018
- Pradhan Mantri Kisan Samman Nidhi Yojana (PM-Kisan)
- Pradhan Mantri Annadata Aay Sanrakshan Abhiyan (PM-AASHA)
- Pradhan Mantri Krishi Sinchai Yojana (PMKSY)
- Model Contract Farming & Services Act 2018
- Electronic National Agriculture Market (eNAM), a unified national market for agricultural commodities since April 2016
- 'SAMPADA' (Scheme for Agro-Marine Processing and Development of Agro-Processing Clusters) with the aim of waste reduction and doubling farmer's income
- Around 60 Agri Export Zones (AEZ) have been set up across the country

3.3.2 *Policies for Entrepreneurship Development in Indian Service Sector*

- Services Exports from India Scheme (SEIS)
- National Digital Communications Policy 2018
- National Tourism Policy 2015
- National Health Policy 2017
- National Education Policy, 2016
- Foreign Direct Investment Policy
- Goods and Service Tax

- Drafted Trade Facilitation in Services (TFS) for addressing the issues pertinent to transparency, streamlining procedures and eliminating bottlenecks[31]
- Association of South-East Asian Nation (ASEAN) and India signed a Free Trade Agreement (FTA), with effect from 1st July 2015
- In terms of promotional measures, India organised Global Exhibition on Services (GEC) in April 2017

3.3.3 *Policies for Entrepreneurship Development in Indian Manufacturing Sector*

- Make in India Initiative
- Skill India Initiative
- Startup India
- National Manufacturing Policy

3.4 Institutional Support for Entrepreneurs in India

Entrepreneurship is impacted by several influencing factors; individual, environmental, socioeconomics and institutional setups. The environment and the institutional setups are exerting direct influence on entrepreneurship. Specifically, an institutional support system helps in guiding entrepreneurship development and facilitates the way entrepreneurs behave.[32] An attempt is made here to perceive entrepreneurship development from the perspective of the institutional support system. Figure 1 depicts the promotional agencies and institutions which are engaged in development of entrepreneurship in India. These institutions are working in the area of technical guidance, financial support and training. In India 93 percent of the workforce are associated with the unorganized sector, thus having such overwhelming number, it will be incumbent on the government to maintain this avenue for their survival.

[31]Ministry of Finance, Government of India. op. cit.

[32]Welter, F. & Smallbone, D. (2011). "Institutional Perspectives on Entrepreneurial Behaviour in Challenging Environments". *Journal of Small Business Management,* 49 (1), 107–125.

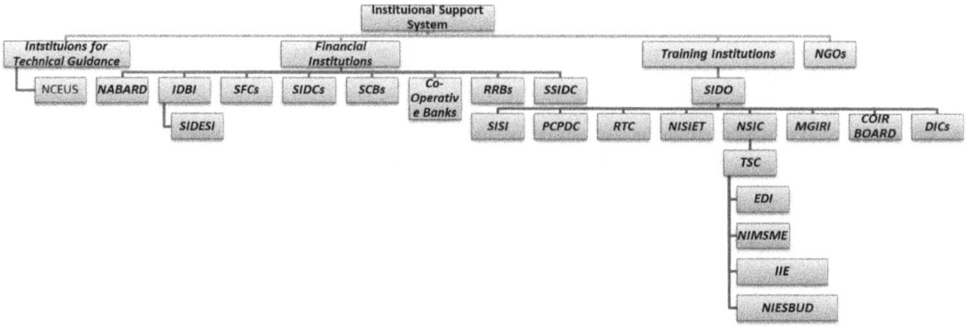

Figure 1: Institutional support system in India

Source: Prepared by author.

The Government of India undertook several initiatives and established a National Commission for Enterprises in the Unorganised Sector (NCEUS) on 20 September,[33] to achieve the goal of a Common Minimum Programme that committed itself "*to ensure the welfare and well-being of all workers, particularly those in the unorganised sector*". It has been recommended by this commission that any enterprise working in the unorganised sector must receive technical, marketing and credit support. Later, financial institutions like the National Bank for Agriculture and Rural Development (NABARD) was designated as an apex development bank in the country. The bank was established in 1982 by a Special Act of Parliament, with a mandate to uplift rural India. It plays a significant role in attracting rural youth, district industrial rural projects (DRIPs) and rural entrepreneurship development programs (REDPs).

Similarly, the Industrial development bank of India (IDBI), through its subsidiary Small Industries Development Bank of India (SIDBI) ensures the flow of financial and non-financial assistance to the small-scale sector. The Small Industries Development Organization (SIDO) was established in 1954 to develop support services for the promotion of small sectors. These autonomous bodies facilitate entrepreneurs by providing them with training, testing facilities, preparation of project proposals and

[33]National Commission for Enterprises in the Unorganised Sector, Academic Foundation (2008). "Report on Conditions of Work and Promotion of Livelihoods in the Unorganised Sector". New Delhi, India.

product profiles, technical and managerial consultancy etc. SIDO has promoted the following institutes and centres and is responsible for their management; *Small Industries Service Institutes* (SISI), *Product-cum-Process Development Centres* (PCPDC), *Regional Training Centre* (RTC). SIDO also controls the affairs of the *National Institute for Small Industries Extension Training* (NISIET) Hyderabad, *National Institute for Entrepreneurship and Small Business Development* (NIESBUD) New Delhi, and integrated training centres at Nilokheri, Haryana. The National Small Industries Corporation (NSIC) Ltd. supplies machinery and equipment, financial assistance, assistance for arranging raw materials, and marketing assistance. For technical support in the small scale sector NSIC established Technical Services Centres (TSC) which include; *Entrepreneurship Development of India* (EDI), *National Institute for Micro, Small and Medium Enterprises* (NI-MSME) in Hyderabad, NIESBUD at New Okhla Industrial Development Authority (NOIDA) in Uttar Pradesh, and the *Indian Institute of Entrepreneurship* (IIE) at Guwahati, as autonomous societies. These institutes undertake training programs, research activities and consultancy for promoting entrepreneurship. Furthermore, for strengthening research and development activities at village level, a separate national level institute was constituted called the Mahatma Gandhi Institute for Rural Industrialization (MGIRI) in association with the Indian Institute of Technology (IIT), Delhi.

3.5 Examples of Entrepreneurial Ventures

From the agriculture and services sector, these entrepreneurs are putting great effort towards the growth of their businesses and are also supporting the growth of entrepreneurship in India, showing a pathway to others.

3.5.1 *Legex*

Legex was founded in January 2019 with a vision to make legal processes accessible to individuals and organisations alike using technical infrastructure and assistance from professionals (Figure 2). In terms of implementation, the startup intends to cover Delhi NCR, after which other major cities will also be covered.

Figure 2: Service provided by Legex

Source: Legex.

The idea of *Legex* was a collective vision of Mr. Vishesh, Mr. Akshit, Mr. Aayush and Mr. Niraj. They feel that the service sector has plenty of challenges, but with right business acumen, they can be channeled into opportunities. The best way to identify opportunities is to observe and discuss. These two abilities help one to connect ideas and perceptions, which is necessary to build something that people need. The founders feel that "*As for the problems, no one can explain the problem in a better way than the actual stakeholder in the process*". So, the most efficient way they have found to date is to identify people who can discuss the problems frankly, the issues, and underlying reasons for those problems, be it existing processes or the product. They believe that problem identification is the first task and later, in handling these problems there can never be 'one' person who can do everything; therefore, start-ups need to understand this as early as possible. So, to solve any major problem, they seek people, friends, connections or even LinkedIn who can help them focus on their work. This also helps them to remaining on-track and getting their developments validated regularly from these external parties.

In recent years, there has been a major push for digital development in India, which in turn has made people more aware and tech-trusting. Even for legal processes, they are witnessing a strong trust factor in the market, which they feel would not have been present four years ago.

As for the legal domain, one of the main hindrances is closed access. It is difficult for those outside of the legal profession to get acquainted with the law and understand the know-how of the market. Also, there has not been much emphasis from the government on reform of the legal sector and processes are not dissimilar to those of a decade or two ago. One of the other biggest hurdles is the recognition of the sector. There are not a lot of government bids or 'Call-for-Proposals' that even consider legal accessibility as a cause for the betterment of society. The same applies to investors as well. If these things are addressed properly, the domain will surely get a technical and infrastructure boost, which is crucial for the ecosystem. There will be a huge upsurge if the government and investors begin taking consideration of the legal-tech domain.

3.5.2 *Raravis Innovations*

Raravis Innovations aims to provide measurement solutions to Out of Home (OOH) advertising agencies using computers and deep learning. They are based in Delhi and operate from a co-working space provided by the Design Innovation Center (DIC), University of Delhi. They started building this venture in March 2019, and so far, have built their beta version of the product. In this journey, they have been supported by HubSpot, General Catalyst and Design Innovation Center and they are enrolled in the prestigious, Y Combinator Startup School. By the end of 2020, they aim to take this venture to international markets. The founders believe in not only deciphering opportunities but that one must look outward with alacrity and assess the market demand for services. The Government of India's initiative, 'Startup India' has been a great concept as well as a few other government schemes that have assisted their journey. These include:

- Registration and recognition policy
- Startup patent filing process (80 percent reduction in fee)
- Startup Hub (they enlist various opportunities, resources and events on a single platform)

The most crucial and important thing any entrepreneur or startup needs are mentorships, capital and infrastructure support to build a better entrepreneurial ecosystem. Governments and/or institutions should focus on providing these things to early-stage startups without any hesitation. There should also be networking opportunities with potential investors, clients, governments and other stakeholders, organising regular events and competitions. As Raravis are building a hardware and SaaS platform for the OOH advertising industry, the major problem they are facing is finding talent in the hardware domain and getting it protected through patent or copyright. They believe the government or other agencies should ensure consultancy to early-stage ventures.

3.5.3 *Apna Haat*

Apna Haat provides free home delivery/instore access of sorted/graded, digitally weighed, farm fresh produce at very competitive prices to consumers in Gaziabad and Bangalore regions of India.

Apna Haat was started in March 2014, by a team of Agribusiness management graduates in India, with Mr Sanjeev and Mr Vibhesh Mishra as founders. Initially, it started with a home delivery model only in the Gaziabad region of India, but after six months of operation, the founders realised that going forward it can only be sustainable by an omni-channel model. They opened their first physical store in December 2015.

Apna Haat believes in the philosophy that "*the hand that grows the crop should be the one to earn from it*". The founders felt that intermediaries in India are taking away the farmers' share and making consumers pay for it. Despite India being an agrarian economy, the political and social system does not benefit the farmers. Therefore, this group of young agribusiness professionals are sensitive towards the needs of farmers and as end consumers witnessing this discrepancy, decided to start a venture that would bring the farmers' products directly to consumers, thereby minimising the chain of intermediaries. At Apna Haat, consumers are getting fresh fruit and vegetables at very reasonable prices, and of extremely good quality and the farmers are getting the real monetary value of their products. The enterprise works on a two-pronged strategy:

1. Developing farmers & their economic well-being:
   — Providing technical know-how to improve crop productivity & quality
   — Encouraging use of technology to improve supply chain efficiency
   — Link to market/consumption to improve per unit return
2. Empowering agri-entrepreneurs & creating opportunities for the socially underprivileged:
   — Develop consolidators at farm level
   — Develop pushcart vendors & small kirana stores
   — Improve their earning capacities

Image 1: Apna haat founders, stores and initiatives

Source: Apna Haat.

Apna Haat strongly believes in environmental sustainability which is reflected in their initiatives like the 'polythene ban' and 'refuelled'. Startups like Apna Haat are serving society and giving a strong message to the government as well as emerging entrepreneurs to take proactive steps towards sustainability and empowerment.

3.5.4 *Wellversed Health*

Wellversed Health is a tech-enabled health food manufacturing company that was started in 2017 and facilitates the production of customised clinical food products specific to the health requirements of demography or an individual. The unique manufacturing framework developed by Wellversed Health allows personalisation of food per clinical, dietary and physiological demands of a particular health condition. This enables creation of precision food with the desired nutrition composition and ingredients in a quality-controlled environment.

The co-founders of Wellversed Health — Aanan Khurma, Aditya Seth & Ripunjay Chachan — are alumni of Stanford Biodesign — a multidisciplinary fellowship for Healthcare Innovation conceived through a collaboration between Stanford University, AIIMS, and IIT Delhi.

This realm of food manufacturing represents a paradigm-shift for it removes the need for large capital and dedicated machinery to manufacture different products with different nutritional composition and ingredients. The team is working towards advanced machine learning algorithms that will determine the right combination of ingredients and the precise ratio of ingredients to achieve the desired nutrition level along with perfect taste profile and texture of the food product.

The founders believe that a preventive health mechanism is required in India to promote a healthy life because a majority of health-related problems arise through the wrong lifestyle choices.

Using demand data for personalised nutrition, the company realised in late 2018 that there is a separate niche in the market for low carb health products that are required by people with diabetes, thyroid and other chronic issues. Wellversed launched a separate brand called **Ketofy**, which is emerging as one of the leading low carb brands in India.

Image 2: Wellversed founders

Source: Wellversed Health.

3.6 Conclusion

Entrepreneurship in India is emerging and the complete ecosystem of the country is in support of it. There is increasing scope for entrepreneurs in the fields of agriculture, food processing, service sector and other industries. The Government of India is also coming up with supportive policies and institutions to align + with the needs of entrepreneurs. Entrepreneurs are finding scope in niche areas of food, technology and sustainability.

https://doi.org/10.1142/9789811212741_0004

Chapter 4

Entrepreneurship in Punjab

Priyanka Sharma and Sandeep Singh

4.1 Introduction

Punjab is one of the most prosperous states in northern India. The State is circumscribed by the Indian states of Jammu and Kashmir toward the north, Himachal Pradesh toward the east, Haryana toward the south and southeast, Rajasthan toward the southwest, and the Pakistani region of Punjab toward the west. It covers a territory of 50,362 sq. km, 1.53 percent of India's total land mass. Punjab is the 20th biggest Indian State by territory. It is the 16th biggest State by population, containing 22 districts at the 2011 enumeration with 27,704,236 occupants. Punjab's geographical reach covers 29.30° North to 32.32° North and longitudes 73.55° East to 76.50° East.[1] Punjabi is the official language of the State and is the most spoken language with Punjabis the primary ethnic group of the State, comprising Sikhs at 58 percent and Hindus at 38 percent. Image 1 shows the Golden Temple in Amritsar, Punjab. The capital of Punjab is Chandigarh, a Union Territory and furthermore the capital of Haryana the neighbouring state. Punjab was established in 1947 when the Partition of India split the previous Raj territory of Punjab between India and Pakistan. The majority Sikh region in the East became India's Punjab State and the majority Muslim representation in the West became Pakistan's, Punjab State. In Punjab, there are 22 regions, 168 statutory

[1]Gosal, G. (2004). "Physical Geography of the Punjab". *JPS*, 11(1), 20.

Image 1: Golden Temple

Source: © 2012 Sanyam Bahga https://commons.wikimedia.org/wiki/File:Khalsa_Heritage_Memorial_176_Edit.jpg Sanyam Bahga [CC BY-SA (https://creativecommons.org/licenses/by-sa/3.0)].

and 69 enumeration towns with an aggregate of 237 towns (or state urban communities). Significant urban areas of Punjab incorporate Mohali, Ludhiana, Amritsar, Patiala and Jalandhar.[2] One of the world's most established and first human advancements, the Indus Valley Civilization spread over a significant part of the Punjab area, with urban communities, for example, Harappa and Mohenjodaro now situated in the cutting edge Pakistani region of Punjab. In the world, Punjab has one of the oldest and richest cultures. Its assorted variety and uniqueness are apparent in Punjabi science, history, philosophy, traditions, spirituality, education, technology, artistry, values, cuisine, poetry, military warfare, architecture, and music. The empathy and liveliness shown in the way of life of individuals of Punjab are difficult to miss. While the individuals of Punjab are known for their solid assurance, their way of life introduces a multi-shaded legacy of ancient civilizations. Image 2 shows Jaliyalwalabagh Massacre Memorial Monument in Amritsar, Punjab.

[2]Government of Punjab, India (2019). "Know Punjab". http://punjab.gov.in/know-punjab 2019. [Accessed 27 July 2019].

Image 2: Jaliyalwalabagh Massacre Memorial Monument

Source: © 2019 Prasanthnaduvath https://commons.wikimedia.org/wiki/File:Jaliyalwalabagh_massacre_memmorial_monument.jpg Prasanthnaduvath [CC BY-SA (https://creativecommons.org/licenses/by-sa/4.0)].

4.2 Historical Overview

Formerly, Punjab has encountered numerous changes and disturbances, which have impacted the way in which it has developed. The area of Punjab has historically experienced unusual changes. During the rule of Akbar (1556–1605 AD) the terminology 'Punjab' was broadly utilized. During the rule of Ranjit Singh in 1799–1839 Punjab was known as the Kingdom of Lahore. In 1849 the British consolidated Delhi and the Hisar division of the previous Northwest State (now Uttar Pradesh) with Punjab in 1858. In 1901, Punjab's outskirt regions arranged over the Indus were removed to frame the Northwest Frontier State. Delhi region was separated from Punjab in 1912. Image 3 shows the map of Punjab province in 1909. Punjab was divided into two sections West Punjab (Pakistan) and East Punjab (India) in 1947 and only 1,52,649 sq. km and 13 districts were left in Indian Punjab out of 3,59,179 sq. km and 29 zones. The two Punjab's were segregated on religious grounds. The generally backward eastern part stayed in India and the most prosperous and creative western

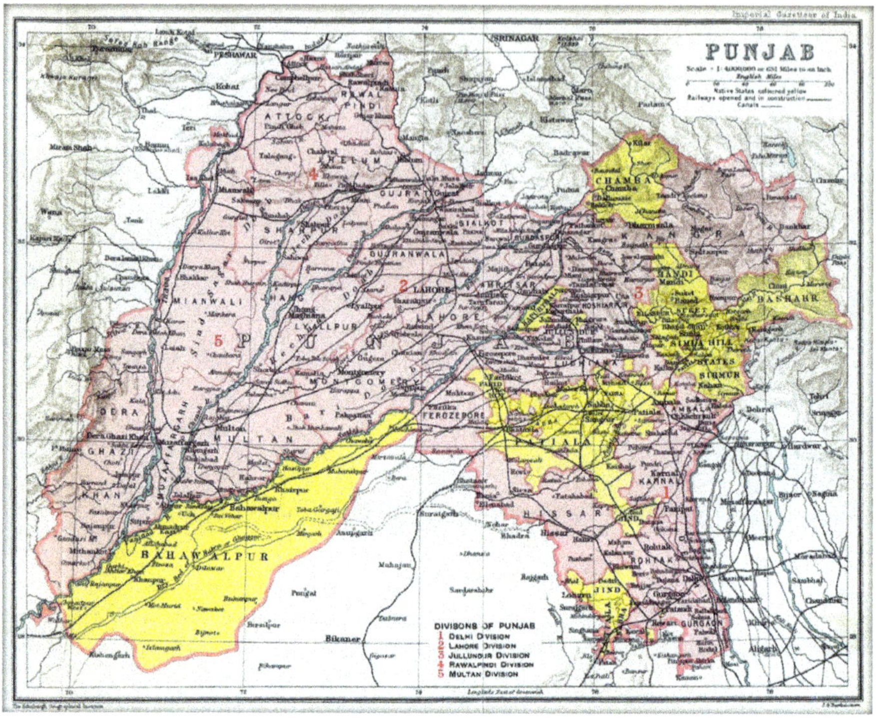

Image 3: Punjab province in 1909

Source: Wikimedia (Public Domain) https://commons.wikimedia.org/wiki/File:Punjab_1909.jpg [Public domain].

part went to Pakistan. Upon revamping of the States based on linguistics in 1956, the previous Patiala and East Punjab States Union (PEPSU) region was merged with Punjab.[3]

Punjab was additionally revamped in 1966 under the Reorganization Act 1966. There was a strong interest in the rearrangement of the State on a linguistic premise so that local sentiment could correspond with the State's advancement. On 1 November 1966, the Punjabi speaking territories were removed from modern Punjab. The Hindi speaking regions in the north were converged with Himachal Pradesh and the southern Hindi

[3]Punjab Development Report (2014). "Profile of Development and Change — Ch 1". http://planningcommission.nic.in/plans/stateplan/sdr_punjab/sdrpun_ch1.pdf. 2014. [Accessed 4 June 2019].

speaking zones were established in another State, Haryana. Punjab turned out to be linguistically homogeneous and fundamentally compact after the rearrangement. In 1966, the Punjabi speaking state comprised 11 areas, including Rupnagar. As stated by Kant,[4] in 1956 the rearrangement reduced Punjab to approximately two-fifths of its size after the merger of PEPSU, and before independence this was one-seventh the zone of Punjab.

The Punjab State cannot take equal pride in industrial advancement as in agriculture (farming). According to Dana[5] an activity which prompted more withdrawals from the business sector during the 1880s was when well established, reputed local firms were defrauded by British partners. At the time of Partition in 1947, the State acquired a weak industrial base, as most of the industrial undertakings and the territories providing crude materials stayed in West Punjab (Pakistan). Image 4 shows the Wagah Border which is located between Amritsar (Punjab) and Lahore (Pakistan), which has

Image 4: Wagah Border, between Amritsar (Punjab) and Lahore (Pakistan)

Source: © 2019 Guilhem Vellut https://commons.wikimedia.org/wiki/File:Wagah_border_ceremony2.jpg Guilhem Vellut [CC BY (https://creativecommons.org/licenses/by/2.0)].

[4]Kant, S. (1988). *Administrative Geography of India*. Rawat Publications, Jaipur.

[5]Dana, L.-P. (2000). "Creating Entrepreneurs in India". *Journal of Small Business Management*, 38(1), 86–91, p. 87.

transformed into the primary border crossing is known for the elaborate ceremony after the Partition of Punjab. Dread and frenzy kept entrepreneurs from putting resources into enterprises in a State with an historically sensitive surrounding and an unfriendly neighbour. Punjab needed to pay for the wars of 1962, 1965 and 1971 and these brought about a further drain of capital from the State. In addition to the revamping of the State, whatever industrial complexes Punjab had gone when Delhi went to Haryana and forest & mineral resources went to Himachal Pradesh in 1966.[6]

At the time of independence, Punjab had only a couple of hundred industrial units primarily handling foodgrains, brick kilns and cotton ginning. The majority of fabricated things, of even basic use originated from outside. Until 1954, private enterprises were not promoted since India's first Prime Minister (Jawaharlal Nehru) did not encourage enterprise in the private sector even after the independence of India.[7] During the post-independence period, industrial improvement in Punjab occurred in stages. Subsequently, in the 1950s, the cycle-parts and hosiery ventures took their foundations, while in the 1960s, with the approach of the green revolution, agri-business related enterprises like farm machinery assembly came up. The focus in the 1970s was around such enterprises as car parts and electronics and during the 1980s on asset-based ventures such as vanaspati, food processing, consumable and non-consumable oils and sugar in a major way. The expansion of industry had begun, with the procedure of advancement and monetary changes, while a considerable amount of built-up processing units, both in the small, medium and large divisions were under pressure. The industrial sector in the State is in the throes of an extremely noteworthy period of progress with serious difficulties and numerous new chances.[8] The State's financial presentation has changed over various periods. According to Department of Planning, during 1965–1966 to 1975–1976, the economy developed at a pace of 4.8 percent as compared to 3.5 percent in the national economy.

Advancement in a State is the result of the interaction of an assortment of elements, for example, geographical, political, financial, and

[6]Punjab Development Report. op. cit.

[7]Dana. op. cit.

[8]Punjab Development Report. op. cit.

statistical. Being an outlying State (Punjab), both internal and external changes have impacted its advancement. The State was initially apportioned in 1947 and then trifurcated into Punjab, Haryana and Himachal Pradesh in 1966. The time of militancy, in the recent past, because of an internal emergency, had its own effect on forming the development pattern of Punjab. In spite of this, it has been able to make astounding progress in achieving conditions for a superior standard of life.[9]

In entrepreneurship, as per Dana and Anderson,[10] the most significant role is played by cultural perception. According to Batra,[11] the improvement of entrepreneurship in Punjab as in numerous parts of the nation has only been quantitative and not subjective, which is a progressively significant part of enterprise. Subjective parts of business enterprise concerns have coupled with the compelling presentation of entrepreneurs in changed financial and administrative fields. A large portion of small units are described by uneven or low-quality production, poor money related administration, low productivity and insufficient marketing know-how. The primary reason for the terrible showing of small entrepreneurs is because of the absence of administrative capability and experience. Dana[12] highlighted that India has a distinctive population base and diverse culture from which it is difficult to single out a business entrepreneurship.

The industrial structure in Punjab is denominated by small scale enterprises. The limitation of advancement in the small sector and its inability to match quality over the large-scale industries are the result of many variables. Punjab does not have numerous rich industrialists to put resources into large-scale industry and investment by the central government has been pitiful. As a result of the proximity with Pakistan, entrepreneurs from government offices and different parts of India have been hesitant to put resources into large industries. What is more, the absence of petroleum derivatives and metallic minerals required for the

[9]ibid.

[10]Dana, L.-P. & Anderson, R.B. (Eds.) (2007). *International Handbook of Research on Indigenous Entrepreneurship*. UK and Northampton, Massachusetts: Edward Elgar, Cheltenham.

[11]Batra, G.S. (2002). *Development of Entrepreneurship*. Deep and Deep Publications. New Delhi.

[12]Dana. op. cit.

establishment of large-scale businesses constrained industrialists in embracing small-scale ventures.[13]

During 1973–1974 small-scale enterprises in Punjab represented more than three-fifths of all industrial production versus two-fifths at the national level and with this, we can assess the power of small-scale industries in Punjab. Since 1966 small-scale enterprises have developed exponentially. As stated by Singh,[14] the total number of small-scale industrial units expanded from 8,023 in 1966 to 2,00,603 in 2000–2001. The workforce utilized in small-scale industries expanded from 56,000 to 8,97,417 during the same period. During 1966–1967 to 2000–2001, production expanded from Rs. 200 crore to Rs. 19,525 crore, fixed investment expanded from Rs. 60 crore to Rs. 4,250 crore, and perunit average fixed investment expanded from Rs. 0.74 lakh to Rs. 1.89 lakh with employment generated per crore rupees invested dropping from 933 to 211. The number of units in the small-scale sector developed at a rate of 9.6 percent per annum, while employment provided expanded at an annual pace of 8.2 percent, with the outcome that the average per unit of people employed declined from seven in 1966–1967 to four in 2000–2001, during the same period. Employment generated per crore rupees contributed was 614 people in the 1980s versus 342 in the 1990s.[15]

According to Singh,[16] large-scale industrial units expanded from 122 in 1966 to 132 in 1974–1975, and from 355 in 1989–1990 to 638 in 2000–2001. The workforce utilized in this segment expanded from 42,735 to 57,891 to 1,69,801 and 2,51,890 respectively during the same period. Average fixed investment per unit in 1989–1990 was Rs. 868.4 lakh, which expanded to Rs. 1,254.6 lakh by 1992–1993. During 1966–1967 to 2000–2001, per unit average fixed investment expanded from Rs. 85.2 lakh to Rs. 2,416.7 lakh, fixed investment expanded from Rs. 104 crore to Rs. 17,000 crore, production expanded from Rs. 93 crore to Rs. 35,600 crore, and the employment generated per crore rupees invested dropped from 411 to less than 15. Since the early 1990s, average fixed investment per unit has begun

---

[13]Punjab Development Report. op. cit.

[14]Singh, H. (2001). *Green Revolution Reconsidered: The Rural World of Contemporary Punjab*. Oxford University Press. New Delhi.

[15]Punjab Development Report. op. cit.

[16]Singh. op. cit.

expanding strongly. Medium to large industries have turned out to be generally more capital intensive in contrast to small-scale enterprises. In the 1980s, employment generated per crore rupees invested resources in large & medium industry was 88 people versus 24 in the 1990s.[17]

As stated by Abbi and Singh,[18] after some time, small-scale enterprises in Punjab are connecting to large-scale industries as ancillaries. Subsequently, their production procedures are becoming increasingly modernized. However, small-scale units are still backward, and as a rule rely upon moderately less skilled workers, willing to accept employment with low compensation and poor working conditions. This makes openings for work unattractive for the educated youth, and because of this unemployment for the educated continues to rise at a disturbing rate despite an amazing rate of development in industrial production. On entrepreneurship, social capital has a major impact as highlighted by Zelekha and Dana[19] and Frese and Gielnik.[20]

Punjab is a great example of a rapidly developing economy with agriculture as its foundation. Image 5 shows agricultural fields of Punjab during the monsoon. The State today contributes almost 40 percent of wheat and 60 percent of rice secured for dispersion through the public distribution system. A dynamic blend of the water system, manure and a high-yielding assortment of seeds established the framework — a procedure, which was further reinforced by agricultural credit societies, village electricity, rural link roads and an assortment of expansion administrations. Likewise, Punjab advanced the 'White Revolution', bringing about the most astounding per capita accessibility of milk to individuals. Another noticeable component of the State's economy is agro-based and agro-situated industrialization. The efforts are no less commendable in

---

[17]Punjab Development Report. op. cit.

[18]Abbi, B.L. & Singh, K. (1997). *Post Green Revolution Rural Punjab: A Profile of Economic and Socio-Cultural Change (1965–95).* Centre for Research in Rural and Industrial Development Publishers, Chandigarh.

[19]Zelekha, Y., & Dana, L.-P. (2019). "Social Capital Versus Cultural Capital Determinants of Entrepreneurship: An Empirical Study of the African Continent". *The Journal of Entrepreneurship*, 28(2), 250–269.

[20]Frese, M. & Gielnik, M.M. (2014). "The Psychology of Entrepreneurship". *Annual Review Organisational Psychology Organisational Behaviour*, 1(1), 413–438.

Image 5: Agricultural fields of Punjab during the monsoon

Source: © 2019 Sanyam Bahga https://commons.wikimedia.org/wiki/File:Punjab_Monsoon.jpg Sanyam Bahga [CC BY-SA (https://creativecommons.org/licenses/by-sa/3.0)].

reinforcing the infrastructure, particularly the water system and power in the State. The combined impact of this is reflected in the highest income per capita being in Punjab since its development in 1966, and with Punjab holding this prestigious position for a majority of years.[21]

Agriculture is the pillar of Punjab's economy and other significant ventures incorporate assembling of scientific instruments, electrical merchandise, finance related administration, machinery, materials, sewing machines and so on. Punjab has gained extensive financial ground after Independence in spite of the mishap it endured in 1947. It contributes about 66 percent of the total production of food grains and 33 percent of milk production of the nation. Punjab is the main producer of wheat, consequently adding to national food security. The 'Green Revolution' (a noteworthy farming activity) has been advanced by individuals of Punjab. Despite the fact that Punjabis represent fewer than 2.5 percent of the Indian population, they are one of the most prosperous ethnic groups in India, and

[21] Punjab Development Report. op. cit.

Image 6: Khalsa Heritage Memorial Complex, Anandpur Sahib

Source: © 2012 Sanyam Bahga https://commons.wikimedia.org/wiki/File:Khalsa_Heritage_Memorial_176_Edit.jpg Sanyam Bahga [CC BY-SA (https://creativecommons.org/licenses/by-sa/3.0)]

their per capita income is double the national average. Punjab is considered to have the best infrastructure in India; incorporating river, rail, road and air transport connections that extend throughout the region. Image 6 shows Khalsa Heritage Memorial Complex, Anandpur Sahib. Punjab likewise has the lowest poverty rate in India and has also won the best State performance award, in view of statistical data accumulated by the Indian Government.[22]

Punjab's economy is the 14th largest State economy in India with ₹5.18 lakh crore (US$75 billion) in gross domestic product (GDP) and per capita GDP of ₹153,000 (US$2,200).[23,24] The State occupies a noteworthy third

---

[22]Government of Punjab, India. op. cit.

[23]Ministry of Statistics and Programme Implementation (MoSPI), Government of India (2019). "MoSPI Gross State Domestic Product", https://en.wikipedia.org/wiki/Ministry_of_Statistics_and_Programme_Implementation. [Accessed 9 June 2019].

[24]Economic and Statistical Organization Government of Punjab (ESO) (2017). "State Wise Data". http://www.esopb.gov.in/Static/PDF/GSDP/Statewise-Data/StateWiseData.pdf. [Accessed 30 June 2019].

Image 7: Qila Mubarak

Source: © 2019 Nitin544 https://commons.wikimedia.org/wiki/File:Qila_Mubarak_In_2015.jpg Nitin544 [CC BY-SA (https://creativecommons.org/licenses/by-sa/4.0)]

place among Indian states in human advancement.[25] Punjab is essentially agriculture-based because of the accessibility and proximity of rich water sources and ripe soil.[26] Other enterprises include manufacturing of scientific instruments, financial services, horticultural merchandise, textiles, tourism, electrical products, mechanical devices, sewing machines, sports merchandise, starch, garments, manure, bicycles and the processing of pine oil and sugar. Minerals and vitamin products also contribute to Punjab's economy but to lesser degree. Punjab has the biggest number of steel rolling factory plants in India, located in 'Steel Town', which is in Mandi Gobindgarh in the Fatehgarh Sahib area. Image 7 shows Qila Mubarak in Bhatinda, Punjab.

[25]Global Data Lab. Institute for Management Research, Radboud University (2018). "Subnational HDI — Area Database". https://globaldatalab.org/shdi/shdi/ [Accessed 15 April 2019].
[26]Overseas Indian Facilitation Centre (2011). "Punjab". https://web.archive.org/web/20111010150641/http://m.oifc.in/Our-Partners/State-Partners/Punjab. [Accessed 10 June 2019].

4.3 Environment for Entrepreneurship and Micro Small and Medium Enterprises (MSME)

Independence was distinguished by a surge in the entrepreneurial sector. With the newly discovered opportunities, entrepreneurs plucked up the courage and conviction to chase their entrepreneurial dreams. The need for work and territorial improvements cleared the route for start-ups. During this period strategies were not detailed with any extraordinary focus on entrepreneurship. Improvement of existing ventures on a large scale was initially the core focus. In developing nations globalization is threatening small businesses. Also, on small business debt, banks charge high loan costs and the absence of capital originates from poverty in India.[27]

The following couple of decades saw critical development in entrepreneurial ventures crossing financial and social divisions. With the evolving situation, entrepreneurship increased in significance. The most recent decade has seen critical improvements in the nature of start-ups in Punjab. Institutions have begun to recognise business and academic enthusiasm for start-ups. Over the last couple of years, they have displayed potential and capability, which has directed global, financial specialists to explore Punjab's start-up ecosystem.

Punjab is a place known for rich green fields and an energetic entrepreneurial culture. It is one of the fastest developing States of the nation. With an amicable industrial atmosphere, dynamic and promotional steps have been taken by the Punjab Government and financial backing has been supported by the Government of India, opening doors for the establishment of MSME ventures that have expanded in complexity in the State. As indicated by Dana,[28] to change the social attitude with respect to entrepreneurship, efforts have been made to encourage entrepreneurs by giving youth the self-assurance to be high achievers.

Punjab is known for the enterprising spirit of its people, which has made the State a focal point for small and medium enterprises. Presently the State needs to adapt to innovation and knowledge driven enterprises

---

[27] Bhensdadia, R.V. & Dana, L.-P. (2004). "Globalisation and Rural Poverty". *International Journal of Entrepreneurship and Innovation Management*, 4(5), 458–468.

[28] Dana. op. cit.

and develop another culture of innovation. For the future development of the State's economy, entrepreneurship and innovation are essential. To build and strengthen the innovation and entrepreneurship ecosystem, Punjab supports a cluster specific, bottom up approach. In order to encourage learning and connections, the State follows an entrepreneur-centric approach. By bringing entrepreneurs together in a domain that catalyzes learning, the State also facilitates networking between entrepreneurs and entrepreneurship support organizations.[29]

Punjab has been named as the place that is known for entrepreneurs and has enlisted in excess of 140 start-ups with the Department of Industrial Policy and Promotion (DIPP) as of August 2018, and the number is increasing every day. As stated by Singal,[30] numerous unregistered start-ups are working in the area, and in order to avail themselves of the incentives offered by the central government, youths are approaching the DIPP to get their ventures listed, Newly enrolled start-ups are exempt of income tax, alongside taxes on investments and capital gains for three years as indicated by the DIPP guidelines. Likewise, they can also obtain 80 percent discount on patent filings alongside other different incentives.

One of the most mainstream start-up areas in Punjab, Mohali has been created as an Information Technology (IT) hub by the Punjab Government, while Chandigarh has seen a blend of start-ups entering the ecosystem. The city is delivering different gems, from education platforms like WizIQ and Edurev to online business start-ups such as Jumbo Basket and Pumpkart. Additionally, to further push their dreams towards the real world, organizations like the Chandigarh Angels Network are approaching and supporting start-ups with development potential. Even though there have been high points and low points in the pursuit of new ventures, the result is what is important.

Today's youth are very aware of open doors in the field of entrepreneurship, and different initiatives by both private associations and

[29]Government of Punjab (2018). "Startup and Entrepreneurship". https://pbindustries.gov.in/static/policy_framework;Key=Startup_and_Entrepreneurship. [Accessed 21 June 2019].
[30]Singal, A. (2019, Jan 4) "Could Chandigarh be the Next Silicon Valley of India?" *Entrepreneur India.* https://www.entrepreneur.com/article/325794. [Accessed 30 May 2019].

government have additionally cultivated the start-up culture in Punjab. One such open door is Franchise India's Startup Summit 2019, which is India's forerunner as a trusted business and tradeshow and is one of the biggest emerging forums for competitors to learn and network.

As per advance estimates, Punjab's industrial sector, which contributes 24.51 percent to GDP expanded by 4.52 percent during 2017–2018, compared to four percent growth in the industrial sector of the national economy. Punjab's Government has instructed the 'Industrial & Business Development Policy-2017' to return the State to the high levels of development and prosperity and give a further lift to the industrial sector in the State. For sustainable industrial growth of Punjab, the policy is an all-encompassing structure with eight key mainstays that the policy is built around, which are: — Start-up and Entrepreneurship, ease of doing business, micro, small and medium enterprises (MSME), power, skill development, infrastructure, fiscal and non-fiscal incentives and stakeholder engagement upheld by sector specific strategies for development. In order to encourage investment in Punjab, the policy offers alluring open doors for organizations. The Punjab Government has also given a power subsidy amounting to Rs. 1440 crore by subsidising power at Rs. 5 per unit to industry.

In the Bathinda district of Punjab, there is a renowned refinery project on more than 200 acres of land with nine million metric tonnes per annum capacity and is the largest investment project with Rs. 21,500 crore, which has been set up by HPCL-Mittal Energy Ltd. (HMEL). It is a single location and this project promotes downstream Polypropylene/Petroleum based small and medium scale enterprises.

As of 31 March 2017, there was around 1.72 lakh enlisted micro, small, medium and large industrial units in Punjab employing about 15.26 people, with a fixed investment of Rs. 86324 crore. In 2016–2017 these industrial units had a total production of Rs. 201590 crore, which included yarn and textiles, hosiery goods, automobile parts, sewing machine parts, hand tools and machine tools, leather goods, bicycles and cycle parts, and sports goods. Recently, Punjab's export performance has been impressive. Total exports from Punjab during the year 2014–2015 to 2016–2017 were Rs. 27,235 crore, Rs. 27,747 crore and Rs. 29,300 crore respectively. (Table 1).

Table 1: The progressive growth of the industrial sector in Punjab from 2011 to 2017

	Units (No.)			Employment (No.)			Investment (Rs. Crore)			Production (Rs. Crore)		
Year	SSU	L&M	Total	SSU	L&M	Total	SSU	L&M	Total	SSU	L&M	Total
2011–12	151977	380	152357	1033553	238589	1272142	9815	50176	59991	56184	92393	148577
2012–13	154421	428	154849	1077616	240293	1317909	11459	53705	65164	62971	77557	140528
2013–14	156518	445	156963	1112858	243820	1356678	12961	55244	68205	74606	91130	165736
2014–15	158655	454	159109	1139126	246087	1385213	14191	64652	78843	84630	87703	172333
2015–16	163460	457	163917	1199577	256641	1456218	15954	67069	83023	92114	95953	188067
2016–17	171450	469	171919	1258214	267625	1525839	16733	69591	86324	96617	104973	201590

Source: Department of Industries, Government of Punjab.

Note: SSU = Small Scale Units and L&M = Large & Medium.

As indicated in Table 1 there were 163,460 small scale industrial units with Rs. 15,954 crore investment generating employment to 12 Lac people with Rs. 92,114 crores turnover during 2015–2016 and these expanded to 171,450 with Rs. 16,733 crore fixed investment, employing 12.58 Lac people with Rs. 96,617 crore production value during 2016–2017. The number of large and medium scale industrial units was 457 with Rs. 67,069 crore fixed investment, employing 2.57 Lac people with Rs. 95,953 crore turnover during 2015–2016 and these units grew to 469 with Rs. 69,591 crore fixed investment, employing 2.68 Lac people with Rs. 104,973 crore turnover during 2016–2017.

The MSME division assumes a significant role in giving huge business openings at relatively lower capital expense and reduces regional imbalances by helping in the industrialization of rural & backward areas. It has also emerged as an engine for socio economic growth. The Central Government established the Micro, Small and Medium Enterprises Development (MSMED) Act 2006, which encourages and upgrades enterprises. Punjab recognizes that MSME has different needs at different stages. In 1956, to serve the recently combined Punjab, the Micro, Small and Medium Enterprises Development Institute was set up at Ludhiana. Presently, in the Punjab and U.T. Chandigarh this institute considers the needs of micro, small and medium enterprises.

Punjab has developed as centre for materials based ventures, for example, hosiery, apparel manufacturing and spinning exports, and another significant contributor to the economy of the State is the engineering sector, which in the course of the most recent decade, has grown 16 percent and contributes 23 percent of the total industrial output. The flourishing ecosystem of well settled MSMEs is the key strength of Punjab. The State has a strong base of MSME (micro, small and medium enterprises) units. Punjab has around 1.6 Lac MSME units, which are significant for industrial development. The industry of Punjab is directed by SMEs and has a rich, modern base of MSME units (auto components, hosiery, bicycle parts, agricultural implements, sports goods etc). For over four decades, until the 1990s, Punjab drove the country's industrial growth and gave rise to some of the prominent industrial houses.[31]

A comprehensive structure laid down by the Reserve Bank of India for recovery and restoration of poorly performing MSMEs, which accommodates other money-related aids, grant of additional assistance, rescheduling of payments, allows the sale of non-core assets of the business and rebuilding of credit benefited by MSME units from the banks. Under the Micro, Small and Medium Enterprises Development (MSMED) Act 2006 the MSE facilitation council has been set up.[32]

Notwithstanding this, the interest of women entrepreneurs in the Indian economy has expanded because of the explosion of microcredit projects and self-help groups, and because of these projects, an increase in women in the political sector. The UN Gender Inequality Index has positioned India underneath a few sub-Saharan African nations. Sexual orientation incongruities are increasingly articulated in financial interest and women's business conditions in India. Women entrepreneurs have differing educational backgrounds.[33] Women's entrepreneurship is progressively common in younger age groups in contrast with older age groups.[34] The majority of women entrepreneurs are in the lower and

---

[31]Industrial and Business Development Policy (2017). http://investpunjab.gov.in/Content/documents/Notifications/Industrial_and_Business_Development_Policy_2017.pdf. [Accessed 6 My 2019].

[32]ibid.

[33]Patole, M. & Ruthven, O. (2002). "Metro Moneylenders–Microcredit Providers for Delhi's Poor". *Small Enterprise Development*, 13(2), 36–45.

[34]Dhameja, S.K. (2002). *Women Entrepreneurs: Opportunities, Performance and Problems*. India: Deep and Deep Publications.

middle income groups[35] and have service oriented enterprises.[36] Women's entrepreneurship is currently advancing from pickles, papads and powders to distinguished fields like engineering.[37] Women entrepreneurs are currently developing as "techpreneurs".[38]

Out of all entrepreneurs, women entrepreneurs are a small percentage. For financial, social and comprehensive development, women entrepreneurs should be supported. Women entrepreneurs face clear difficulties in formal and informal parts of the economy identified by the State, which includes rural and urban areas and should facilitate conditions for women entrepreneurs to add to financial improvement. In different states and centrally supported schemes, the State encourages and creates awareness among women entrepreneurs. Women who have business ideas and are keen to begin their business ventures in Punjab are supported by the State providing specific schemes for women entrepreneurs.

The participation of women in management/ownership in the small-scale industries (SSIs) sector in Punjab is 30,190 and the number of women enterprises is 29,068. The number of female employees in the registered SSI sector is 11,757 and the unregistered sector is 36,013 with the percentage of female employment out of the total employment of Punjab at 5.26 percent.[39] (Development Commissioner — Ministry of MSME — Participation of Women in SSI Sector).

Indian women entrepreneurs have gone up against plenty of difficulties. Gaining access to simple and practical accounts and advertising is acknowledged as one of the more obvious obstacles by a large portion of women entrepreneurs.[40] High costs of raw materials, ponderous systems of permissions, enlistment and avoidance from banking and budgetary

---

[35]Vinze, M.D. (1987). *Women Entrepreneurs in India: A Socio-Economic Study of Delhi*, 1975–85. India: Mittal Publications.

[36]Gupta, D.D. (2013). "The Effect of Gender on Women-led Small Enterprises: The Case of India". *South Asian Journal of Business and Management Cases*, 2(1), 61–75.

[37]Munshi, S., Munshi, A., & Singh, V.P. (2011). "A Study on Trends Visible in Women Entrepreneur in India and Globally". *Asia Pacific Business Review*, 7(3), 155–166.

[38]Charantimath, P.M. (2005). *Entrepreneurship Development and Small Business Enterprise*. India: Pearson Education.

[39]Development Commissioner, Ministry of MSME (2019). "Participation of Women in SSI Sector". https://www.dcmsme.gov.in/ssiindia/census/ch11.htm. [Accessed 16 July 2019].

[40]Panandikar, S. (1985). "Women Entrepreneurs: Problems and Potentials". *The Economic Times*, p. 5. 26 December 1985.

administrations create hurdles for women entrepreneurs.[41] Women entrepreneurs are regularly tormented by fragile money related status. Absence of social and family collaboration and ignorance about different government plans and projects obstruct the advancement of women entrepreneurship.[42] Women entrepreneurs regularly report difficulties related to money, work and showcasing issues.[43] According to Das,[44] absence of income and working capital, lack of manufacturing knowledge and weight of family unit obligations represent a genuine test to women entrepreneurs in India.

4.4 Toward the Future — Government Initiative

For supporting development and start-ups the State has launched 'Start-up Punjab' to provide a solid ecosystem. With different central and state programs, Punjab will guarantee the necessary synergy and convergence, promoting start-ups, innovation and entrepreneurship. Punjab has a significant number of reputable, national level academic and research institutions. In order to leverage research and expertise capabilities, Punjab will connect with leading institutions of the State.[45]

Punjab supports setting up of incubation centres in academic institutions and universities. To promote an entrepreneurial culture in students, these incubation centres play a significant part. Additionally, Punjab promotes and provides essential support and offer different fiscal and non-fiscal incentives to accelerators and incubation centres led by the private sector. In order to boost the innovation ecosystem, Punjab facilitates creating adequate infrastructure, which would be formed in all districts across various sectors in the State. The Punjab Government, as with other State governments advanced their start-ups by means of offering waivers in electricity duty and stamp obligations for a period of seven years. The start-ups are additionally being given exclusion from payments of change

---

[41] Vinze. op. cit.

[42] Rao, C.H. (1991). "Promotion of Women Entrepreneurship". *Sedme*, 18(2), 21–28.

[43] Chandra, K.S. (1991). *Development of Women Entrepreneurship in India: A Study of Public Policies & Programmes*. New Delhi: Mittal Publications.

[44] Das, M. (1999). "Women Entrepreneurs from Southern India: An Exploratory Study." *Journal of Entrepreneurship*, 8(2), 147–163.

[45] Industrial and Business Development Policy. op. cit.

of land-use (CLU), and a property tax and investment subsidy by way of repayment of State Goods and Services Tax (SGST).

To support the start-up ecosystem in Punjab, innovative steps are being taken by the State Government. The Punjab Government is offering appealing incentives to start-ups in addition to the 'Start-up Punjab' initiative. To promote start-ups in Punjab the incentives offered are start-of-the-art infrastructure, seed grants, interest rate subsidies for loans, setting up of dedicated start-up cells and creating incubators with plug and play facilities. Likewise, the State expects to set up 10 accelerators and incubators, encourage 1,000 start-ups in five years, construct a start-up centre at Mohali, and in State-colleges, develop 50 entrepreneurship centres by setting up solid connections with significant establishments. The 'Start-up India' mobile van travels to many locations in Punjab to spread awareness and capture innovative ideas, in order to discover talented entrepreneurs. Also, in Punjab, bootcamps followed by pitching sessions are conducted at prominent educational institutions.[46]

As of now, Punjab has a start-up network which is naturally formed, and the underlying foundations of a genuine start-up ecosystem have been laid. The State is currently on a change of culture to advancement and innovation driven enterprise. First class infrastructure, brilliant connectivity, premium educational establishments and a helpful government approach add to the qualities of the State. In order to give important administrative and technical help to the start-up coordination committee, a start-up cell has been created in Punjab Infotech, where start-ups can perform their ventures and connect with government departments. On behalf of the Punjab Government, on different occasions, Punjab Infotech participates as a State partner to create awareness about the incentives being offered to start-ups and incubators.

In 1966, Punjab State Industrial Development Corporation (PSIDC), was set up in Chandigarh to advance medium and large-scale industries and for developing new industries, acting as an institutional entrepreneur in Punjab. In the State, PSIDC provides financial help in the form of

---

[46]Department of Industries and Commerce (2017). https://startup.punjab.gov.in/startup-resources/yatra-bootcamps/. [Accessed 12 June 2019].

Image 8: STPI Incubation Centre Mohali

Source: Justdial.com https://www.justdial.com/photos/stpi-incubation-center-mohali-mohali-sector-74-chandigarh-q9o2d44p3e-pc-139997415-sco-19uaauqqqeq.

preference share capital, direct participation and under-writing of equity to the projects promoted by private entrepreneurs.

The Start-up Punjab Hub is proposed to be housed in the Software Technology Parks of India (STPI), Mohali, Punjab as shown in Image 8, which is a newly constructed facility with a mandate to launch and promote the flagship program of Start-up and Entrepreneurship in the State of Punjab. STPI has come up with its state-of-art Incubation Centre in Mohali with a 1.40 Lac square foot facility, Tier 3 Data Centre with 160 racks, and a floor dedicated to skills development.[47]

The Start-up Punjab Hub will be the single point of contact for the entire start-up ecosystem and enable knowledge exchange and access to funding, in partnership with Start-up India Hub, which will be a key partner in the emerging dynamic ecosystem with the hubs working together. It will be a hub and spoke model with both government (central & state), legitimate partners, advisors, banks, angel investor networks, Indian and offshore venture capitalists, colleges, incubators and research and

---

[47]ibid.

development establishments. Start-up India Hub is a guide, friend and mentor to all young Punjabis who have the courage to enter the risk environment. It helps start-ups throughout their life with the explicit spotlight on significant viewpoints like management assessment, acquiring finance, marking skills enhancement, feasibility testing, innovation commercialization, and business organization advisory. Start-up Punjab Hub arranges mentorship programs in partnership with incubation centres, educational institutions, private associations and government associations who wish to encourage development.

The State clearly recognizes the need for business incubation and co-working spaces for small entrepreneurs and new graduates. A start-up corpus of INR 100 cr. for scale up subsidizing with an extraordinary emphasis on women and SC entrepreneurs has been set up with Start-up 2019 Yatra and Bootcamps, Technology and Innovation Support for Budding Entrepreneurs.[48] In addition to the training camps, a Start-up India Yatra Van will go to different urban areas of Punjab with accompanying goals such as spreading mindfulness about Start-up India and the policies and schemes of the Punjab Government for start-ups, providing an opportunity to pitch an idea to be selected for accelerating the program. A few colleges have also been selected and the Van will stop at said colleges for multiple day-long training camps alongside an hour and a half Van Stop.

The Department of Industrial Policy and Promotion, Start-up India, the Government of Punjab and Department of Industries and Commerce have resolved to make a world class innovation start-up ecosystem by encouraging entrepreneurship and a culture of development, which adds to expanded information, riches and work for the general public. Through innovation and motivating start-ups, the government intends to make an ecosystem that creates an entrepreneur in every group in the State. Entrepreneurs to be contacted number over five thousand, with 19 Van Stops and eight Bootcamp destinations. The day long training camp in every city will incorporate introductions on Start-up India and Policies and Schemes of the Punjab Government, followed by a broad ideation

---

[48]ibid.

workshop. A thought pitching session will be held after each bootcamp to choose the premier ideas and start-ups for the Grand Finale.[49]

Punjab would set up MSME Punjab in order to address countless challenges which are being faced by MSMEs and provide the required support to MSME units like access to market, skills, credit, technology etc. as part of Punjab industrial and business development authority for further development of MSMEs in the state. In addition, to deliver different services to stakeholders, professional agencies will be assisting MSME. For the development of the MSME sector, Punjab will follow the cluster approach and for upgrading and developing different MSME clusters, Punjab will focus on optimum utilization of central government schemes as per the Industrial and Business Development Policy 2017.[50] Punjab will set up a strong and effective single window system which will provide various services like access to infrastructure, mentoring, finance, technology, support to start-ups, self-employment, regulatory services etc. to support MSME units at the district level.

For each major industrial cluster, Punjab will aim to set up one technology centre which will act as a centre of incubation and training, design services and innovation, demonstration and research of latest tools, prototyping, technological knowhow, calibration and testing. In each main industrial cluster, Punjab will also set up one Common Facility Centre (CFC). As per the requirement of the concerned cluster, CFC will offer marketing centres, supportive capacity, and testing labs. In order to support the MSME sector, revamping of IDCs as CFCs and QMCs (Quality Marking Centres) as technology centres on a public private partnership model will be undertaken. In Punjab, there are 20 existing IDCs and 13 QMCs catering to various sectors like machine tools, sports goods, textile, engineering, paints, leather etc. For MSMEs, Punjab would guarantee adoption of modernization and technology upgrading schemes such as Lean manufacturing, quality technology tools, zero effect zero defect, credit linked capital subsidy schemes, quality management standards and technology and quality up-grading schemes.[51]

---

[49]ibid.

[50]Industrial and Business Development Policy. op. cit.

[51]ibid.

In order to encourage technology adoption by MSME units, Punjab will incentivize audits for safety, energy and water. To expand marketing and export support to MSME units, a number of measures will be taken by the State such as annual 'buyer and seller meets' programmes for showcasing MSME products at international, national and local events with financial assistance provided by the State for online marketing and trading of products, encourage e-commerce portals, vendor development programmes etc. For MSME units across the districts of Punjab 'plug and play' infrastructure, developed sheds and flatted factories will be provided by the State. To make the SME units available on the exchange platform, necessary incentives will also be provided by the State. For MSME units' growth, accelerator services will be provided by Punjab State. In order to encourage MSMEs to attain higher growth, Punjab will associate with internationally established agencies to train and appoint growth managers. Finally, in different MSME clusters, the State will help in setting up of common environment infrastructure like CETPs according to the Industrial and Business Development Policy 2017.[52]

[52]ibid.

https://doi.org/10.1142/9789811212741_0005

Chapter 5

A Woman's Perspective of Entrepreneurship in MSME Family Businesses

Navneesh Tyagi, Geetika Shukla and Priya Singh

5.1 Introduction

Women in India represent an important segment of the entrepreneurship movement emerging from the transition period. They have achieved a high level of equality in both education and employment and therefore it is expected that they would also take on a crucial role in family firms, but the reality is somewhat different. Their real contribution seems to be undervalued due to male domination and conservative traditions in the country, and the full potential of women is still underutilised. However, the role of women in family firms should be further supported for the benefit of their importance in economic and social roles, family well-being and the improved prospects of the development of family firms for the next generation. Fitzgerald and Muske[1] identified that women generally hold second-level managerial positions and rarely act as CEOs in family firms. Danes and Oslon[2] reported that women are modestly represented in the ownership structure of family businesses and consider this issue to be fairly unimportant. Women's views of transitional issues of their family

[1]Fitzgerald, M.A. & Muske, G. (2002). "Copreneurs: An Exploration and Comparison to Other Family Businesses". *Family Business Review*, 15 (1), 1–16.

[2]Danes, S.M. & Oslon, P.D. (2003). "Women's Role Involvement in Family Businesses, Business Tensions, and Business Success". *Family Business Review*, 16 (1), 53–68. https://doi.org/10.1111/j.1741-6248.2003.00053.x [Accessed on March 2019].

firms are different from men's views.[3] Women in family firms exercise a different, 'feminine' style of management due to differences in their values, personal traits and experience.[4] While there are differences in the gender roles and rewards in family firms, this situation is not perceived by both sexes as a pressing case of discrimination that would demand immediate action.[5,6] The vast majority of businesses are in the ownership and control of the family, managed mostly by men in CEO positions. Generally, the women are younger than the men in family firms and women tend to have significantly higher levels of formal education than the men.

5.2 Background

The family business literature is sparse on this topic and empirical research contributions are even less.[7] Women family members are one category of stakeholders with a vested interest in the viability of the business, next to owners and employees[8] and they can have an important impact on the business. While women tend to enhance their presence as female entrepreneurs, research on women in family businesses have suggested that the majority of women continue to remain in the background, staying 'invisible'[9,10] contradicting the level of feminism. However, for some authors,[11,12] occupying a subdued role has provided them with a

---

[3]Sharma, P. (2004). "An Overview of the Field of Family Business Studies: Current Status and Directions for the Future". *Family Business Review*, 17 (1), 1–36.

[4]Poza, E.J. & Messer, T. (2001). "Spousal Leadership and Continuity in the Family Firm". *Family Business Review*, 14 (1), 25–36.

[5]Danes & Olson. op. cit.

[6]Rowe, B.R. & Hong, G.S. (2000). "The Role of Wives in Family Business: The Paid and Unpaid Work of Women". *Family Business Review*, 13 (1), 1–13.

[7]ibid.

[8]Davis, J. & Tagiuri, R. (1991). "The Influence of Life Stage on Father-Son Work Relationships in Family Companies". *Family Business Review*, 2 (1): 47–74.

[9]Cole, P.M. (1997). "Women in Family Business". *Family Business Review*, 10 (4), 353–371.

[10]Fitzgerald & Muske. op. cit.

[11]Dumas, C. (1998). "Women's Pathways to Participation and Leadership in the Family-Owned Firm". *Family Business Review*, 11 (3), 219–228.

[12]Lyman, A., Salganicoff, M., & Hollander, B. (1996). "Women in Family Business: An Untapped Resource". In Aronoff, C.E. Astrachan, J.H., & Ward, J.L. (Eds.). *Family and Business Sourcebook II.* Marietta, GA: Business Resources, 460–463.

unique vantage point, allowing a rich understanding of the prevailing issues and relationship dynamics where they might make a highly valuable input to the efficient conduct of the business and the management of relationships among family members. Sharma[13] even says that, if used astutely, wives' observations, intuition and emotional capital can make a difference between the success and failure of a family firm.

5.3 Literature Review

5.3.1 *Females in Family Owned Businesses*

Poza and Messer[14] described six different types of roles adopted by spouses of successful family firms: jealous spouse; chief trust officer; partner or 'copreneur'; vice-president; senior advisor; and free agent. Curimbaba[15] reported that women occupied either a professional, invisible or anchor role in their firms. However, it is mostly expected that women occupy the second rank or head up one of the business functions, traditionally finance and accounting or sales. Danes and Olson[16] found 42 percent of wives as major decision-makers even in family firms owned and managed by men. Moreover, spouses and other female family members are often just paid employees in family firms: Danes and Olson[17] found 57 percent of working spouses even in family firms owned by their husbands, with 47 percent being paid, which may suggest a certain level of discrimination among them. Some authors analyse the advantages and disadvantages for women in family firms,[18] including flexible work hours, access to positions in traditionally male-dominated industries, job security, professional challenges, and opportunities for personal growth.[19] However,

---

[13]Sharma. op. cit.

[14]Poza & Messer. op. cit.

[15]Curimbaba, F. (2002). "The Dynamics of Women's Roles as Family Business Managers". *Family Business Review*, 15 (3), 239–246.

[16]Danes & Olson. op. cit.

[17]ibid.

[18]Frishkoff, P.A. & Brown, B.M. (1993). "Women on the Move in Family Business". *Business Horizons*, 36, (2), 66–70.

[19]Barnett, F. & Barnett, S. (1988). *Working Together: Entrepreneurial Couples*. Berkeley, CA: Ten Speed Press.

family firms can also involve gender stereotyping and discrimination found in society at large,[20,21] like the popular view that the male partner is the entrepreneur while the female partner does the bookkeeping in the back room.[22] This attitude leads to the fact that even an important contribution of women to family businesses may not be properly recognised in terms of job titles or salaries.

5.3.2 *Females as Co-preneurs: Just as the Counterparts*

Alcorn[23] suggested the prevalence of the dominant father figure and a subordinate mother figure throughout family businesses. Lyman *et al.*[24] stated that the work environment in family businesses displayed cultural traditions that placed women and men in different social positions and different work and family responsibilities. According to Ponthieu and Caudill,[25] these characteristics apply to wives, mothers and daughters. The evaluation of the true contribution to the family's economic well-being therefore encounters a different mix of paid employment and unpaid family work between men and wives.[26] Wicker and Burley[27] found that wives influence on the business increases when they work in the family business.

---

[20] Jaffee, D.T. (1990). *Working with the Ones You Love: Conflict Resolution & Problem-Solving Strategies for a Successful Family Business*. Berkeley: Conari Press.
[21] Salganicoff, M. (1990). "Women in Family Business: Challenges and Opportunities". *Family Business Review*, 3 (2), 125–138.
[22] Dumas. op. cit.
[23] Alcorn, P.B. (1982). *Success and Survival in the Family-Owned Business*. New York: McGraw-Hill Book Company.
[24] Lyman *et al.* op. cit.
[25] Ponthieu, L.D. & Caudill, H.L. (1993). "Who's the Boss? Responsibility and Decision. Making in Copreneurial Ventures". *Family Business Review*, 6 (1), 3–17.
[26] Voydanoff, P. (1990). "Economic Distress and Family Relations: A Review of the Eighties". *Journal of Marriage and the Family*, 52 (4), 1099–1115.
[27] Wicker, A.W. & Burley, K.A. (1991). "Close Coupling in Work-family Relationships: Making and Implementing Decisions in a New Family, Business and at Home". *Human Relations*, 44 (1): 77–92.

5.3.3 *Females Recognition and Beliefs*

Danes and Amarapurkar[28] noticed that women are not being adequately recognised and involved in running the business and making business decisions creates tensions out of the dissatisfaction and clashes of values and beliefs about the operation of the business and the involvement, tasks and rewards for family members. Prolonged and unresolved tensions eventually affect the achievement, health and fellowship of the business.[29] However, as Danes and Olson[30] discuss, tensions and conflicts can either foster a constructive climate that focuses resources on targeted goals, leading to growth and/or continued success[31,32] or they could create an environment of a lack of trust and fellowship.[33]

5.3.4 *Gender Discrimination and Unacceptance*

Gender roles in family firms are changing but, when a female chooses a non-traditional role, tensions often surface.[34,35] As entrepreneurship has emerged as a career choice for both men and women, that choice has disrupted traditions about how they manage their work lives and negotiates the overlap of their entrepreneurship endeavours and family obligations.[36]

---

[28]Danes, S.M. & Amarapurkar, S. (2001). "Business Tensions and Success in Farm Family Businesses". *Family Economics and Resource Management Biennial*, 4, 178–190.

[29]ibid.

[30]Danes & Olson. op. cit.

[31]Cosier, R.A. & Harvey, M. (1998). "The Hidden Strengths in Family Business: Functional Conflict". *Family Business Review*, 11 (1), 75–79.

[32]Danes, S.M., Zuiker, V.S., Kean, R., & Arbuthnot, J. (1999). "Predictors of Family Business Tensions and Goal Achievement". *Family Business Review*, 12 (3), 241–252.

[33]Danes & Amarapurkar. op. cit.

[34]Hollander, B.S. & Bukowitz, W.R. (1996). "Women, Family Culture and Family Business". In Aronoff, C.E., Astrachan, J.H., & Ward, J.L. (Eds.), *Family and Business. Sourcebook II*. Marietta, GA: Business Resources, 451–459.

[35]Lyman *et al.* op. cit.

[36]Greenhaus, J.H. & Callahan, G. A. (1994). *Career Management (2nd ed.)*, Ft. Worth: Dryden Press.

5.3.5 *Conflict of Issues*

Work-family issues at the intersection of the business and family systems within family businesses are a particularly fertile area for conflict,[37] with the content of conflict arising from five categories: justice, role, work-family, identity, and succession conflict.[38,39] The existence of more than one decision-maker in a family business will, over time, create some level of disagreement and tension.[40] This certainly depends on the situation as to whether: (1) spouses are partners so they should have a say in family business decisions; or (2) husbands are in control of the family business and the views of their wives may not be taken seriously.[41] According to Danes *et al.*,[42] men and women use different conflict styles and conflict begins to subside when women try to avoid tensions.

5.4 Need for the Study

In today's scenario women are walking hand to hand with men and are considered equal to men in all respects. Women in employment are also on the increase, but there is still a low rate of women's participation in family businesses. Women are continually facing great problems and restrictions to join or work in family businesses in India where people give more importance to societal factors. These factors observed as an obstacle or hurdle in the enhancement of women's participation and growth in the family business. Women from time immemorial are considered to be

---

[37]Harvey, M.R. & Evans, E. (1994). "Family Business and Multiple Levels of Conflict". *Family Business Review*, 7 (4), 331–348.

[38]Danes, S.M., Leichtentritt, R., Metz, M.E., & Huddleston-Casas, C. (2000). "Effects of Conflict Styles and Conflict Severity". *Journal of Family and Economic Issues*, 21 (3), 259–286.

[39]McClendon, R. & Kadis, L.B. (1991). "Family Therapists and Family Businesses: A View to the Future". *Contemporary Family Therapy*, 13 (6), 641–651.

[40]Kaye, K. (1991). "When the Family Business Is a Sickness". *Family Business Review*, 9 (4): 347–368.

[41]Rosenblatt, P.C., de Milk, L., Anderson, R.M., & Johnson, P.A. (1985). *The Family in Business: Understanding and Dealing with the Challenges Entrepreneurial Families Face*. San Francisco: Jossey-Bass.

[42]Danes *et al.* (2000). op. cit.

responsible for domestic issues and taking care of their family, for which professional careers take second place. Irrespective of the industry they work in, women face similar pressures to juggle multiple roles, and the major reason they leave jobs is when they are promoted with more responsibilities. In spite of these obstacles women's participation is on the increase in family businesses. This paper reveals the influential factors, inspiring women, to enter into family businesses especially in the MSME sector.

5.5 Methodology

Since the nature of the study is empirical it has been completed with the help of primary data. For this study, data was drawn largely from a primary survey conducted with 184 female entrepreneurs and females in managerial positions in different areas of India. The sample was selected through snowball sampling technique for the study to present women's perspectives of entrepreneurship in MSME family businesses. Secondary information was used for the explanation and discussion of findings through the review of existing literature pertaining to the study and using relevant documents published in articles, journals, dissertations books, and databases.

5.6 Objectives of the Study

1. To explore the values and attitudes of female family members as owners and in managerial-level positions.
2. To investigate women's perspectives about possible gender discrimination and influential factors in entrepreneurship.

5.7 Data Analysis and Interpretation

As the study presents women's perspectives of entrepreneurship in MSME family businesses, therefore respondents chosen here were females either working in managerial positions or owners in MSME family firms. A selection of the sample was done by asking relevant people about females involved in family firms as owners or as managers because neither the sampling frame nor the area frame was available. Moreover, the size of the sector is not clear. A total of 250 questionnaires were sent directly to the respondents, of which 184 were completed and returned, showing a response rate of 73.6 percent. Before sending the questionnaire, a pilot questionnaire was performed using 40 females working in different firms to measure internal consistency and reliability. The value of Cronbach alpha was 0.73 which was above the threshold value for reliability of the questionnaire.

5.8 Women's Association to the Business

5.8.1 *Women's Standing in Family Businesses*

Woman-owned family businesses are flourishing and changing the face of family firms all over the world. More women are entering family business today, and their number is likely to grow in the future.[43,44] Table 1 shows that 94 percent of women agree that the top position is occupied by the male member of the family while only 5.4 percent women agree that the top position is held by females. 4.8 percent of women agree that the secondary position is occupied by the male member of the family while 86.9 percent of women agree that the secondary position is held by females. When asked about the supportive role, 0.5 percent of women agreed that the supportive role is performed by the male member of the family while only 7.6 percent of women agree that the supportive role is performed by females. There are lots of opportunities for women in family businesses as nearly 60 percent of all family owned businesses have women in top management team positions. Female ownership and leadership have increased the level of participation of women family members as full-time employees of their family businesses. In more recent times, daughters have not just inherited the business; they have been involved in running it with contributions of women now respected in the family business.

---

[43]Danco, K. (1981). *From the Other Side of the Bed: Women Looks at Life in the Family Business.* Cleveland: Ohio, Centre for Family Business University Press.

[44]Mancuso, J.R. & Shulman, N. (1991). *Running a Family Business.* New York: Prentice Hall.

Table 1: Perceptions of women in MSME family businesses

Gender		Perceptions		
	Women Association to the Business	**Position in Family Business**		
		Top Position	Secondary Position	*Supportive Role*
Man		174 (94.5)	9 (4.8)	*1 (0.5)*
Woman		10 (5.4)	160 (86.9)	*14 (7.6)*
		Education		
		Higher Education	Vocational	*None*
Man		160 (86.9)	14 (7.6)	*10 (5.4)*
Woman		179 (97.2)	5 (2.7)	*0 (0%)*
		As a Career Choice		
		Primary	Secondary	*Tertiary*
Man		167 (90.7)	14 (7.6)	*3 (1.6)*
Woman		90 (48.9)	70 (38)	*24 (13)*
		Role of Entrepreneur's Spouse		
		Primary	Secondary	*Tertiary*
		179 (97.2)	3 (1.6)	*2 (1)*
		Loyalty		
		Man	Woman	*Both*
		20 (10.8)	160 (86.9)	*4 (2.1)*
	Ownership Issues and Transition from Past Status	**Social Change**		
		Major Acceptance	Minor Acceptance	*No Acceptance*
		90 (48.9)	80 (43.4)	*14 (7.6)*
		Invisibility and Visibility		
		Significantly Visible	Slightly Visible	*Invisible*
		79 (42.9)	100 (54.3)	*5 (2.7)*
		Dilemma vs. Priority to Choose Between Business and Family		
		Priority to Business	Priority to Family	*Both*
Man		138 (75)	40 (21.7)	*6 (3.2)*
Woman		70 (38)	101 (54.9)	*13 (7)*

(*Continued*)

Table 1: (*Continued*)

Gender		**Perceptions**		
		Priority in Role Allocation		
	Gender-Based Roles in Family Firms	Important Positions	Secondary Position	*No Involvement*
Man		174 (94.5)	9 (4.8)	*1 (0.5)*
Woman		10 (5.4)	160 (86.9)	*14 (7.6)*
		Opening Doors for Growth and Recognition		
		Higher Salary	Lower Salary	*Similar Salary*
Man		115 (62.5)	40 (21.7)	*29 (15.7)*
Woman		69 (37.5)	85 (46.1)	*30 (16.3)*
		Managerial Styles		
		A Blend of Manifold	Similar to Men	*Specific to Female*
		123 (66.8)	25 (13.5)	*36 (19.5)*
		Legal Right in Inherited Business/Property		
		Justified	Unjustified	*Neutral*
Woman		16 (8.7)	112 (60.8)	*56 (30.4)*

Source: Compiled by author.

Women today are challenging the stereotype and assumption that men are the best and most qualified candidates for taking over the family business. Women are identified as having specific characteristics and qualifications as well as a rational outlook on business which has enabled them to become successors in family businesses and run them successfully.

However, a look at the business functions occupied by women partly downplays this extreme position. It shows that a number of women with a formal managerial role are in fact doing supportive tasks. Women have well-designated business functions, mostly in finance, and administrative tasks that usually cover everything needed to run a micro business and are also in the supportive role. There seems to be a pattern whereby men take on the top positions, as women primarily handle finance and accounting functions. They also play a key role in performing the functions of HR activist as part of their managerial/administrative tasks. This allocation of business areas is not only a matter of traditions, beliefs, attributes and chance but also relies on educational background.

5.8.2 *Education*

Table 1 suggests that both males (86.9 percent) and females (97.2 percent) have acquired higher education. While the education level is generally low in family firms,[45] the second generation is improving[46] and women have a higher formal education. However, they differ significantly in the area of education and therefore in their business expertise.

Globalisation, liberalisation, and a growing importance of education have helped to raise the status of women in family businesses. Education and exposure have led to greater societal acceptance of women participating in various walks of life, including business.

Perhaps the biggest change in the past couple of decades has been the increasing importance of educational qualifications. Holding professional degrees and qualifying from some of the best business schools, many young females are carving out a rightful position for themselves in the family business. Children in the families whether sons or daughters are educated abroad and bring a wealth of outside influences, breaking down barriers. The female members are well and equally qualified, and able to take on the responsibility of running the business. Institutions of higher education are now claiming larger female student populations than ever with men only accounting for 42 percent of enrolment on professional courses. With the increase in the importance of educational qualifications in the past couple of decades, the distinction between female and male members of a family is also declining. This has led to greater women's involvement in family businesses.

5.8.3 *As a Career Choice*

Mostly in an entrepreneurial family, the natural trend is to think in terms of a family business career and to push a son or daughter, either openly or discreetly in that direction. Little thought may be given to the basic issues involved, which include their talent, aptitude and temperament. Many women see family

---

[45]Glas, M., M. Coh, A. Visnar, J. Vadnjal (2003), "Transgenerational Views on the Success and the Future Development of Family Firms", *Paper Presented at the EFMD Conference. Barcelona, IESE.*

[46]Glas, M., Herle, J., Lovsin, F., & Vadnjal, J. (2006). "The State of Family Firm Management in Slovenia". *Paper Presented at 2nd Workshop on Family Firm Management Research*, Nice, 1–2 June 2006.

businesses as a great career, as they are able to get better positions, higher incomes and more flexibility in work schedules. Women may join family businesses for many reasons, either to help the family, fill the position that no other family member wanted or dissatisfaction from another job. Table 1 shows that the majority of women perceive males (90.7 percent) rather than females (48.9 percent) choosing family business as their primary choice of career. Family business offers women abundant opportunities.[47]

Family businesses offer women access to male-dominated industries and provide more job security and scope for personal growth. Some women see jobs in the family business as merely one possibility among many career options to be considered after completing their studies. In any case, a family business offers another doorway to entrepreneurship for those women whose families are involved in their own businesses. Women are more determined to make a mark for themselves. They are a lot more career-oriented than in the past and more assertive about their rights and status.

5.8.4 *The Entrepreneur's Spouse*

Table 1 shows that the majority of women perceive that the role of entrepreneur's spouse is very important in family business. If a spouse joins the family business, he or she plays a supporting role in the entrepreneur's career. The entry of women in family businesses is recognition of a social change from two perspectives: one, acknowledging the capability of women, and two, assuring that ownership and control do not go away even if there are problems with in-laws. There is also a huge change in attitudes of society toward girls, with the number of children in many families decreasing, and families sometimes only having one or two girls.

5.8.5 *Loyalty*

Women have some unique gender characteristics such as being emotional, sensitive and loyal, which are often reflected when they join family businesses. Table 1 shows the perception regarding loyalty to the family is higher in females (86.9 percent) compared to males (10.8 percent). They

---

[47] Salganicoff. op. cit.

are more concerned for other family members and are more sensitive to the needs of others. Women in family businesses are more capable of solving problems or conflicts among family members.

5.9 Ownership Issues and Transition from Past Status

5.9.1 *Social Change*

Table 1 proves that due to awareness and societal and legal changes more and more women are being accepted in a major (48.9 percent) or minor way (43.4 percent) in the business realm; a place where women were traditionally seen as outsiders or as a resource to help build a business alliance. With the increase in women's education, there is greater economic participation of women in society due to sheer lack of 'man' power. Now, daughters are also inheriting the family business. Some women still continue the identity of their family by retaining their names even after marriage and due to changes in society norms by accepting divorce, this means son -in- laws are no longer for life. The increasing role women are playing as business owners is part of the overall impact on the leadership position when their husbands have died. Many recognizable businesses today are owned and operated by the wife or daughter of the founder.

5.9.2 *Invisibility and Visibility*

Table 1 shows that women feel that they are slightly visible (54.3 percent) to stakeholders. Many women in family businesses feel that they are not viewed by others in the same way as male members whether inside the business or outside. This happens mostly with female partners in husband and wife businesses.[48] The assumption by the outside world is that women hold important positions, because they are married to the boss. Sometimes clients ignore the women in family businesses.

Even if the wife is more capable than the husband, these women find that others sidestep them and look to their spouse for the final decision. Salganicoff[49] believes that invisibility of women in family businesses can

---

[48] Hollander & Bukowitz. op. cit.

[49] Salganicoff. op. cit.

be due to continued stereotyping and discrimination that are the result of prejudices in society and are reflected and expressed within the family business system.

5.9.3 *Dilemma vs. Priority to Choose Between Business and Family*

Table 1 show that women give more priority to family interests (54.9 percent) while men give more priority to business interests (75 percent). When a woman joins the family business it is difficult for her to make a balance between work and family life. If any woman is asked, what comes first, the family or the business, the majority of women will go for the family. Though most of the women are motivated by the sense of family responsibility, sometimes they are so engrossed in the business that they are not able to spend enough time with their children. Many women in family businesses make minor sacrifices for the good of the business. However, the clash of family interest and business interest is so constant that women in the family business need to decide which comes first. Even when the stakes are high, some choose business over family but for others family becomes first priority. For the survival of the family business, its interests cannot be unduly compromised to satisfy family wishes. Family firms must recognize that for growth, professional management is needed, and that family interest must sometimes be secondary. The health and survival of family business requires proper attention to business and family interests, as well as proper balancing of those interests. Otherwise, in the long run at least, results will be unsatisfactory for both.

Today's generation of women are fast taking the place of sons in running the family business empire. According to the Indian Family Business Survey, the number of female CEOs or presidents has doubled every five years since 1997. The most recent survey, done in 2007, indicates that 24 percent of the businesses surveyed currently have a female CEO or president — up from about five percent in 1997. This growth should continue as 31 percent of those surveyed indicated that they may have a female successor. Over the past few years there has been a steady increase in active participation by female family members in the family business. Since families have been getting smaller and if there are not enough male members to lead the growing business, families might need to choose between grooming daughters to head the business or selling off the family business. Sometimes women become successors in family businesses in neither extreme situations as they are neither planned nor the result of grooming. For some business families, the process of turning to women started because they had no choice. All over the world we can find examples of wives or daughters entering into business in crisis situations such as when the head of the family meets an untimely death or due to prolonged illness or a traumatic incident such as divorce. Even in today's world of professionalism the family still believes in trusting a female family member rather than an outsider. Women have made great progress in the business world, and they are building on their successes at a remarkable speed. More and more, women are playing a larger role in the leadership of family businesses.

Some of the best-known names from India include Meghna Modi, Umesh Modi's daughter, who is handling the family's Revlon cosmetics business. Similarly, Prakash Chauhan's Parle Agro venture, which makes the mango drink Frooti, is now being managed by his daughters Schauna, Alisha and Nadia, and Chennai-based Apollo Hospitals are run by promoter Prathap Reddy's daughters Suneeta, Preetha, Sangeeta and Shobana. Also, Adi Godrej's consumer products are run by daughters Nisa and Tina.

5.10 Gender-Based Roles in Family Firms

Men take the top position when the question arises of heading businesses in top positions such as CEO, VP, MD etc. This may simply follow on from the fact that they have dominated and taken over top positions with women left out and not considered for the same. The dilemma still remains as to how women feel in their role. Do they perceive it as a case of gender discrimination in the family firm?

5.10.1 *Priority in Role Allocation*

Table 1 show that 94.5 percent of women agree that the important positions are occupied by the male member of the family while only 5.4 percent women agree that important positions are held by females. 4.8 percent of women agree that secondary positions are occupied by the male member of the family while 86.9 percent of women agree that the secondary position is held by females. When asked about involvement, 7.6 percent of women agree that females are not involved in the family business. When succession is the concern, primogeniture (rights of the first-born son) still seems to be the default and it remains that in some family businesses, women's chances of running the company remains slight because the first-born son usually inherits the business. The women in the family are often overlooked completely, regardless of their skills, accomplishments or desires. Many women in family businesses suffer from the problem of a 'glass ceiling'. Being female, they do not advance as quickly as men and remain in lower level positions. Women in family businesses are subject to the constraints of traditional female roles. In most of the family businesses, wives are often kept in the dark about the business and its finances. Daughters, daughters-in-law, granddaughters, sisters and nieces are often relegated to the position of non-contributing members. Even as employees and company leaders, women face challenges establishing and maintaining authority, as well as sustaining a work/life balance. Despite the challenges, women are proving to be a key source of talent in family businesses.

5.10.2 *Opening Doors for Growth and Recognition*

Referring to Table 1, 62.5 percent of women perceive that men are paid higher while only 37.5 percent of women perceive that women are paid higher. Women also come across a situation where they face a tougher time when it comes to receiving a salary hike, appraisal or promotion. Such discrimination however has no base because women are not considered as doing less demanding or responsible work and no gender-specific views were found concerning this traditional comment that seeks to justify their lower salaries.

5.10.3 *Managerial Styles*

Table 1 describes women's perceptions that the majority (66.8 percent) see a managerial style of women that is a blend. A number of studies recognise several specific features of female managerial styles and the differences are not considered as a disadvantage that may prevent women from taking top positions in family firms. The managerial style of women in operations and decision-making often plays a complementary role in bringing some 'softness' vis-a-vis tough male managers. The female attitudes to equal ownership shares prove that they do not perceive the current dominant male ownership as just and that there is room to improve their satisfaction within their role in family firms. It is evident that women in family firms perceive their situation in a significantly more critical way than the male CEOs. These differences are probably partly due to their different experiences, opinions and attitudes related to their roles and to the different characteristics of women belonging to different groups.

5.10.4 *Legal Rights in Inherited Business/Property*

Table 1 show that the majority of women (60.8 percent) view their legal rights in inherited business/property as unjustified and unfair. The differences of opinions of male CEOs may reflect some traditional concepts about women, and male CEOs tend to neglect the meaning of equal treatment of women to enhance their satisfaction and motivation. Women do perceive their share in management, ownership and rewards as inherently unjust and find their dual role in the family and firm as consistently more demanding on time and energy spent than the role of men.

5.11 Concluding Remarks About Different Traits of Women Holding Family Businesses in India

5.11.1 *Women Are Ambitious*

A successful woman is a dreadfully strong-minded one, has an inner urge or drives to change contemplation into realism. Knowledge from her previous occupancy as an employee, relying on educational qualifications or lessons learnt from inborn business, she is ready to grab opportunities, sets goals, possess clear vision, steps confidently forward and is ambitious to be successful. Every successful businesswoman is determined to achieve goals and make her business prosper. Thorough knowledge of the field is indispensable to success. She comes with new innovative solutions to old problems to overcome issues.

5.11.2 *Women Are Confident*

A successful woman owner is confident in her ability. She is ready to learn from others, search for help from experts if it means adding value to her goals. She is positive in nature and is keener to take risks. A winning woman entrepreneur uses common sense to make sound judgments when encountering everyday situations. This is gleaned from past experience and information acquired over the years. It is essential not to get aggravated and give up when faced with obstacles and trials. The aptitude to explore uncharted territory and take bold decisions is the hallmark of a successful businesswoman. A successful woman usually loves what she does. She is extremely fervent about her tasks and activities. Her high energy levels motivate her to contribute intensely towards building, establishing and maintaining a prosperous business.

5.11.3 *Women Are Open and Willing to Learn*

A successful businesswoman keeps an eye on change, as she is fully conscious of the importance of evolving situations. She is ahead of her competitors and thrives on change. She adapts her business to changes in technology or service expectations of her patrons. She is inquisitive, eager to learn and accommodating to innovation.

5.11.4 *Women Are Cost Conscious*

An intelligent woman prepares pragmatic budget estimates. She provides cost-effective quality service to her clients. With minimized operating costs, she is able to force her team to capitalize on profits and reap its benefits.

5.11.5 *Women Value Cooperation and Allegiance*

A woman has the ability to work with all levels of the populace. She is keen to maintain associations and communicates evidently and efficiently.

This helps her to negotiate even complex issues without difficulty. She is sympathetic to people around her and has good networking skills that help her to get better contacts and utilize opportunities.

5.11.6 *Women Can Balance Home and Work*

A woman engaged in business is good at balancing varied aspects of life. Her multitasking aptitude combined with support from spouse and relatives enables her to bring together business priorities with domestic responsibilities competently and efficiently.

5.11.7 *Women Are Aware of Legal Responsibilities to the Social Order*

A successful woman is eager to share her achievements with society. She is dedicated to assist others and enjoys her liability.

5.11.8 *Women Focus on Their Plans*

Women taking care of businesses plan their work and work with to the plan. Set long-term and short-term goals and take consistent actions in moving toward them.

5.11.9 *Women Are Resourceful*

Women governing business take full advantage of coordinating the available factors and resources such as mentoring, training and coaching and build a strong base of education, training and experience which can help lead to success.

5.12 Implications

On the basis of this study it is understood that a large number of women are taking part in the growing entrepreneurial sector, showcasing their worth by holding their own businesses. Working with family members and avoiding stress and uncertainty by leaving the leadership role to their male partners seems more attractive to women than facing business challenges as sole owners. On the other side, the formal role of women on boards and in managerial ranks is often recognised as a supporting role to confirm stability. Moreover, women are also exercising their influence on the decision-making process in the office and during family time. This advantage of interlocking family and business supports the highlighted issue of the formal role of women in family firms that does not reach beyond the role of women in non-family businesses. Considering that female family members share second-rank managerial roles in a large share of family businesses where men dominate as CEOs, their share in ownership certainly understates their role in running the family business. However, women do not seem to oppose the existing situation and often consider their informal influence as powerful enough to support their personal satisfaction.

The Companies Act, 2013 Section (149) has made a provision for employing women directors on the boards of certain classes of companies, making it compulsory to appoint at least one female director, which will open doors for their entry in family businesses too. Moreover, an amendment in the Hindu Succession (Amendment) Act, in 2005, removed gender discrimination in inheritance in Hindu joint families. Previously, only the male line, down to the great-grandson, had inheritance rights. The amendment gives women an equal share in the family business. In addition, even women married before 1994 can claim equal rights into the family business as well as inherited assets.

The 'feminine' style of women in family firms is very important for creating good internal relationships and the themes of trust, oneness and an overall supportive climate in the business to promote employees' satisfaction and morale. Hence this will positively contribute to the financial performance of family firms showcasing the well-being and acceptance of employees even if not materialised in improved balance sheets. This contribution by women is often benevolently recognised but not adequately rewarded in well accepted monetary or social recognition terms. While holding major responsible positions in business, women are more aware of their feminine-focused managerial roles. As women acquire the top position, a series of changes in management style are witnessed whereby adding their softer feminine approach to the business adding a new quality to the existing style.

Women consider their role in the family business very differently to male members. It can be assumed that women are frustrated by the existing formal structure of family firms. However, they seem reluctant to raise these issues in the family and are not radical in demanding changes. The feminist movement never had deep roots and radicalism has mostly been calmed by legislation that formally supports (full) gender equality, but no mechanisms to ensure this equality have been devised. Women desperately need confirmation of their roles from bread bakers to bread earners. They do expect some changes and improvements in the existing acknowledgement of their status to induce some open and varied acceptance of their multitasking roles.

In conflict-resolution programmes, women can play an enormously positive role in reducing the conflict which appears mostly among men. Their psychological, emotional, decisional, behavioural traits make them stand apart and contribute robustly and capably for any issue.

There are many opportunities for further research in the field. Researchers should be encouraged to use more sophisticated analytical approaches; however, they should provide larger samples in order to arrive at reliable assessments. A more multidisciplinary approach is recommended because the complex family and partnership relationship combined with pressures of day-to-day business activities demands much broader research skills and knowledge than is usually available to and provided by business science researchers.

https://doi.org/10.1142/9789811212741_0006

Chapter 6

Financing Businesses in India: An MSME Sector Viewpoint

Robin Thomas

6.1 Introduction

Financing decisions in organizational management deals with the arrangement of funds and allocation of funds. It is considered crucial as it involves decisions about finance mix, channels of finance, use of funds, and repayment of borrowed funds decisions, which are crucial and bear long term impact on any organization. When an entrepreneur decides to start-up a business, he/she will require a primary investment, also termed as start-up capital; the initial investment an entrepreneur needs to begin operations of the firm. There are various ways to fund the initial investment; owner's personal money, borrowed money from varied sources, borrowings from family members, friends or money raised from private individuals or private investors. This initial capital is also termed as Seed Capital or Seed Money, which is defined as the initial funding requirement of a start-up enterprise to begin operations.

A newly started enterprise usually undergoes four phases of capital requirement; 1) Seed Capital, 2) Venture Capital, 3) Mezzanine Capital and 4) Initial Public Offering (IPO). Venture Capital is interchangeably used with Seed Capital. Seed Capital is used in common parlance for newly started enterprises with relatively lower capital requirement but with a distinct and unique idea proposition. Seed Capital grows the enterprise, funding the idea up-to that extent where its formation is complete and subsequent Venture Capital is required to fuel its growth. Sometimes it may happen that the Seed Capital has only helped to develop the viability of the unique idea proposed by the entrepreneur and actual operations might not yet have started. Venture capitalists may pour in Venture Capital to further explore such an idea even though the actual product or service is not yet at the delivery phase. Mezzanine Capital financing is high interest rate financing required to support introductory businesses with an available preliminary track record. The IPO is the process where the shares of the enterprise are made open for the public; to raise funds from the capital markets for businesses with a proven track record and which have faced the analytical eyes of the market and investors.

The MSME sector contributes about 29 percent of India's Gross Domestic Product (GDP).[1] Estimates show that India has 633.88 Lakh MSME units, out of which 31 percent are in the manufacturing sector, 36 percent in trade and the remaining 33 percent are in other services, whereas 51 percent of the MSME enterprises are in rural areas and the other 49 percent are in urban areas.[2] It is also important to know that the Micro sector comprises 99 percent of the total MSME enterprises. The MSME sector creates an estimated 11.10 Crore jobs in the country.[3] It goes without saying the importance of financing decisions and arrangement of financial resources in the MSME sector given the position it enjoys in the Indian economy.

It is however also important to note that Indian MSMEs operate in an exigent environment; they struggle on multiple fronts, primarily financing and credit availability, which are some of the major hindrances they face.[4] The availability of funds and the role of finance has been cited as a significant feature for the growth of the MSME sector worldwide.[5] This chapter details the various sources of financing available to Indian MSME sectors

---

[1]Ministry of MSME, Govt. of India, Annual Report 2017–18, https://msme.gov.in/sites/default/files/MSME-AR-2017-18-Eng.pdf [Retrieved on 22 July 2019].

[2]National Sample Survey (NSS) 73rd round, conducted by National Sample Survey Office, Ministry of Statistics & Programme Implementation during the period 2015–16.

[3]ibid.

[4]Rao, P., Kumar, S., & Madhavan, V. (2019). "A Study on Factors Driving the Capital Structure Decisions of Small and Medium Enterprises (SMEs) in India". *IIMB Management Review*, 31(1), 37–50.

[5]Cook, P. (2001). "Finance and Small and Medium-Sized Enterprise in Developing Countries". *Journal of Developmental Entrepreneurship*, 6(1), 17–40.

including the various standard operating procedures (SOPs) and schemes which the Government of India has initiated for the development of the sector.

6.2 MSME Finance in India: The Present Scenario

It is estimated that the total demand for credit in the MSME Sector is ₹37 Lakh Crore, whereas the total supply of credit from formal sources is assessed to be ₹14.5 Lakh Crore. As a result, the total finance gap in the MSME sector is assessed to be approximately ₹24 Lakh Crore.[6]

Chart 1 shows the total outstanding credit to the MSME sector from the formal financial sector at the end of FY2019, which amounts to Rs. 17.4 Lakh Crores. The Public Sector Banks (PSBs) contribute Rs. 9.3 Lakh Crores to MSME finance, followed by Private Banks (PVTs) at Rs. 5.7 Lakh Crores.

Chart 2 shows the trend in total outstanding credit to the MSME sector from the formal financial sector for the period 2014–2019. It is noteworthy that except FY2017, the credit extended by PSBs has been above Rs. 8 Lakh Crores and the PVTs credit extension to MSMEs significantly increased in FY2017 to Rs. 4 Lakh Crores and is touching Rs. 6 Lakh Crores in FY2019.

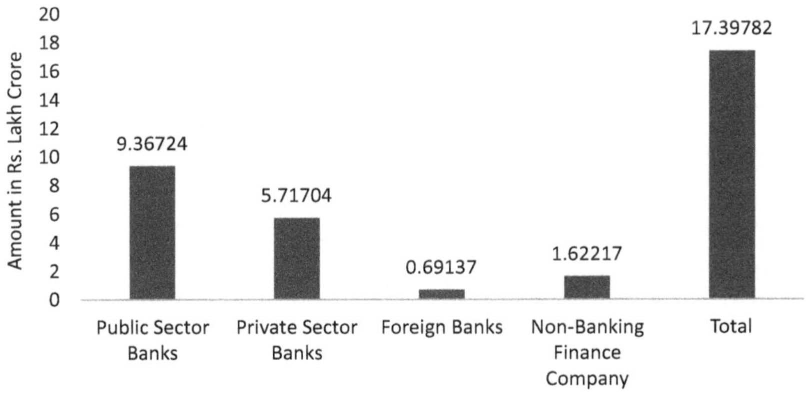

Chart 1: Total formal outstanding credit to the MSME sector, March 2019

Source: RBI Expert Committee Report, 2019 on MSME Enterprises.

[6]IFC Report 2018, RBI Report on MSME Sector June 2019.

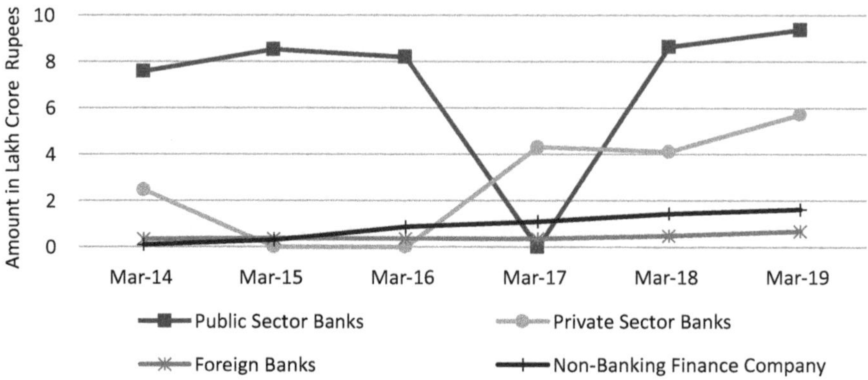

Chart 2: Trend of source-wise formal outstanding credit to MSMSE sector

Source: RBI Expert Committee Report, 2019 on MSME Enterprises.

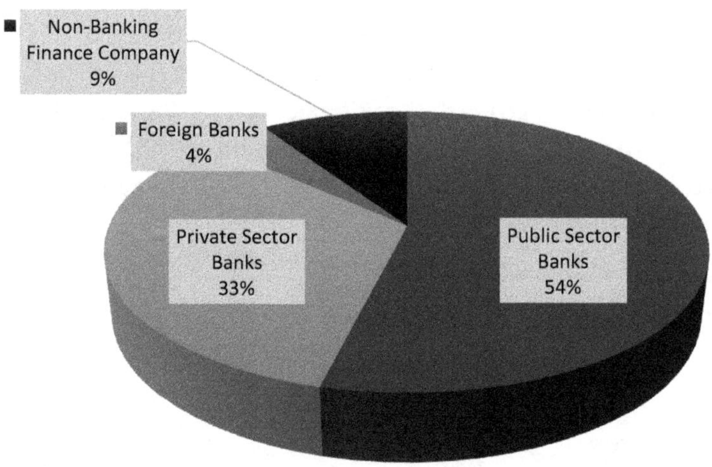

Chart 3: Share of financial institutions in MSME finance, March 2019

Source: RBI Expert Committee Report, 2019 on MSME Enterprises.

Chart 3 shows the percentage share of various lending institutions towards MSME finance at the end of FY2019. PSBs have a 54 percent share of MSME credit, followed by PVTs at 33 percent. Foreign banks and Non-Banking Finance Companies (NBFCs) contribute four percent and nine percent respectively.

6.3 Challenges in MSME Lending

The gap in the demand for MSME credit and its supply through the formal sector is quite evident from the RBI data. Apart from the demand supply mismatch there are certain other barriers to MSME lending. Banks consider MSME lending as riskier lending due to the higher percentage of nonperforming assets in MSME loans. MSMEs have almost nil capital buffers and in cases of genuine business risk, MSMEs fall vulnerable to factors such as payment delays, supply chain bottlenecks and changing consumer preferences. Another important factor for inevitable credit losses is the lack of risk mitigation system availability to MSMEs.

MSMEs are comparatively tough to assess on financial fundamentals due to the lack of authentic, certified and relevant financial information, unlike publicly traded companies. Heavy information asymmetry in the MSME segment makes it difficult for lenders to review their financial performance. Higher operating and monitoring costs are borne by lenders if substantial collateral security is not provided by the enterprise. Another reason for the demand supply mismatch in the MSME segment is inadequate formal financial sector coverage of operational locations of MSMEs.

Essentially, it can be said that as MSMEs have an informal nature, financial institutions and banks find it difficult to assess the credit risk of MSMEs due to dearth of appropriate financial information data. Also, only a handful of MSMEs can draw equity support and venture capital financing.

Conventionally, MSMEs face stark information asymmetry difficulties. MSMEs are also less aware of government support, SOPs and schemes. This results in MSMEs' deprivation of credit facilities and other non-financial formal support. MSMEs in effect have inefficient access to market intelligence knowledge and other opportunities. In significant cases they also lack administrative, legal and procedural expertise and the required ability to function effectively.

Another problem hindering the competitiveness of MSMEs is infrastructural bottlenecks. These deprives MSMEs' access to global markets. MSMEs suffer from lack of basic requirements such as tool rooms, sheds, testing labs, power, internet access, access to innovative ideas and guidance on finance and credit access. Also, government intended development of MSME clusters and traditional artisan clusters has been limited and confined to government and government aided agencies and institutions with very little participation of private investment.

Undoubtedly the role of MSMEs in employment generation, entrepreneurship development and development of supply chains is critical and crucial. Thus, the need to assist, foster and fund pioneering commercial ideas and form them into business enterprises is unquestionable. One of the other related challenges which MSMEs face is the lack of entrepreneurial development centres, and because of this, the innovative spirit of the MSME environment is not progressing.

Chart 4 exhibits the Turnaround Time (TTD) in number of days for MSME Loans processed by lenders. TTD is the time in number of days required to complete the process of MSME loan processing. Banks assess the credit risk of the enterprise primarily through a dual model system: 1) minimum cut-off marks model for small loans, and 2) detailed risk assessment financial models for large loans. Such financial models are bank specific and incorporate the risk appetite of the individual banks. Such traditional models yield higher turnaround times for appraisal and sanctioning. It is noteworthy that the NBFCs' log lowest average TTD for the period FY2016–2018 is about 20 days, followed by PVTs at 30 days

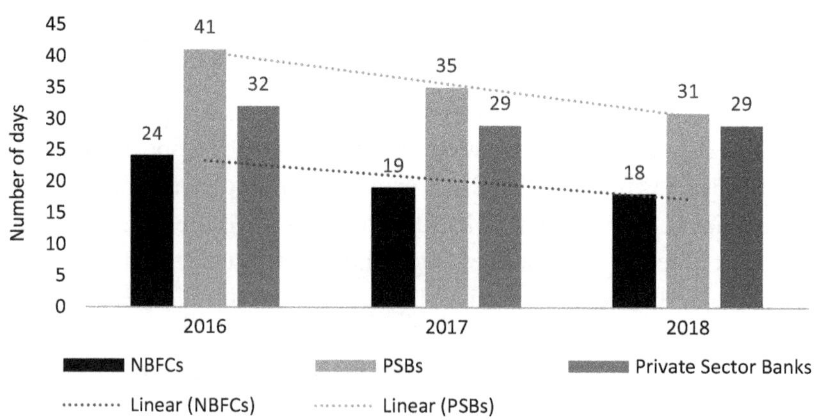

Chart 4: Turnaround time for MSME lending

Source: RBI Expert Committee Report, 2019 on MSME Enterprises, MSME Pulse Report by SIDBI-TransUnion CIBIL.

and the highest by PSBs at almost 36 days. It is however noteworthy that since 2016 there has been a significant reduction of 10 days in TTD of PSBs and in FY2019 the TTD of PSBs and PVTs have a difference of only two days. The NBFCs have a significantly lower TTD than PSBs and PVTs at 18 days in FY2019.

6.4 Financial Assistance Schemes for MSME Entrepreneurs

6.4.1 *MUDRA Loan Scheme*

MUDRA is an acronym that stands for Micro-Units Development & Refinance Agency Ltd. MUDRA was conceived in April 2015 under the aegis of the Small Industries Development Bank of India (SIDBI) as a wholly owned subsidiary of SIDBI. MUDRA's objective is to cultivate and refinance India's MSME sector by backing-up the financial institutions lending to MSMEs. MUDRA therefore collaborates with banks, MFIs, and other lending institutions and supports financial institutions at State and regional levels.

MUDRA has a three-tier credit extension system, for varying amounts and varying interest rates which is offered as a refinancing tool to financial institutions, banks, rural banks and cooperative banks:

1. Shishu Loans for amounts up to Rs. 50,000, at an interest rate of 10–12 percent;
2. Kishor Loans for amounts between Rs. 50,000 and Rs. 5 Lakh, at an interest rate of 14–17 percent;
3. Tarun Loans for amounts between Rs. 5 Lakh and Rs. 10 Lakh, at an interest rate of more than 16 percent.

MUDRA also extends business loans up to Rs. 1 Lakh through Micro-Finance Institutions (MFIs) under its Micro Credit Scheme (MCS). MUDRA covers varied MSME needs such as loans to vendors, to traders, to shopkeepers, to the services sector MSMEs, including working capital credit, equipment finance transport vehicle finance etc. An individual can apply for a MUDRA business loan either by approaching a bank or on their website.

Chart 5 shows the total amount disbursed through various financial institutions under MUDRA. PTCs are debt instruments that enable investors to draw interest from securitised assets. Another form is 'Direct Assignment', in which direct sale of loans is carried out.

Chart 6 displays the percentage share of MUDRA refinance to various financial institutions for FY2018. 59 percent of MUDRA refinance is provided by banks, followed by NBFCs at 13 percent. Interestingly PTCs

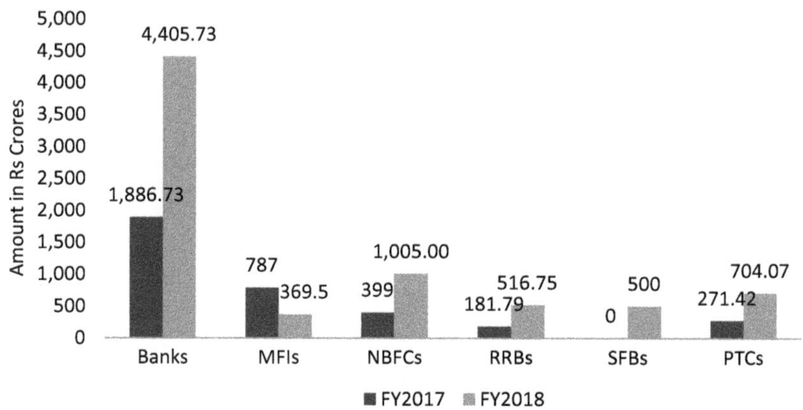

Chart 5: Refinance disbursal under MUDRA

Source: MUDRA Annual Report 2017–18 (MFI — Microfinance Institutions, NBFC — Non-Banking Finance Companies, RRB — Regional Rural Banks, SFB — Small Finance Banks, PTC — Pass Through Certificates).

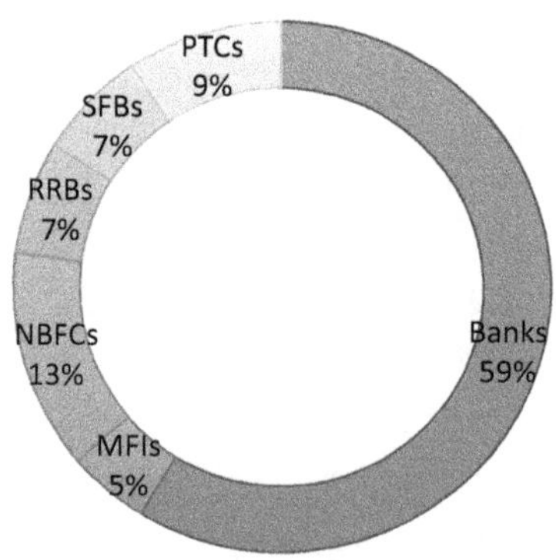

Chart 6: Share in MUDRA scheme, FY2018

Source: MUDRA Annual Report 2017–18.

received nine percent refinance. The RRBs and SFCs received seven percent each while MFIs received five percent of MUDRA refinance.

6.4.2 *Stand-Up India Scheme*

The Stand-Up India Loan Scheme is an initiative of the Government of India targeted at MSMEs run by women and so-called ‘socially backward’ entrepreneurs. The objective is to ensure easy and fair access of financial resources to these entrepreneurs. The scheme was launched in April 2016 and envisages easy bank finance access of loans between Rs. 10 Lakh and Rs. 1 crore for registered castes/tribes and women entrepreneurs for the setting-up of new greenfield businesses in the manufacturing, trading or services sector but excluding the farm sector.

Stand-Up India is envisaged to cover 75 percent of the total initial credit requirements of greenfield projects including the term loan portion and the working capital portion of the enterprise. Such loans are conceived to be free from collateral requirements, however the issuing bank can secure the loan through guarantees under the Credit Guarantee Fund Scheme for Stand-Up India Loans (CGFSIL). Banks can decide about the interest rate portion to be charged for such loans and at present it is calculated at three percent above the Base Rate/MCLR plus the tenure premium. The loan tenure at present is seven years with a maximum moratorium period of 18 months. Loan applications can be applied in person or through an online handholding support system.

6.4.3 *59-Minute Loan Scheme*

Loans under one hour or the 59-minute loan scheme was launched in November 2017, with an objective of faster approval of loans and actual disbursals within a week of approval, starting from Rs. 1 Lakh to 5 Crore. The initiative targets computerization and digitization of several procedures of Commercial Loans (Term Loan/Working Capital Loan) in such a way that a debtor gets an in-principle support (entitlement) letter in less than 59 minutes. The borrower has been given the flexibility to choose lender which mainly consists of SIDBI, State Bank of India, other PSBs and a couple of private banks. The rate of interest starts from 8.5 percent onwards. The Platform is integrated with Credit Guarantee Fund Trust for Micro and Small Enterprises (CGTMSEs) to check eligibility of borrowers.

6.4.4 *Scheme of Fund for Regeneration of Traditional Industries (SFURTI)*

SFURTI, launched in August 2014 aims to organize the traditional artisans and related industry manpower into clusters so that these clusters may become more competitive, sustainable and may create and provide sustainable employment, with better marketing options for their products/services. The other objective of SFURTI is skills enhancement of traditional artisans, to provide better common facilities for such artisans clubbed into clusters, and equip these artisans with improved tools, techniques and equipment. The scheme also aims to strengthen, develop and improve the cluster governance system under this scheme through participation of stakeholders, increasing the skillset of artisans and ultimately replicating similar redundant and less efficient cluster systems. SFURTI provides financial assistance for any project to a maximum of Rs. 8 Crores to individual clusters.

Eligible individuals/institutions to apply to include state/central government institutions and field functionaries, Non-Government Organizations (NGOs), semi-government institutions, institutions under Panchayati Raj System, Cluster Specific Special Purpose Vehicle's private sector, Corporate Social Responsibility (CSR) foundations with expertise in cluster development.

SFURTI nodal agencies are KVIC, Coir Board, NIMSME Hyderabad, NIESBUD Noida, IIE Guwahati, all MSME Development Institutions of Centre and State Governments.

6.4.5 *Coir Udyami Yojana*

The scheme is intended at assisting the establishment of coir units. Banks will extend term loans for capital expenditure and cash credit loans for working capital requirements. Loan proposals may be composite in nature including capex and working capital finance proposals. Financial assistance in this scheme is limited to Rs. 10 Lakh, plus a maximum of Rs. 2.5 Lakh for one cycle of working capital requirements. The government subsidises 40 percent of the total project amount and banks extend 55 percent credit and the remaining five percent is the owner's contribution. The subsidy does not include working capital requirements. This scheme envisages a maximum tenure of seven years for loan repayment and a rate of interest on par with the bank's base rate.

Eligibility for loans and subsidies consists of individuals, companies, self-help groups, NGOs, institutions registered under the Societies Registration Act 1860, production co-operative societies, joint liability groups, and charitable trusts. MSMEs registered with the Coir Board under the Coir Industry (Registration) Rules, 2008, are eligible for this scheme. No MSME will receive subsidies under this scheme if it has already received other subsidies under any other central/state government scheme.

6.4.6 *SIDBI's 'Make in India' Soft Loan Fund for MSMEs (SMILE)*

This scheme of SIDBI was launched in 2015. MSMES in greenfield manufacturing and services sectors are eligible to apply. While current enterprises undergoing extension, modernisation, technological upgradation, or similar growth-oriented projects are also covered and eligible to apply. The objective of this scheme is to provide easy loans, in the category of quasi-equity, and term loans on reasonably lenient terms to MSMEs to meet the prerequisite debt-equity ratio for the formation of new MSMEs and to allow the development of existing ones. The scheme also provides more lenient loan conditions to entrepreneurs of SC/ST communities. The credit amount available under this scheme is as under:

1. General category entrepreneurs — 10 percent of the project cost (maximum limit of Rs. 20 Lakh)
2. For entrepreneurs belonging to SC/ST communities, PWDs and Women entrepreneurs — 15 percent of the project cost (maximum limit of Rs. 30 Lakh); also, such individuals compulsorily owning a controlling stake (51 percent or more)

On completion of three years from the date of the first disbursement, the remaining soft loan, plus any other dues remaining, will turn into a secured term loan. The rate of interest will be based on the borrowers' rating. The loan repayment period is generally up to seven years, inclusive of a moratorium of up to 18 months for the term loan and up to 24 months for the soft loan.

6.4.7 *Sustainable Finance Scheme (SFS)*

SFS is a scheme promoted by SIDBI and is focused for industries in Green energy, non-renewable energy, technology hardware and renewable energy. In particular, projects such as solar electricity generation plants, wind power generators, mini hydel electricity generation projects, biomass-based power plants, and other related projects, for both captive and non-captive use are eligible under this scheme. SFS also provide assistance to potential cleaner production investments including waste management, appropriate assistance to original equipment manufacturers (OEMs), which produce energy efficient or cleaner production or green machinery and equipment, subject to the condition that either the OEM should be an MSME or it should be supplying its products to a substantial number of MSMs. The rate of interest will be applicable on the basis of credit rating of MSMEs.

6.4.8 *Financial and Credit Assistance Schemes of the Ministry of MSME, Government of India*

1. Prime Minister's Employment Generation Programme (PMEGP)
   Khadi and Village Industries Commission (KVIC) is the implementing agency for this scheme, which executes the scheme through State KVIC Directorates, State Khadi and Village Industries Boards (KVIBs) and District Industries Centres (DICs) with the cooperation of banks. The maximum project cost under this scheme is limited to Rs. 25 Lakhs in the manufacturing enterprises and Rs. 10 Lakh for service enterprises. PMEGP scheme is applicable to green-field projects only. Eligible individuals include, Self Help Groups, Institutions registered under Societies Registration Act, 1860; Production Cooperative Societies, and Charitable Trusts.

2. Credit Linked Capital Subsidy Scheme (CLCSS) for the Manufacturing Segment
   As the name of the scheme suggests, this is an incentivised capital subsidy scheme of 15 percent with a ceiling of maximum Rs. 15.00 Lakhs on formal institutional finance served to them with an objective of new technological adoption. The maximum amount eligible for such subsidy is capped at Rs. 1 Crore. The scheme is aimed at 51 manufacturing sub-sectors and is applicable to new and existing Micro & Small Enterprises (MSEs). There are 12 Nodal Agencies/ Banks of implementing this scheme under the MSME Development Commissioner. An individual MSE may approach online to a PLI from where the MSEs availed term loan for up-gradation of technology. The PLI then sends the application to the Nodal Agency which in-turn sends it to Development Commissioner's office for approval of subsidy. Funds are subsequently sent from the Development Commissioner to the Nodal Agency, which in turn send it to PLI.
3. Credit Guarantee Fund Trust for MSEs (CGTMSE) — UDAAN — Provision of Collateral Free Credit for MSMEs
   The scheme is applicable to new and existing micro and small enterprises with loans amounting up to Rs. 2 Crores. The CGTMSE extends credit guarantees to lending institutions including NBFCs to extend loans (term loans and working capital loans) with any collateral. CGTMSE provides guaranteed cover of 75 percent for loans amounting to Rs. 50 Lakhs, 85 percent cover for loans amounting to Rs. 5 Lakh and 80 percent cover for loans to women and entrepreneurs in the North East Region with a uniform cover of 50 percent for loans between Rs. 50 Lakh and Rs. 2 Crores. CGTMSE charges an annual guarantee fee of 1.0 percent per annum of the loan amount sanctioned, however this charge is 0.75 percent for loans up to Rs. 5 Lakh and 0.85 percent for loans above Rs. 5 Lakh and up to Rs. 2 Crores for women entrepreneurs, north-eastern region units and all micro units.

6.5 Role of NSIC in MSME Credit

National Small Industries Corporation (NSIC) functions under Government of India's Ministry of Micro, Small and Medium Enterprises. NSIC works to support, help and nurture the progression of micro, small and medium enterprises. NSIC functions via a nationwide network of bureaus and Technical Centres. NSIC has also set up a Training cum Incubation Centre managed by expert manpower. NSIC has the mission "*To promote and support Micro, Small & Medium Enterprises (MSMEs) Sector*". NSIC's vision is "*To be a premier Organization fostering the growth of Micro, Small and Medium Enterprises (MSMEs) Sector*".

NSIC offers credit aid for raw material procurement by making the disbursement directly to suppliers/creditors in the Raw Material Assistance scheme against a bank guarantee. NSIC also aids financing by providing support to MSMEs under schemes such as Tender Marketing, Exports and Bill Discounting. NSIC has also entered into a Memorandum of Understanding (MoU) with Nationalized and Private Banks. NSIC aids credit arrangements through syndication with these banks (fund or non-fund-based limits) without any cost/fee to MSMEs. Credit facilitation of Rs. 6,373 Crore was made during the FY2017–18.

NSIC assists MSMEs to gain credit access through an association of some public and private sector banks. Entrepreneurs can also switch their bank accounts to a different bank through NSIC's help. The corporation helps MSMEs prepare loan application documents and negotiate on their behalf for a liberal rate of interest. The MSMEs can directly approach any of NSIC's branches and submit their application for credit requests from any of the banks in NSIC's tie-ups. The authorized personnel at the office will deliver a handholding provision to the MSME unit by assisting them in concluding all papers as a prerequisite for final proposal to the bank. Under the Bank Credit Facilitation Scheme, the MSME(s) may avail loan facilities form individual banks based on their credit policies. Closer attention is paid to the loan proposals supported by NSIC.

The several types of loans and credit assistance through NSIC comprise Term Loans for purchase of fixed assets (land/building, plant/machinery, other fixed assets) for installing and setting up new units and for extension, modernization and diversification in case of existing units. Working Capital loans are also available to encounter the working capital needs of the MSME units such as cash credit, overdraft against book debts and bill discounting facilities. Non fund-based limits such as guarantees, letters of credit, foreign bank guarantees, foreign letters of credit etc.

MSMEs also face a dual problem of 1) access to quality raw material and 2) access to markets for the finished product. NSIC facilitates MSMEs via its market assistance scheme to ascertain markets for their products. The Government e-Marketplace (GeM) gateway has empowered MSMEs to unite with buyers from Public Sector Undertakings and Government Departments. The GeM portal has 38,609 registered MSMEs on the platform as of 12 June 2019.

6.6 Role of SIDBI in MSME Sector

The Small Industries Development Bank of India (SIDBI) came into existence on 2nd April 1990 with the mandate for promotion, financing and development of the MSME sector. SIDBI also acts as a coordinator for institutions engaged in similar activities. SIDBI aims to enable and reinforce credit flows to MSMEs. SIDBI has a two-fold credit portfolio. Its engaged in Indirect lending and Direct lending. Indirect lending includes refinance to Banks and Financial Institutions, Micro Finance Institutions and NBFCs; while the direct lending includes direct loans and advances and trade receivable financing.

6.6.1 *Major Functions of SIDBI*

1. Refinancing loans extended by Primary Lending Institutions, such as commercial banks and NBFCs, to the MSME sector.
2. Financing activities include bill discounting and rediscounting. Also offering services such as factoring and leasing to industrial concerns.
3. Promoting marketing channels for MSME in domestic and international markets.
4. Initiatives for technological upgrading of MSME units.

SIDBI claims to have a three-pronged strategy for the MSME sector; 1) Bridging the MSME credit gap in MSME lending, 2) Promotion of non-financial support to MSMEs and 3) Increased focus on MSME data access.

Some of the non-financial activities of SIDBI includes credit counselling for MSMEs, trade fairs, buyer-seller meet, workshops, vendor development feasts/meets, entrepreneurial guidance for development of new businesses and case-studies of successful start-ups.

Chart 7 exhibits the composition, trend and position of the credit portfolio of SIDBI's loan portfolio. At the end of FY2018 the total outstanding portfolio of SIDBI stood at Rs. 95.3 Thousand Crores while it stood at Rs. 68.3 Thousand Crores at the end of FY2017. At the end of

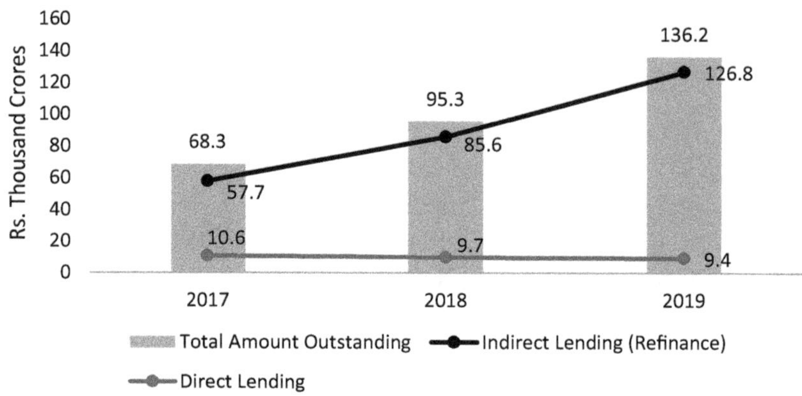

Chart 7: SIDBI's outstanding credit portfolio

Source: SIDBI Annual Reports, 2017–2019.

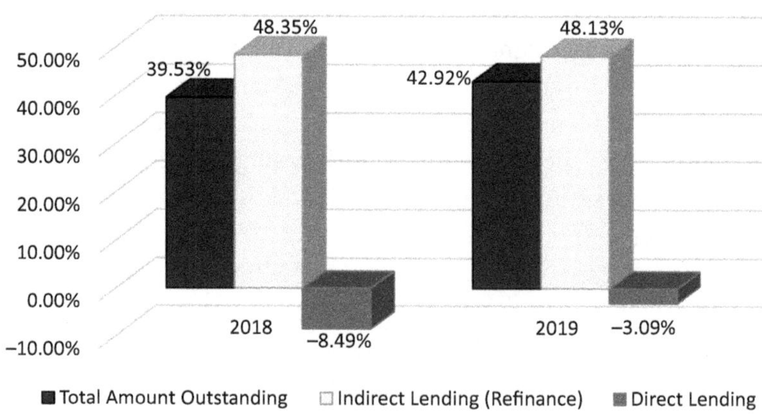

Chart 8: YoY growth in SIDBI credit portfolio

Source: SIDBI Annual Reports, 2017–2019.

FY2019, the total outstanding portfolio of SIDBI stood at Rs. 1.36 Lakh Crores. It is clear from the chart that much of the growth in the total credit portfolio comes from indirect refinancing activities of SIDBI and in-effect the direct lending activities are shrinking in terms of total direct outstanding credit.

Chart 8 exhibits the year-on-year (YOY) growth of SIDBI's lending portfolio. In FY2018 the total credit portfolio of SIDBI grew at a rate of almost 40 percent compared to FY2017, while in FY2019 this growth rate was almost 43 percent. A major portion of the total credit portfolio comprised of indirect refinance which saw a rise of 48.3 percent in FY2018 and 48.13 percent in FY2019. The direct lending channel of SIDBI has however registered a decline consecutively in FY2018 and FY2019.

https://doi.org/10.1142/9789811212741_0007

Chapter 7

Bank's Contribution Towards Financing MSMEs in Assam

Maumita Choudhury

7.1 Introduction

Finance is an important factor for the growth of the MSME sector. The more formal finance for MSMEs, the easier it is to bring the sector under the formal economic system. Banks are the most important mediator for finance to MSMEs for various reasons, which has been discussed in subsequent sections of this chapter. The MSME sector generally requires funds of two types, firstly long-term funds for investment in fixed assets for setting up new units or expansion/modernization of existing units and secondly, working capital or short-term funds to manage day-to-day operations of their businesses. Long-term credit funds are mainly provided by institutions like the Small Industries Development Bank of India (SIDBI), Commercial Banks, State Financial Corporations (SFCs), Non-Banking Financial Companies (NBFCs), NEDFI, etc. and in a limited measure, from other sources like Foreign Direct Investment, Venture Capital/Private Equity funds, etc. Similarly, the working capital needs of the sector are largely met by the banking sector, including Scheduled Commercial Banks (SCBs), Regional Rural Banks (RRBs), Urban Co-operative Banks (UCBs), National Small Industries Corporation (NSIC), factoring companies, etc. The National Commission on Enterprises in the Unorganised Sector (NCEUS) had estimated the credit gap only for microenterprises in the unorganised sector at 6.31 lakh crore (73 percent) as at end March 2012. As *The Economic Times* reported on 1 July 2015, even with banks' lending around Rs. 8 trillion to the MSME sector, the sector is still undercapitalised. According to the International Finance Corporation (IFC), the MSME sector faces a severe capital shortage of Rs. 32.5 trillion. Out of this, the debt shortfall is Rs. 26 trillion. This is the shortfall that the organised financial sector will have to provide to MSMEs to ensure that MSMEs are properly capitalised and can continue to grow. For the banks, the challenge is to reach the MSME segment and for small business owners to access finance. The challenges faced by MSMEs in accessing finance is lack of comprehensive formal documentation relating to accounts, income and business transactions. This chapter documents the extent of contribution of commercial banks towards MSME financing in Assam. Secondary data from various sources such as SLBC websites, the SLBC handbook, annual reports of banks and DIC, journals, books, etc. have been used for the study. The study includes only those public, private and co-operative banks for which data has been available since 2012.

7.2 Importance of Banks as a Source of Finance for MSMEs

The importance of adequate finance for MSMEs has been sufficiently highlighted. It is also understood that the source of finance is equally important for the sector. The more formal finance for MSMEs, the easier it is to bring the sector under the formal economic system. Banks are the most important mediator for finance to MSMEs due to various reasons out of which the most relevant are:

i. Easy accessibility
ii. Convenient locations
iii. Intermediary for majority of government schemes
iv. Regulated interest rates
v. Ethical conduct
vi. Professional handling of the process

7.3 Data Available on Banks as a Source of Finance for MSMEs

An executive summary on 'Sub-Group on Flow of Private Sector Investments for MSME Sector' prepared by Working Groups/Steering

Table 1: Limitation of MSME credit data availability

Data Type	Status of Availability with Sources
1 Working capital	Credit outstanding to MSE sector from banks — Available from 2008 Credit outstanding to medium enterprises — available from 2010 Factoring data for MSMEs — Not available Data on NBFCs support to MSMEs — Available for total, not for SMEs
2 Term loans	Data from banks — Available from 2008 Data on VC funds for SMEs — not available Long term support to MSMEs through FDI, securitization, NBFCs are not available.
3 Credit outstanding in break-up of term loans and working capital	Not available
4 Share of MSMEs in GDP	Not available in absolute terms

Source: Planning Commission, Government of India.

Committees for the 12th Five Year Plan (2012–2017) under the Planning Commission of India has delineated the availability of data related to MSME credit as shown in Table 1.

As per the available literature, data on estimation of the credit gap for the MSME sector is not available in India. However, the National Commission on Enterprises in the Unorganised Sector (NCEUS) had estimated the credit gap for microenterprises in the unorganised sector at Rs. 6.31 lakh crores (73 percent) as at end March 2012, with the caveat that the number of such unorganised microenterprises was estimated at 70 million with an average credit offtake of Rs. 1.23 lakh per enterprise. This is in contrast to the MSME sector, which is estimated to have Rs. 32.2 million enterprises with an average credit offtake of Rs. 7.16 lakhs as at end March 2012, based on scheduled commercial banks data on a number of MSME accounts. Some data related to credit linkages of the MSME sector are available in the 4th Census on MSMEs in 2006–07. According to the Census, based on available data for 1.5 million MSMEs, formal financial institutions contributed 11.2 percent of the total credit with only 5.2 percent of total enterprises outstanding.

7.4 Government Guidelines and Measures for Credit to MSME Sector Classification of MSME Sector

As per the Master Direction, lending to the Micro, Small & Medium Enterprises (MSME) Sector issued the following criteria by RBI to be recognised under the category of MSMEs with regard to bank lending policies:

i. Manufacturing Enterprises as recognised under MSMED Act, 2006.
ii. Service Enterprises as recognised under MSMED Act, 2006.
iii. Khadi and Village Industries Sector (KVI).
iv. Other categories as follows:
   a. Loans to entities involved in assisting the decentralized sector in the supply of inputs to and marketing of outputs of artisans, village and cottage industries.
   b. Loans to co-operatives of producers in the decentralized sector viz. artisans, village and cottage industries.
   c. Loans sanctioned by banks to MFIs for on-lending to MSME sector as per the conditions specified in the extant Master Direction on 'Priority Sector Lending — Targets and Classification'.
   d. Credit outstanding under General Credit Cards.
   e. Overdrafts extended by banks after April 8, 2015 up to Rs. 5,000/- under Pradhan Mantri Jan Dhan Yojana (PMJDY) accounts provided the borrower's household annual income does not exceed Rs. 100,000/- for rural areas and Rs. 1,60,000/- for non-rural areas.
   f. Outstanding deposits with SIDBI and MUDRA Ltd.

7.5 Credit Directives Administered by RBI for MSME Sector

The RBI has administered a set of credit directives to be followed by banks in order to protect the interests of the MSME sector.[1] These guidelines are:

---

[1]Reserve Bank of India (2015). *Master Circular — Lending to Micro, Small, & Medium Enterprises (MSME) Sector*. https://rbi.org.in/Scripts/BS_CircularIndexDisplay.aspx?Id=9877 [Accessed May 18, 2019].

7.5.1 *Targets for Lending to Micro and Small Enterprises (MSE) Sector by Domestic Commercial Banks and Foreign Banks Operating in India*

i. Advances to Micro and Small Enterprises (MSE) sector shall be reckoned in computing achievement under the overall Priority Sector target of 40 percent (32 percent for Foreign Banks operating in India with less than 20 branches) of Adjusted Net Bank Credit (ANBC) or credit equivalent amount of Off-Balance Sheet Exposure, whichever is higher.
ii. In terms of the recommendations of the Prime Minister's Task Force on MSMEs, banks are advised to achieve a 20 percent year-on-year growth in credit to micro and small enterprises and a 10 percent annual growth in the number of microenterprise accounts.
iii. In order to ensure that sufficient credit is available to microenterprises within the MSE sector, banks should ensure that:
    a. 40 percent of the total advances to the MSE sector should go to micro (manufacturing) enterprises having investment in plant and machinery up to Rs. 10 lakh and micro (service) enterprises having investment in equipment up to Rs. 4 lakh.
    b. 20 percent of the total advances to the MSE sector should go to micro (manufacturing) enterprises with investment in plant and machinery above Rs. 10 lakh and up to Rs. 25 lakh, and micro (service) enterprises with investment in equipment above Rs. 4 lakh and up to Rs. 10 lakh. **Thus, 60 percent of MSE advances should go to microenterprises**.
    c. While banks are advised to achieve the 60 percent target, in terms of the recommendations of the Prime Minister's Task Force, the allocation of 60 percent of the MSE advances to microenterprises is to be achieved in stages; 50 percent in FY2010–11, 55 percent in FY2011–12 and 60 percent in FY2012–13.
iv. The target for lending to Micro Enterprises within the MSE sector (i.e. 60 percent of total lending to the MSE sector should go to microenterprises) will be computed with reference to the outstanding credit to MSE sector as on the preceding March 31st.

Additionally, a sub target of 7.5 percent of ANBC or Credit Equivalent Amount of off-Balance Sheet.

Exposure, whichever is higher also exists for all commercial banks in India, only for microenterprises.

7.6 Committees and Guidelines to Promote Credit to MSME Sector

7.6.1 *Banking Codes and Standard Board of India (BCSBI)*

The Banking Codes and Standard Board of India (BCSBI) has formulated a Code of Bank's Commitment to Micro and Small Enterprises. This is a voluntary code, which sets minimum standards of banking practices for banks to follow when they are dealing with Micro and Small Enterprises (MSEs) as defined in the Micro, Small and Medium Enterprises Development (MSMED) Act, 2006. It provides protection to MSEs and explains how banks are expected to deal with MSEs for their day to-day operations and in times of financial difficulty. The objectives of the BCSBI Code are:

a) Give a positive thrust to the MSE sector by providing easy access to efficient banking services.
b) Promote good and fair banking practices by setting minimum standards in dealing with MSEs.
c) Increase transparency so to encourage a better understanding of what can be reasonably expected of the services.
d) Improve understanding of business through effective communication.
e) Encourage market forces, through competition, to achieve higher operating standards.
f) Promote a fair and cordial relationship between MSEs and banks and also ensure timely and quick responses to banking needs.
g) Foster confidence in the banking system.

7.6.2 *Specialised MSME Branches*

Public sector banks have been advised to open at least one specialised branch in each district. Further, banks have been permitted to categorise their general banking branches having 60 percent or more of their advances to the MSME sector as specialized MSME branches in order to encourage them to open more specialised MSME branches for providing better service to this sector as a whole.

7.6.3 *Structured Mechanisms for Monitoring the Credit Growth to the MSE Sector*

In view of the concerns emerging from the deceleration in credit growth to the MSE sector, an Indian Banking Association (IBA)-led Sub-Committee (Chairman: Shri K.R. Kamath) was set up in 2013 to suggest a structured mechanism to be put in place by banks to monitor the entire gamut of credit related issues pertaining to the sector. An e-tracking of MSE loan applications, monitoring the loan application disposal process in banks, giving branch-wise, region-wise, zone-wise and State-wise positions has been proposed. The position in this regard is to be displayed by banks on their websites.

7.6.4 *Cluster Approach*

All SLBC Convenor banks have been advised to incorporate in their Annual Credit Plans, the credit requirement in the clusters identified by the Ministry of Micro, Small and Medium Enterprises, Government of India. As per the Ganguly Committee recommendations (4 September 2004), banks have been advised that a full-service approach to cater to the diverse needs of the SSI sector (now MSE sector) may be achieved through extending banking services to recognized MSE clusters by adopting approaches namely, Customer Focus, Cost Control, Cross-Sell and Contain Risk. A cluster-based approach to lending may be more beneficial: (a) in dealing with well-defined and recognized groups; (b) availability of appropriate information for risk assessment and (c) monitoring by the lending institutions.

7.6.5 *Committees on Flow of Credit to MSE Sector*

The Reserve Bank of India had appointed a one-man High-Level Committee (30 June 1998) headed by Shri S L Kapur, (IAS, Retd.), Former Secretary, Government of India, Ministry of Industry to suggest measures for improving the delivery system and simplification of procedures for credit to the SSI sector. The Committee made 126 recommendations covering a wide range of areas pertaining to financing of the SSI Sector out of 88 recommendations were accepted and implemented. Another committee to examine the Adequacy of Institutional credit to SSI Sector (now MSE) and related aspects (Nayak Committee). The Committee was constituted by Reserve Bank of India in December 1991 under the Chairmanship of Shri P. R. Nayak, examined the issues confronting SSIs (now MSEs) in the matter of obtaining finance. The Committee submitted its report in 1992 and all the major recommendations of the Committee have been accepted. A 'Working Group on Flow of Credit to SSI sector' was constituted under the Chairmanship of Dr. A. S. Ganguly in 2003–04 and the Committee made 31 recommendations covering a wide range of areas pertaining to financing of the SSI sector of which eight recommendations were accepted so far and commended to banks for implementation. A High-Level Task Force was constituted by the Government of India (Chairman: Shri T. K. A. Nair), in January 2010, to consider various issues raised by Micro, Small and Medium Enterprises (MSMEs). The Task Force recommended several measures having a bearing on the functioning of MSMEs; credit, marketing, labour, exit policy, infrastructure/technology/skill development and taxation. This was a paradigm shifting change to the issue of lending to the MSME sector that covers legal and regulatory structures and recommendations for the North-Eastern States and Jammu & Kashmir.

7.7 Branch Network in the State of Assam

The number of bank branches bank-wise (sub categorised as public, private and rural banks) for the year ending 2017–18 is presented in Table 2.

7.8 Disbursement of Credit to MSME Sector (Micro, Small or Medium) by Commercial Banks in Assam for the Year 2016–17

For the secondary data collection, only those banks for which data on credit towards MSME sector is available since the year 2012–13 have

Table 2: Bank Branch's network in Assam for the year ending 2017–18

Sl No	Bank Name	Rural (R)	Semi Urban (SU)	Urban (U)	Total (R+SU+U)
1	Allahabad Bank	41	22	13	76
2	Andhra Bank	1	1	7	9
3	Bank of Baroda	8	13	15	36
4	Bank of India	14	19	16	49
5	Bank of Maharashtra	0	5	5	10
6	Canara Bank	18	34	22	74
7	Central Bank of India	60	33	29	122
8	Dena Bank	2	3	6	11
9	Industrial Development and Bank of India	3	16	11	30
10	Indian Bank	9	15	12	36
11	Indian Overseas Bank	9	11	10	30
12	Oriental Bank of Commerce	0	10	11	21
13	Punjab National Bank	30	19	14	63
14	Punjab and Sind Bank	2	1	11	14
15	State Bank of India	186	100	81	367
16	Syndicate Bank	8	12	16	36
17	United Bank of India	169	57	31	257
18	UCO Bank	71	42	25	138
19	Union Bank of India	26	22	21	69
20	Vijaya Bank	3	8	13	24
21	Corporation Bank	0	9	8	17
Public Total		660	452	377	1489
1	HDFC Bank	9	27	27	63
2	Federal Bank	0	2	10	12
3	ICICI Bank	6	30	30	66
4	Indusind Bank	3	14	15	32
5	AXIS Bank	4	34	24	62
6	YES Bank	0	4	7	11

(Continued)

Table 2: (*Continued*)

Sl No	Bank Name	Rural (R)	Semi Urban (SU)	Urban (U)	Total (R+SU+U)
7	Kotak Mahindra Bank	0	2	2	4
8	South Indian Bank	0	0	2	2
9	Karnataka Bank Ltd	0	0	2	2
10	Bandhan Bank	41	16	13	70
Private Total		63	129	132	324
1	Assam Gramin Vikash Bank	311	83	20	414
2	Langpi Dehangi Rural Bank	52	7	0	59
RRB Total		363	90	20	473
1	Assam Co-op. Apex Bank	18	20	29	67
AACB Total		18	20	29	67
Grand Total		1104	691	558	2353

Source: State Level Bankers' Committee.

been included for MSME disbursals for the state of Assam. The State Level Bankers' Committee, North East (SLBC-NE) data showing the credit disbursals towards the MSME sector by commercial banks in Assam for the year 2016–17 as a percentage of their total credit disbursements does not paint a favourable picture for the MSMEs. The majority of the banks' (77 percent) MSME credit disbursal as a proportion of total credit disbursals ranges between 1 to 10 percent. This is presented in Table 3.

From Table 4, it can be seen that the following percentages of banks were able to achieve their sub-targets as advised by RBI (7.5 percent of total credit to Micro and 60 percent of MSME credit to micro).

From Table 4, it shows that apart from Bank of India, United Bank of India and Corporation banks, public sector banks are directing a significantly lower proportion of aggregate credit being disbursed towards the MSME sector, when compared to private sector banks. It is also interesting to note from Table 5 that less than 50 percent of banks were able to

Table 3: Credit disbursals towards MSME sector segregated by unit type by commercial banks in Assam during 2012–18 (amount in lakhs)

	2012–13				
	Disbursal Amt of Micro	**Disbursal Amt of Small**	**Disbursal Amt of Medium**	**SME Disbursal During the Year**	**Total Disbursal by Bank for the Year**
ALB	10854.18	12945.17	141.56	23940.91	441002.4
AND	0	0	0	0	43809.82
BOB	3963.56	1368.24	60.85	5392.65	230851
BOI	385.6	75	2400	2860.6	82660.42
BOM	138.52	78.82	0	217.34	7220.24
CAN	688.61	977.65	7699.11	9365.37	501214.9
CBI	3541	3590	280	7411	381540
DEN	0	59	0	59	28842
IDBI	271	1267	4227.9	5765.9	396960.5
IND	321	2826	5431	8578	148816.9
IOB	1310.27	2568.97	0	3879.24	121898.3
OBC	26	649.82	20	695.82	29878.56
PNB	472.34	678.66	0	1151	530189.5
PSB	195	0	0	195	15528.61
SBI	5404.08	12452.33	3060.54	20916.95	4648362
SYN	1085.21	910.81	349.01	2345.03	80300.06
UBI	47395	23635	820	71850	1382398
UCO	701	492	0	1193	476976.6
UNI	1716.53	711.53	4.12	2432.18	178740.5
VJB	80.53	155	0	235.53	68575.58
HDFC	11365.7	26491.81	2329.3	40186.81	373083.9
FED	430	1682.1	944.94	3057.04	80971.94
ICICI	0	457	0	457	191221
INDUS	0	0	0	0	100390.9
AXIS	69	2015	3545	5629	271838
AGVB	43859.29	3451.86	210	47521.15	1144523
LDRB	1124.67	0	0	1124.67	73755.23

(Continued)

Table 3: (*Continued*)

	2013–14				
	Disbursal Amt of Micro	**Disbursal Amt of Small**	**Disbursal Amt of Medium**	**SME Disbursal During the Year**	**Total Disbursal by Bank for the Year**
ALB	23137.86	26943.81	0	50081.67	536816.7
AND	291.21	741.64	189	1221.85	35279.23
BOB	13789.84	0	0	13789.84	253913.9
BOI	19591.91	7397.67	0	26989.58	139371.2
BOM	130.84	76.74	0	207.58	6624.63
CAN	10731.5	12396.5	2714.83	25842.83	399795.1
CBI	4651	3290	19	7960	503825
DEN	0	702	0	702	24700
IDBI	1476.22	4512.16	6293.01	12281.39	397522.1
IND	1009.9	2624.65	879.84	4514.39	156512.3
IOB	1082.74	2860.02	228.3	4171.06	135274.3
OBC	6	726	0	732	25559.34
PNB	20470.32	11680	23726	55876.32	585462.2
PSB	823.28	626.28	0	1449.56	32371.93
SBI	7700	17700	15700	41100	5155117
SYN	0	357.78	1359.26	1717.04	62755.29
UBI	41360	32465	2000	75825	1600421
UCO	553	1559	122.99	2234.99	539177.2
UNI	1875.97	1700.62	0	3576.59	197318.4
VJB	3340.75	1773.23	0	5113.98	84718.42
HDFC	22305.75	20158.34	4541.86	47005.95	574333.9
FED	55.14	76.04	220.1	351.28	86930.9
ICICI	3117	6349	0	9466	145819
INDUS	11640.47	13223.68	0	24864.15	182071.1
AXIS	1388	2423	1725	5536	223560
AGVB	50040.96	8233.43	2260	60534.39	1372751
LDRB	571.52	0	0	571.52	84301.81

Table 3: *(Continued)*

	2014–15				
	Disbursal Amt of Micro	**Disbursal Amt of Small**	**Disbursal Amt of Medium**	**SME Disbursal During the Year**	**Total Disbursal by Bank for the Year**
ALB	14515	21543	0	36058	502483.5
AND	556.91	1408.47	0	1965.38	101891.4
BOB	6293.72	0	0	6293.72	239292.8
BOI	4428	921	600	5949	121792.5
BOM	92.87	267.57	13.4	373.84	123339.8
CAN	4202	9386.06	924.91	14512.97	503015.2
CBI	6780	5310	867	12957	461580
DEN	2	2092	178	2272	146289
IDBI	1631.35	2388.79	1455	5475.14	356015.9
IND	4243.72	5208.63	375	9827.35	158029.1
IOB	3071.11	3189.71	0	6406.82	96728.95
OBC	1730.08	0	0	1730.08	182695.3
PNB	7003.74	10606.5	146	25442.49	483279.5
PSB	922.38	1485.12	0	2407.5	21337.32
SBI	16300	33900	23300	73500	4024468
SYN	1782.46	3051.2	33	4866.66	476079
UBI	33739	18672	36	52447	1444693
UCO	1250	1861	0	3111	513248.4
UNI	4486	1687.21	222.33	6395.54	197710.7
VJB	4619.58	4357.93	0	8977.51	72266.35
HDFC	19517.74	7995.38	3174.49	30687.61	684631.2
FED	4367.21	6262.76	3078.42	13708.39	94375.29
ICICI	22772.82	19138.96	3406.2	45317.98	185763.1
INDUS	9145.98	17146	750.42	27042.4	218606.7
AXIS	70.96	359.32	1961.7	2391.98	403803
AGVB	61029.92	8830.12	2607.84	72467.88	1508218
LDRB	386.87	27	0	413.87	94127.22

(Continued)

Table 3: (*Continued*)

	2015–16				
	Disbursal Amt of Micro	**Disbursal Amt of Small**	**Disbursal Amt of Medium**	**SME Disbursal During the Year**	**Total Disbursal by Bank for the Year**
ALB	21117.29	20199.56	4638.62	45955.47	685169.3
AND	1192.44	2821	0	4013.44	56478.67
BOB	9600.34	0	0	9600.34	299773.5
BOI	7021	4674	0	11695	179874.8
BOM	1698	1025.13	1111.33	3834.46	19536.28
CAN	7558.99	7858.79	1701.98	17119.76	585596.5
CBI	5562	3091	131.58	8784.58	729422
DEN	0	0	0	0	52091
IDBI	12322.41	24616.7	13591.46	50530.57	451116.3
IND	5231.4	8841.25	3000	17072.65	278321.8
IOB	2037	7898	139	10074	98840.52
OBC	0	0	0	0	43660.82
PNB	16956	15583	3340	35879	766946.1
PSB	325.77	579.63	0	905.4	42874.95
SBI	27800	43200	4880	75880	7582375
SYN	7916.71	4711.9	675	13303.61	129799.5
UBI	23159	363	26	23548	1997085
UCO	907.26	1579.67	518.18	3005.11	628716.2
UNI	3001.7	1582.57	1818.83	6403.1	302584
VJB	5481.03	2825.43	0	8306.46	108172
HDFC	32697.12	15589.27	0	48286.39	935862.5
FED	10831.56	14839.82	4693.81	30365.19	108755.8
ICICI	31425.81	21446.53	6146.84	59019.18	246763.8
INDUS	8991.4	10284.38	2281.63	21557.41	139641.1
AXIS	565.63	0	0	565.63	512802.7
AGVB	50901.49	11095.04	2163.99	64160.52	1633199
LDRB	1212.24	2.17	0	1214.41	112996.2

Table 3: (*Continued*)

	2016–17				
	Disbursal Amt of Micro	**Disbursal Amt of Small**	**Disbursal Amt of Medium**	**SME Disbursal During the Year**	**Total Disbursal by Bank for the Year**
ALB	16992.45	16993.61	1480	35466.06	764337.2
AND	298.11	705.25	0	1003.36	71263
BOB	6573.4	0	0	6573.4	317009.1
BOI	29248	27055	2354	58657	190445
BOM	592.33	40	55	687.33	18481.86
CAN	15166	27298	3659	46123	617822
CBI	4604	1972	3469	10045	720636
DEN	1127.46	1055	2	2184.46	50695
IDBI	12650	1634	88	14372	375590.1
IND	12495	5241	1430	19166	344686.9
IOB	533	2825.5	650	4008.5	164761.9
OBC	340	574	0	914	49597
PNB	12931	3514	9780	26225	853390.3
PSB	978	678	51	1707	44211.23
SBI	25700	30100	7200	63000	7585763
SYN	2083	3285	0	5368	140872.8
UBI	22670	14110	410	37190	1657132
UCO	1802.65	953.67	812.24	3568.56	652712.8
UNI	2649.39	743.23	95.78	3488.4	323979.1
VJB	5498.46	2358.22	98	7954.68	152151.5
HDFC	54964.09	22628.26	7049.14	84641.49	1143191
FED	10959.98	12081.1	7203.33	30244.41	120755.8
ICICI	49732	19618	6883	76233	325348.3
INDUS	3795	11834	529	16158	281363.1
AXIS	2989.41	2623	363	5975.41	578617.4
AGVB	41749.5	11872.31	1904	55525.81	1627673
LDRB	1058	0	0	1058	138095.9

(*Continued*)

Table 3: (*Continued*)

	2017–18				
	Disbursal Amt of Micro	**Disbursal Amt of Small**	**Disbursal Amt of Medium**	**SME Disbursal During the Year**	**Total Disbursal by Bank for the year**
ALB	17295.78	14658.8	1575	33529.58	839151.1
AND	2175	1353	1551	5079	32630.86
BOB	10705.64	5893.9	2264.84	18864.38	277029.9
BOI	66272	32690	2512	101474	236250
BOM	24	20	48	92	23511.41
CAN	10225.82	11538.82	6190.65	27955.29	647034.6
CBI	4292	2758	85	7135	722233.7
DEN	2413	213	0	2626	25188
IDBI	14886.1	1889.62	2076.96	18852.68	317910.5
IND	1777.14	8162.19	3213.63	13152.96	324128.9
IOB	5421	2921	643	8985	201874.7
OBC	19944.81	8673.95	619.73	29238.49	62431.64
PNB	3726.54	632.42	5155.06	9514.02	915371.5
PSB	1669.78	765.38	5	2440.16	51667.37
SBI	10105	3422	5946	19473	8383618
SYN	11433.96	2992.51	0	14426.47	145967.4
UBI	17479	13752	1450	32681	1687687
UCO	3116	1322	0	4438	698355.5
UNI	8225.26	1797.58	216.42	10239.26	474974
VJB	7016.79	3989.28	37.5	11043.57	153495.3
HDFC	65555.66	37571.96	6761.14	109888.8	1511616
FED	13546.83	17228.48	4353	35128.31	144370.7
ICICI	56766.46	30442.93	11535.73	98745.12	425700
INDUS	5957.14	16612.8	12.73	22582.67	374809.4
AXIS	8904.23	12827.4	6652.08	28383.71	791927.2
AGVB	48983.26	20275.43	4229	73487.69	1596108
LDRB	2264.17	764.53	0	3028.7	156780.9

Source: State Level Bankers' Committee Reports.

Table 4: Proportion of MSME out of total credit and proportion of micro out of total credit and total MSME credit (in percentage)

	2012–13			2013–14		
Bank	**% of Micro Out of Total Disbursals**	**Micro as % of Total MSE Disbursal**	**MSME as % of Total Disbursements**	**% of Micro Out of Total Disbursals**	**Micro as % of Total MSE Disbursal**	**MSME as % of Total Disbursements**
ALB	2.46	45.61	5.43	4.31	46.20	9.33
AND	0.00	0.00	0.00	0.83	28.19	3.46
BOB	1.72	74.34	2.34	5.43	100.00	5.43
BOI	0.47	83.72	3.46	14.06	72.59	19.37
BOM	1.92	63.73	3.01	1.98	63.03	3.13
CAN	0.14	41.33	1.87	2.68	46.40	6.46
CBI	0.93	49.66	1.94	0.92	58.57	1.58
DEN	0.00	0.00	0.20	0.00	0.00	2.84
IDBI	0.07	17.62	1.45	0.37	24.65	3.09
IND	0.22	10.20	5.76	0.65	27.79	2.88
IOB	1.07	33.78	3.18	0.80	27.46	3.08
OBC	0.09	3.85	2.33	0.02	0.82	2.86
PNB	0.09	41.04	0.22	3.50	63.67	9.54
PSB	1.26	100.00	1.26	2.54	56.80	4.48
SBI	0.12	30.26	0.45	0.15	30.31	0.80
SYN	1.35	54.37	2.92	0.00	0.00	2.74
UBI	3.43	66.73	5.20	2.58	56.02	4.74
UCO	0.15	58.76	0.25	0.10	26.18	0.41
UNI	0.96	70.70	1.36	0.95	52.45	1.81
VJB	0.12	34.19	0.34	3.94	65.33	6.04
HDFC	3.05	30.02	10.77	3.88	52.53	8.18
FED	0.53	20.36	3.78	0.06	42.03	0.40
ICICI	0.00	0.00	0.24	2.14	32.93	6.49
INDUS	0.00	0.00	0.00	6.39	46.82	13.66
AXIS	0.03	3.31	2.07	0.62	36.42	2.48
AGVB	3.83	92.70	4.15	3.65	85.87	4.41
LDRB	1.52	100.00	1.52	0.68	100.00	0.68

(*Continued*)

Table 4: (*Continued*)

Bank	2014–15			2015–16		
	% of Micro Out of Total Disbursals	Micro as % of Total MSE Disbursal	MSME as % of Total Disbursements	% of Micro Out of Total Disbursals	Micro as % of Total MSE Disbursal	MSME as % of Total Disbursements
ALB	2.89	40.25	7.18	3.08	51.11	6.71
AND	0.55	28.34	1.93	2.11	29.71	7.11
BOB	2.63	100.00	2.63	3.20	100.00	3.20
BOI	3.64	82.78	4.88	3.90	60.03	6.50
BOM	0.08	25.77	0.30	8.69	62.35	19.63
CAN	0.84	30.92	2.89	1.29	49.03	2.92
CBI	1.47	56.08	2.81	0.76	64.28	1.20
DEN	0.00	0.10	1.55	0.00	0.00	0.00
IDBI	0.46	40.58	1.54	2.73	33.36	11.20
IND	2.69	44.90	6.22	1.88	37.17	6.13
IOB	3.17	49.05	6.62	2.06	20.50	10.19
OBC	0.95	100.00	0.95	0.00	0.00	0.00
PNB	1.45	39.77	5.26	2.21	52.11	4.68
PSB	4.32	38.31	11.28	0.76	35.98	2.11
SBI	0.41	32.47	1.83	0.37	39.15	1.00
SYN	0.37	36.88	1.02	6.10	62.69	10.25
UBI	2.34	64.37	3.63	1.16	98.46	1.18
UCO	0.24	40.18	0.61	0.14	36.48	0.48
UNI	2.27	72.67	3.23	0.99	65.48	2.12
VJB	6.39	51.46	12.42	5.07	65.99	7.68
HDFC	2.85	70.94	4.48	3.49	67.71	5.16
FED	4.63	41.08	14.53	9.96	42.19	27.92
ICICI	12.26	54.34	24.40	12.74	59.44	23.92
INDUS	4.18	34.79	12.37	6.44	46.65	15.44
AXIS	0.02	16.49	0.59	0.11	100.00	0.11
AGVB	4.05	87.36	4.80	3.12	82.10	3.93
LDRB	0.41	93.48	0.44	1.07	99.82	1.07

Table 4: (*Continued*)

	2016–17			2017–18		
Bank	**% of Micro Out of Total Disbursals**	**Micro as % of Total MSE Disbursal**	**MSME as % of Total Disbursements**	**% of Micro Out of Total Disbursals**	**Micro as % of Total MSE Disbursal**	**MSME as % of Total Disbursements**
ALB	2.22	50.00	4.64	2.06	54.13	4.00
AND	0.42	29.71	1.41	6.67	61.65	15.57
BOB	2.07	100.00	2.07	3.86	64.49	6.81
BOI	15.36	51.95	30.80	28.05	66.97	42.95
BOM	3.20	93.67	3.72	0.10	54.55	0.39
CAN	2.45	35.71	7.47	1.58	46.98	4.32
CBI	0.64	70.01	1.39	0.59	60.88	0.99
DEN	2.22	51.66	4.31	9.58	91.89	10.43
IDBI	3.37	88.56	3.83	4.68	88.74	5.93
IND	3.63	70.45	5.56	0.55	17.88	4.06
IOB	0.32	15.87	2.43	2.69	64.98	4.45
OBC	0.69	37.20	1.84	31.95	69.69	46.83
PNB	1.52	78.63	3.07	0.41	85.49	1.04
PSB	2.21	59.06	3.86	3.23	68.57	4.72
SBI	0.34	46.06	0.83	0.12	74.70	0.23
SYN	1.48	38.80	3.81	7.83	79.26	9.88
UBI	1.37	61.64	2.24	1.04	55.97	1.94
UCO	0.28	65.40	0.55	0.45	70.21	0.64
UNI	0.82	78.09	1.08	1.73	82.07	2.16
VJB	3.61	69.98	5.23	4.57	63.75	7.19
HDFC	4.81	70.84	7.40	4.34	63.57	7.27
FED	9.08	47.57	25.05	9.38	44.02	24.33
ICICI	15.29	71.71	23.43	13.33	65.09	23.20
INDUS	1.35	24.28	5.74	1.59	26.39	6.03
AXIS	0.52	53.26	1.03	1.12	40.97	3.58
AGVB	2.56	77.86	3.41	3.07	70.73	4.60
LDRB	0.77	100.00	0.77	1.44	74.76	1.93

Source: Table 3.

Table 5: Percentage of banks in Assam which have achieved sub-targets to micro sector classified by public, private and RRBs

	2010–11		2011–12		2012–13		2013–14		2014–15		2015–16	
Banks	**% of Micro Out of Total Disbursals**	**Micro as % of Total MSME Disbursal**	**% of Micro Out of Total Disbursals**	**Micro as % of Total MSME Disbursal**	**% of Micro Out of Total Disbursals**	**Micro as % of Total MSME Disbursal**	**% of Micro Out of Total Disbursals**	**Micro as % of Total MSME Disbursal**	**% of Micro Out of Total Disbursals**	**Micro as % of Total MSME Disbursal**	**% of Micro Out of Total Disbursals**	**Micro as % of Total MSME Disbursal**
Public sector banks	0%	30	5%	25%	0%	25%	0%	40%	5%	50%	35%	75%
Private sector banks	0%	0%	0%	0%	20%	20%	40%	40%	40%	40%	40%	40%
RRBs	0%	100%	0%	100%	0%	100%	0%	100%	0%	100%	0%	100%

achieve the sub-target of at least 60 percent of total credit to the MSME sector towards the micro sector.

7.8.1 *Targets and Achievement of Credit to MSME Sector Over the Years in Assam*

To evaluate the scenario in a more detailed manner, a study of the targets and achievements bank-wise for the MSME sector credit disbursal that has been completed in Assam is shown in Table 6.

The bank-wise disbursal of credit to the MSME sector from 2011 to 2018 separated by public sector, private sector and regional rural banks has been presented graphically in Figures 1–3.

From Table 6, average targets and achievements can be calculated as well as the percentage of target that has been achieved as shown in Table 7.

The average targets and achievements of banks in Assam over the years are presented in Figures 4–6.

From Figures 4–6, it can be seen that overall average targets over the years have been fluctuating, while overall average achievements show steady growth and in two instances average achievements were seen to surpass average targets in 2012–13 and in 2016–17. Average achievement seems to show a growing trend for public sector and private sector banks but comparatively, private banks show a steeper growth compared to public sector banks. RRBs show a consistent growth although average achievement seems to have declined post 2015. Table 8 shows the percentage of banks that were able to achieve their targets.

It can be seen from Table 8 that private banks have been able to achieve their targets of year on year growth at 20 percent as recommended by the Prime Minister's Task Force towards the MSME sector which is significantly better when compared to public sector banks and RRBs. However, when corroborated with Table 5, it is found that private banks have marginally failed to achieve the sub-target of 7.5 percent credit towards microenterprises when compared to public sector banks and RRBs. It implies that private sector banks have neglected the microenterprises within the MSME sector.

Table 6: Targets and achievement of MSME sector credit over the years bank-wise in Assam (amt. in lakhs)

Bank Name	Target	Achievement	Target	Achievement	Target	Achievement	Target	Achievement	Target	Achievement	Target	Achievement	Target	Achievement	Target	Achievement
YR	**2010–11**		**2011–12**		**2012–13**		**2013–14**		**2014–15**		**2015–16**		**2016–17**		**2017–18**	
ALB	4786	3675	4786.67	10405.94	3143	11526.84	21399	22770	7653	16577	10000	21168.89	10120	18582	13897	10060.01
ANB	105.58	49	105.58	1.86	136	346.93	518	692	900	1002.36	1200	1003.36	1140	137	428	1693
BOB	700	522	783.33	357.87	847	3284.8	6549	6842.98	3601	1977.45	5000	4236.53	4990	2769.3	4276	7062.46
BOI	440.84	1150	440.84	895.99	742	1212.5	4665	9932	5515	2260	8000	2563	7120	17150.01	6842	26919
BOM	184.14	18	184.14	62.52	163	137.02	71	26.18	1125	177.69	1200	2766.01	1420	268.14	855	23
CNB	2703.27	583	2703.27	2707.98	1422	7831.27	9699	6636.63	5965	8678.51	8000	8451.5	8550	12086	11545	3222
CBI	3315.12	706	3315.12	891	6373	5080	11054	4203	13842	2316	20000	1954.06	15680	3064	20097	3952
DNB	106.13	55	106.13	83	132	16	726	517	1013	619	1500	355	1420	1046	1497	740
IDBI	3213.36	41	3213.36	97.9	335	1238	23884	4623.3	2701	6672	3700	4767.85	3700	8048.5	4062	8969.94
INB	1900.85	1910	1900.85	227	1479	334	4531	3895.39	3826	3310.5	5500	6722.65	4990	7938.5	4704	2344.32
IOB	3900	2604	2170.29	249.65	1025	1964.13	7838	373.26	3151	2607	4500	150	4130	2811.6	4276	5309
OBC	234.54	74	234.54	80	269	86	1195	96	1463	865.04	1800	913	1710	914.36	2138	8697.64
PNB	1706.1	9900	1706.1	468.34	2814	223.55	34649	18168.32	8778	13093	9000	17970	12970	8970.29	10690	2810.52
PSB	285.53	224	285.53	144.5	290	65	200	434.93	788	553.86	1200	147.28	1140	709.28	428	353.1
SBI	9962.14	6815	9962.14	5900	18341	7300	102000	16900	36913	19600	50000	18200	40630	4200	50789	251
SYB	801.68	275	801.68	383.72	559	469.25	3517	1270	2476	2077	3500	2286	3700	1497.94	4490	2031.81

UNI	16142.52	11124	16142.52	18900	10673	24215	53001	11185	27122	9890	35000	7507	30220	14329	26395	6091
UCO	3409.21	283	3409.21	407.07	5238	553	7308	165	16543	1458	22000	2077.65	20670	2629	17153	1250
UNI	1850	459	1850	2998.49	3484	777.25	9160	313.63	7090	1561.31	1000	2453.39	7890	30382	10476	1501.84
VB	607.49	11	607.49	21	908	74.03	435	2085.46	1913	2928.2	2500	2321.69	2560	3060.4	2566	2811.34
HDFC	6842	6191.05	1449.52	11449.68	5500	16708.3	12807	19503.89	4840	10021.74	7000	26146.32	7120	39204.35	6842	31217.19
FB	201	3	209.6	756	216	1058.51	4916	274.9	1350	2757	1800	6415.77	1710	8726.27	641	9244.76
ICICI	8124	9722.41	573.43	2587	727	100	275	6278	5740	12158.98	8000	24392	6410	20259	8124	27346.44
INDUS	177.48	2820	177.48	5641	182	3327	597.5	6104.36	1013	9883.78	1200	13098	1420	11509	2352	10313.89
AXIS	1093.61	5.67	1093.61	11.34	935	2401	20409	2026	4051	8226	5200	14768	7790	4528	6628	56594
AGVB	8874.51	5112	8874.51	13138	16864	21275.67	39043	28450.64	44566	31475.54	62000	26414.23	8120	25009.44	54236.6	21162.73
LDRB	596.91	78	596.91	502.74	742	475.5	307	189.13	6415	171.28	9000	618.43	6700	283.01	12614	877.67

Source: Compiled from State Level Bankers' Committee Reports.

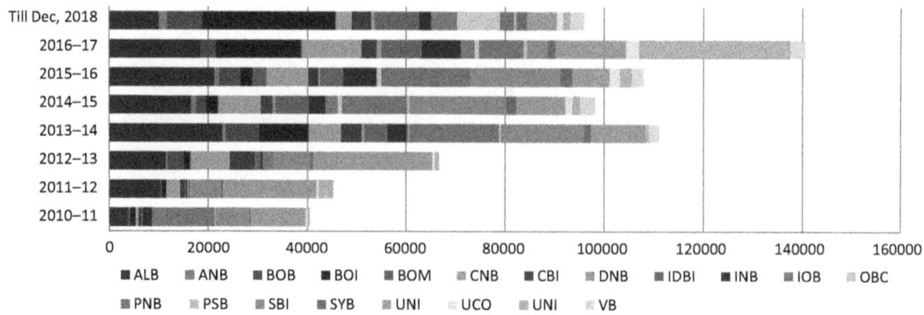

Figure 1: Chart showing bank-wise disbursal of credit to the MSME sector during 2011 to 2018 for public sector banks in Assam

Source: Table 6.

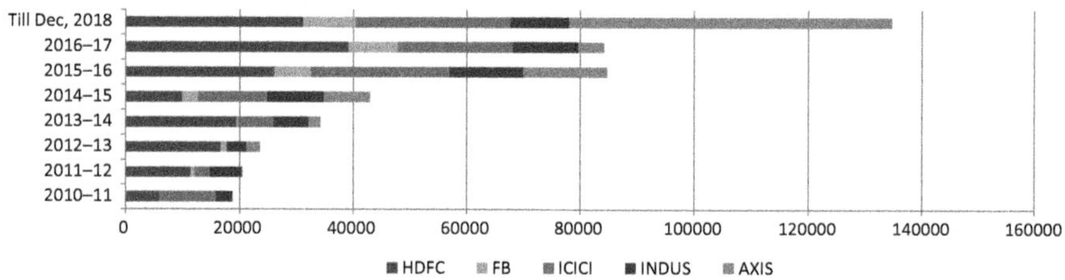

Figure 2: Chart showing bank-wise disbursal of credit to the MSME sector during 2011 to 2018 for private sector banks in Assam

Source: Table 6.

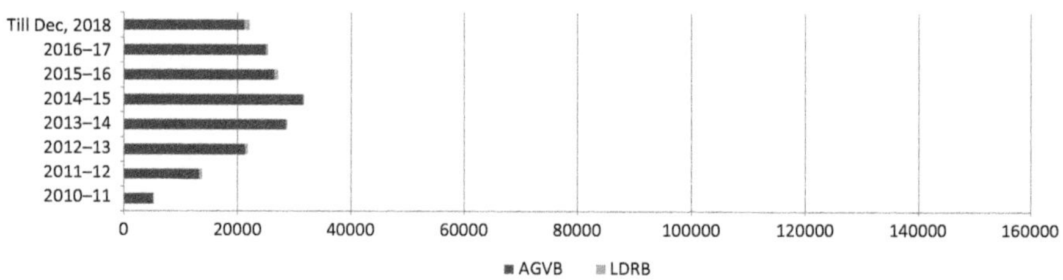

Figure 3: Chart showing bank wise disbursal of credit to MSME sector during 2011–18 for RRBs in Assam

Source: Table 6.

Table 7: Average targets and achievements (MSME Sector) and performance in Assam

Period	**2010–11**	**2011–12**	**2012–13**	**2013–14**	**2014–15**	**2015–16**	**2016–17**	**2017–18**
Average Target (in lakhs)	2938.00	2417.28	2983.54	13560.14	8139.04	10660.71	8240.00	10613.07
Average Achievement (in lakhs)	2199.45	2417.69	3871.67	6213.79	6232.24	7861.31	8936.09	9043.92
Bank Name	**Proportion of target achieved each year by individual banks (in %) (Achievement/Target)**							
ALB	76.79	217.39	366.75	106.41	216.61	211.69	183.62	72.39
ANB	46.41	1.76	254.41	133.5	111.37	83.61	12.02	395.56
BOB	74.57	45.69	387.82	104.49	54.91	84.73	55.50	165.17
BOI	260.87	203.25	163.41	212.90	40.98	32.04	240.87	393.44
BOM	9.78	33.95	84.06	36.87	15.79	230.50	18.88	2.69
CNB	21.57	100.17	550.72	68.43	145.49	105.64	141.36	27.91
CBI	21.30	26.88	79.71	38.02	16.73	9.77	19.54	19.66
DNB	51.82	78.21	12.12	71.21	61.11	23.67	73.66	49.43
IDBI	1.28	3.05	369.55	19.36	247.02	128.86	217.53	220.83
INB	100.48	11.94	22.58	85.97	86.53	122.23	159.09	49.84
IOB	66.77	11.50	191.62	4.76	82.74	3.33	68.08	124.16

(*Continued*)

Table 7: *(Continued)*

Period	**2010–11**	**2011–12**	**2012–13**	**2013–14**	**2014–15**	**2015–16**	**2016–17**	**2017–18**
Bank Name	**Proportion of target achieved each year by individual banks (in %) (Achievement/Target)**							
OBC	31.55	34.18	31.97	8.03	59.13	50.72	53.47	406.81
PNB	580.27	27.45	7.94	52.44	149.16	199.67	69.16	26.29
PSB	78.45	50.6	22.41	217.47	70.29	12.27	62.22	82.50
SBI	68.41	59.22	39.80	16.57	53.10	36.40	10.34	0.49
SYB	34.30	47.86	83.94	36.11	83.89	65.31	40.48	45.25
UNI	68.91	117.08	226.88	21.10	36.46	21.45	47.42	23.08
UCO	8.30	11.94	10.56	2.26	8.81	9.44	12.72	7.29
UNI	24.81	162.08	22.31	3.42	22.02	245.34	385.07	14.34
VB	1.81	3.46	8.15	479.42	153.07	92.87	119.55	109.56
HDFC	90.49	789.89	303.79	152.29	207.06	373.52	550.62	456.26
FB	1.49	360.69	490.05	5.59	204.22	356.43	510.31	1442.24
ICICI	119.68	451.14	13.76	2282.91	211.83	304.90	316.05	336.61
INDUS	1588.91	3178.39	1828	1022.44	975.69	1091.50	810.49	438.52
AXIS	0.51	1.04	256.79	9.93	203.06	284.00	58.13	853.86
AGVB	57.60	148.04	126.16	72.87	70.63	42.60	308.00	39.02
LDRB	13.07	84.22	64.08	61.61	2.67	6.87	4.22	6.96

Source: Table 4 and author.

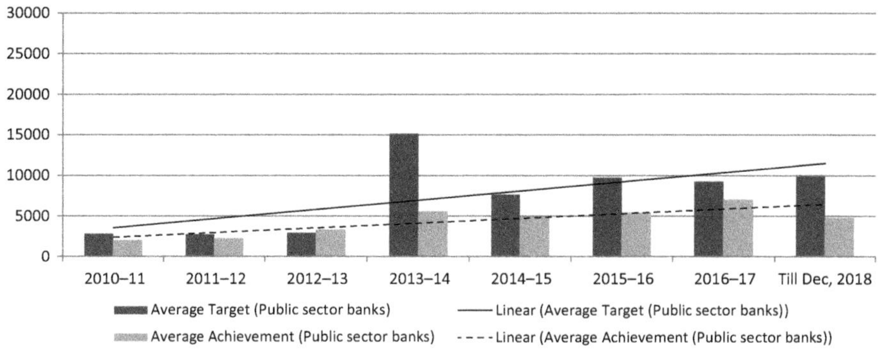

Figure 4: Average annual targets and achievements of MSME sector (public sector banks)
Source: Table 7.

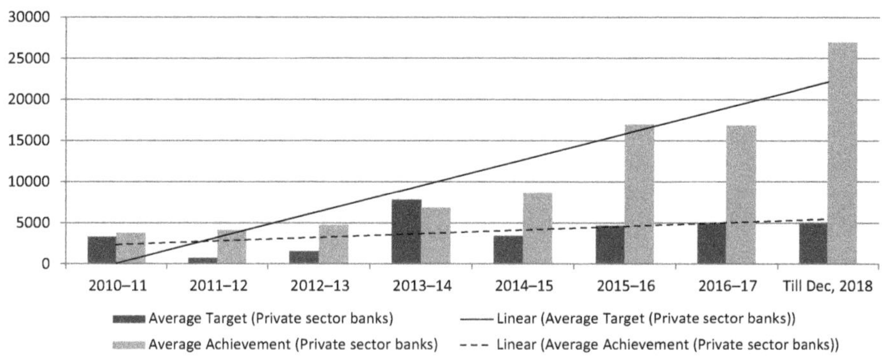

Figure 5: Average annual targets and achievements of MSME sector (private sector banks)
Source: Table 7.

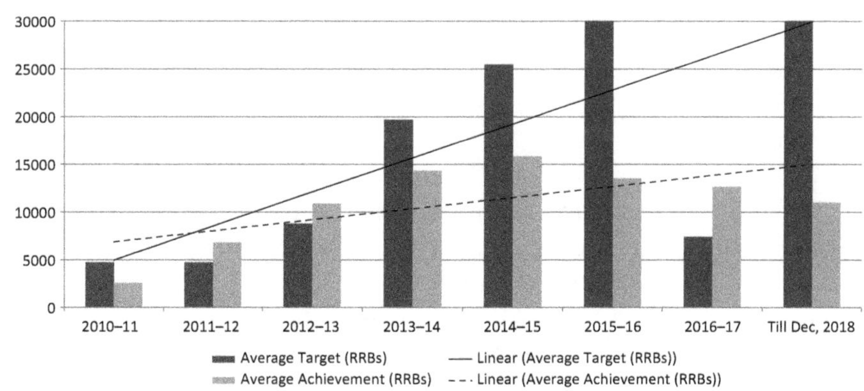

Figure 6: Average annual targets and achievements of MSME sector (RRBs)
Source: Table 7.

Table 8: Percentage of targets achieved by banks in Assam classified as public, private and RRBs as prescribed by RBI

Banks	2010–11	2011–12	2012–13	2013–14	2014–15	2015–16	2016–17	2017–18
Public sector banks	15%	25%	40%	30%	30%	35%	35%	35%
Private sector banks	40%	80%	80%	60%	100%	100%	80%	100%
RRBs	0%	50%	50%	0%	0%	0%	50%	0%

Source: Table 7.

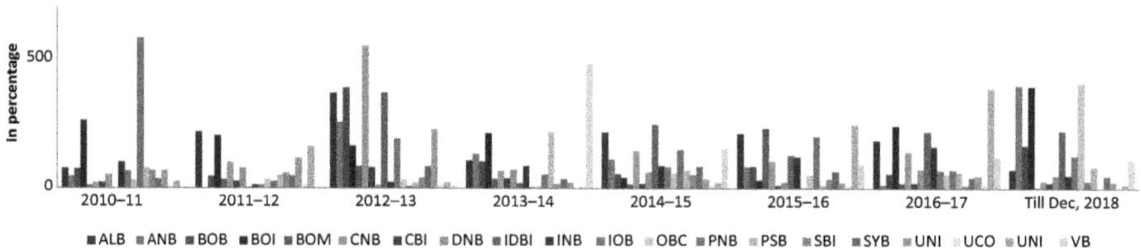

Figure 7: Proportion of targets achieved by public sector banks in Assam

Source: Table 7.

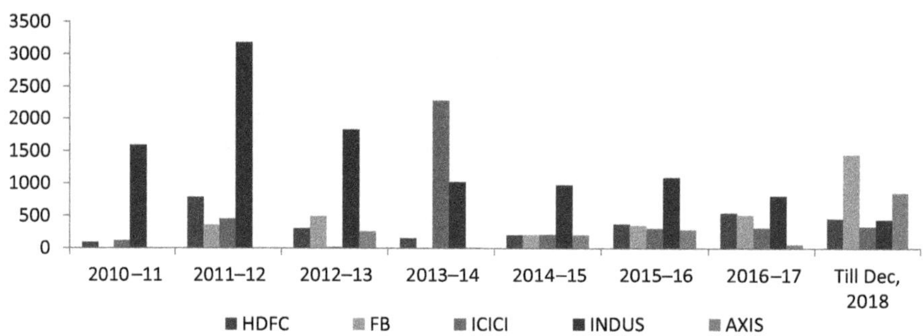

Figure 8: Proportion of targets achieved by private sector banks in Assam

Source: Table 7.

Further, the percentage of target achieved each year by individual banks has been plotted separately for public sector banks, private sector banks and RRBs as shown in Figures 7–9.

From Figures 7–9, the major observation is that private banks like HDFC, ICICI, INDUS and AXIS were seen to have achieved comparatively higher than public sector banks. Most of the public sector banks are

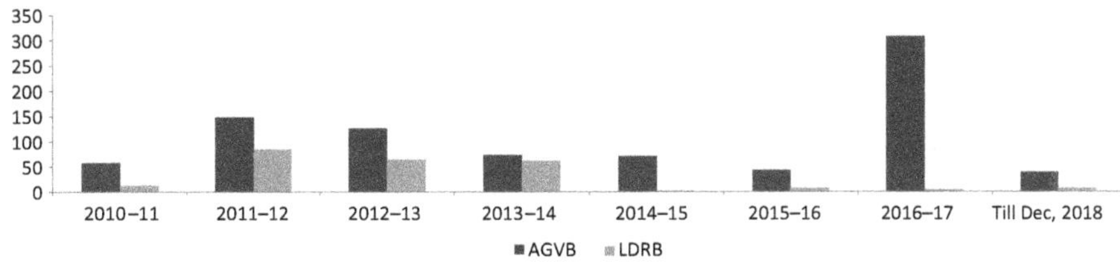

Figure 9: Proportion of targets achieved by RRBs in Assam

Source: Table 7.

seen to struggle to achieve a 100 percent of targets over the years. In the case of RRBs, AGVN has been observed to be doing reasonably well compared to LDRB.

7.9 Comparison of Trends of Flow of Credit to MSME Sector in Assam and Pan India

7.9.1 *Comparison of Flow of Bank Credit in Assam and India*

In order to find out the status of aggregate credit flow to the MSME sector in comparison to aggregate credit flow, reports published by the State Level Bankers Committee, Reserve Bank of India reports and Annual Reports by the Ministry of MSME were used. Table 9 shows the flow of credit to the MSME sector as well as aggregate flow of credit to the state as well as the country as a whole. Table 10 shows the year on year growth as calculated from Table 9.

The data from the table has been represented using bar graphs and line charts from Figures 10–14.

From Table 10 and Figures 11–14, it is observed that though both aggregate credit by banks in Assam and aggregate credit by banks in India are increasing, credit to the MSME sector remains proportionately and almost consistently lower. But if compared, proportion of credit to MSMEs as compared to aggregate credit, in Assam, has been higher than for all of India since 2013. As seen in Figure 13, the share of MSME credit to total credit in Assam has started to improve post 2013 in contrast to total India levels. Also, from Figure 14, it is observed that

Table 9: Aggregate credit and MSME credit by banks in India and Assam

Year	Aggregate Credit to MSME Sector by Banks in Assam (in crores)	Aggregate Credit by Banks in Assam (in crores)	Aggregate Credit to MSME Sector by Banks in India (in crores)	Aggregate Bank Credit in India (in crores)	Proportion of MSME Credit by Banks to Total Credit by Banks in Assam (in %)	Proportion of MSME Credit by Banks to Total Credit by Banks in India (in %)	Proportion of MSME Credit by Banks in Assam to MSME Credit by All India Banks (in %)
2008	686	12990	151137	1361595	**5.28**	**11.1**	**0.45**
2009	1018	16082	191408	1693876	**6.33**	**11.3**	**0.53**
2010	1282	17751	276319	2109076	**7.22**	**13.10142**	**0.46**
2011	1460	20911	369430	2493498	**6.9**	**14.81573**	**0.39**
2012	2054	25605	368600	4491200	**8.02**	**8.207161**	**0.55**
2013	2029	27401	409000	4964200	**7.40**	**8.238991**	**0.49**
2014	3417	31743	456500	5447100	**10.76**	**8.380606**	**0.74**
2015	4332	36477	506500	6102300	**11.87**	**8.300149**	**0.85**
2016	7480	46852	485800	6650000	**15.96**	**7.305263**	**1.53**
2017	6907	38621	474500	7134700	**17.88**	**6.650595**	**1.45**

Source: Compiled from slbcne.com, RBI, Ministry of MSME Annual Reports (percentages are author calculated).

Table 10: Year-over-year growth in Aggregate credit and MSME credit by banks in India and Assam (in %)

Year	Y-o-Y Growth in Aggregate Credit to MSME Sector by Banks in Assam (in %)	Y-o-Y Growth in Aggregate Credit by Banks in Assam (in %)	Y-o-Y Growth in Aggregate Credit to MSME Sector by Banks in India (%)	Y-o-Y Growth in Aggregate Bank Credit in India (in %)
2008				
2009	48.40	23.80	26.65	24.40
2010	25.93	10.38	44.36	24.51
2011	13.88	17.80	33.70	18.23
2012	40.68	22.45	–0.22	80.12
2013	–1.22	7.01	10.96	10.53
2014	68.41	15.85	11.61	9.73
2015	26.78	14.91	10.95	12.03
2016	72.67	28.44	–4.09	8.98
2017	–7.66	–17.57	–2.33	7.29

Source: Calculated from Table 9.

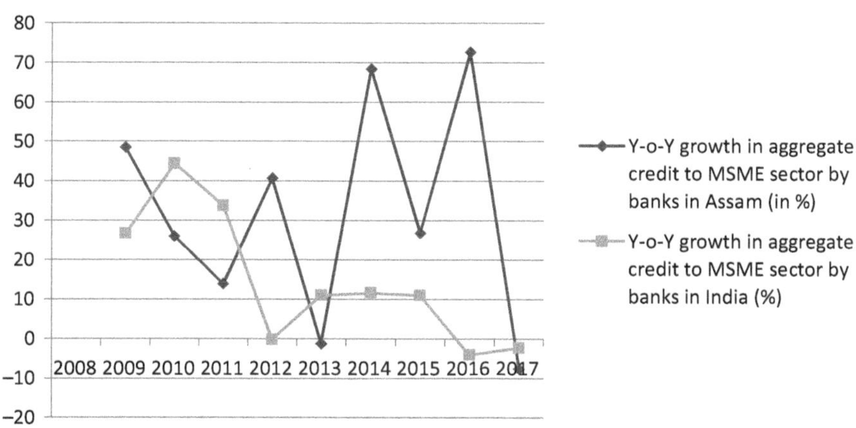

Figure 10: Year over year growth in aggregate credit to MSME sector by banks in Assam and banks pan India

Source: Table 10.

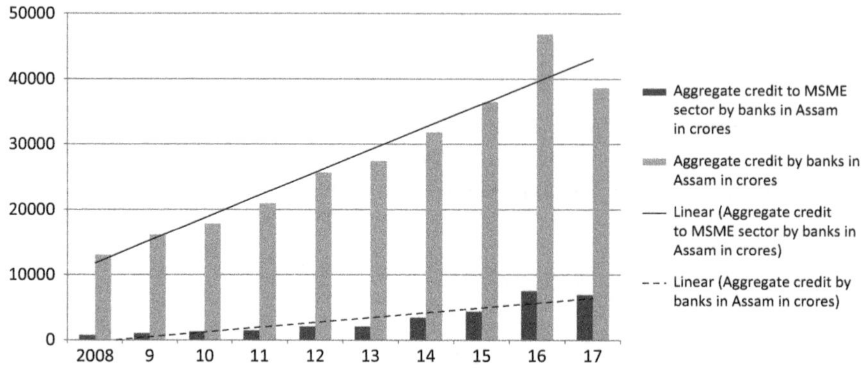

Figure 11: Bank credit in Assam (in crores)

Source: Table 10.

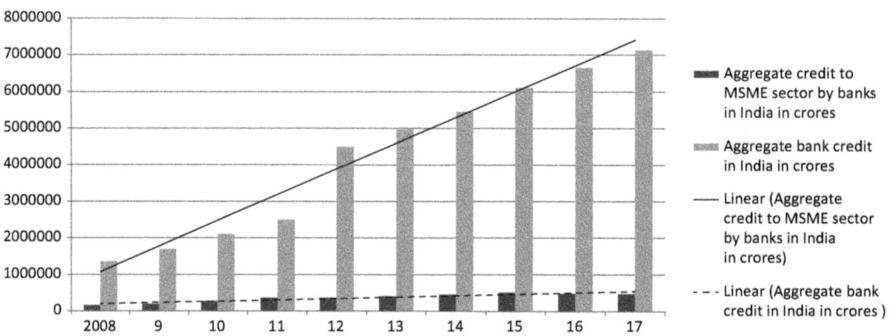

Figure 12: Bank credit in India (in crores)

Source: Table 10.

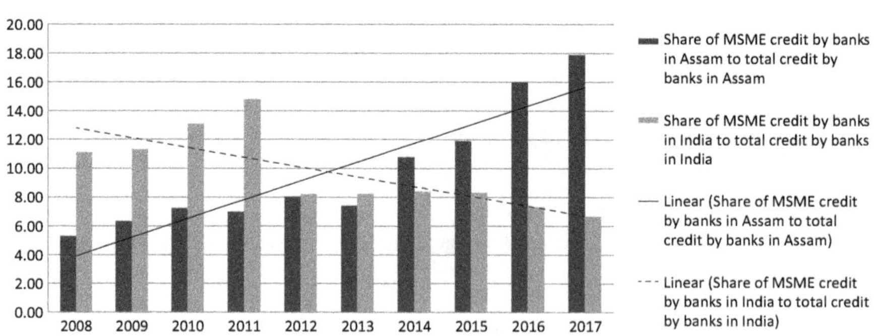

Figure 13: Share of MSME credit to aggregate credit (in %)

Source: Table 10.

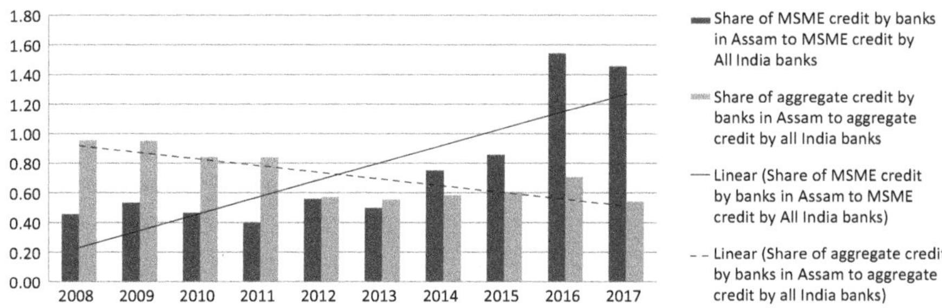

Figure 14: Share of credit disbursed in Assam to credit disbursed in India

Source: Table 10.

the share of MSME credit by banks in Assam to MSME credit by all India banks has started increasing compared to the share of aggregate credit by banks in Assam to aggregate credit by all India banks after 2012.

7.10 Conclusion

When individual contributions are compared, private sector banks as well as RRBs seem to take the cake by a huge margin over public sector banks in Assam in terms of lending to the MSME sector. In the case of public sector banks, only United Bank of India, Allahabad bank and Bank of India have been observed to give sizeable contributors. It is also observed that for the year 2016–17 less than 50 percent of banks were able to achieve the sub-target of at least 60 percent of total credit to the MSME sector towards the micro sector as implemented by RBI. The proportion of MSME credit out of total credit by banks in Assam has been consistently lower than the proportion of MSME credit out of total credit by banks in India till 2012, after which it seems to have increased. Though it shows a positive picture the year on year growth of MSME credit and total credit gives a more detailed insight. After 2015 the aggregate credit to the MSME sector all over India has decreased, whereas the aggregate credit to all sectors has increased. On the other hand, in 2017 it is observed that aggregate credit to the MSME sector by banks in Assam has decreased and the aggregate credit to all sectors has also decreased. Moreover, the proportion of MSME credit by banks in Assam to MSME credit by banks in India has been increasing over the years but the absolute figure still remains very low ranging from 0.45 percent to 1.45 percent. Average achievements (in lending to MSMEs) of banks over the years seem to be increasing for all banks. But only private sector banks seem to have increased average achievements at a steep rate compared to public sector and regional rural banks. Also, only private sector banks' average achievements seem to have surpassed the average targets post 2012, while public sector and regional rural banks failed to do so. When the proportion of targets to the MSME sector that has been achieved is compared, it can be seen that only private sector banks have been able to achieve the targets set for the MSME sector as prescribed by RBI. The public sector banks have fluctuated highly in their performance and no consistent trend has been observed. Private banks such as HDFC, ICICI, INDUS and AXIS have achieved greater targets compared to their counterparts. These four banks have almost achieved consistently well over their prescribed targets. Public sector banks Allahabad Bank, Bank of Baroda, Bank of India, IDBI and Indian Bank seem to have performed reasonably well compared to their counterparts. Assam Gramin Bikash Bank has performed considerably better than Langpi Dehangi Rural Bank.

The most apparent finding from this chapter is that aggregate credit as well credit to the MSME sector seems to be increasing over the years for Assam as well as all India. But the question is, is it enough? The average growth in achievement of targets for MSME disbursal from 2012–13 to 2014–15 was Rs. 20 lakhs (from Table 6) and in the same year new MSME units that were registered were 2,629 units (from MSME Annual Reports[2]). However, statistics show that only negligible proportions of MSMEs actually get registered. It is evident that growth in average MSME disbursal is not sufficient to meet the growth in number of MSMEs. The Prime Minister's Task Force has issued certain guidelines to be adhered to by banks with regard to prescribed lending to the MSME sector, which is implemented and monitored by the RBI. But wide fluctuations were

[2]Government of India, Ministry of Micro, Small and Medium Enterprises. "Annual Report 2013–14". http://dcmsme.gov.in/ANNUALREPORT-MSME-2013-14P.pdf [Accessed May 1, 2019].

observed in the target setting of these banks. The MSME sector is inherently disliked as an investment option because of the associated risks. But over time MSMEs have proved to be quite a lucrative investment destination and because of this, it can be seen that private sector banks have higher credit disbursed to the sector when compared to public sector banks. With time MSMEs have proved to be booming investment hubs and therefore, with proper screening, it is advisable that banks increase their investment in the sector.

In recent years, the public sector banks have been observed to turn conservative in their approach in lending to the MSME sector, possibly as an outcome of rising bad loans under MUDRA scheme and capital constraints. As confirmed by 2nd Edition of MSME Pulse Report[3] by SIDBI-TransUnion CIBIL for June 2018, private banks have increased their market share in Micro and SME lending from 27.5 percent in March 2017 to 30.3 percent in March 2018, while share of public sector banks has fallen from 57 percent to 50.4 percent in the same period throughout India. Banks, especially public sector banks need to improve their attitude towards the sector. MSME lending can prove to be a potential sector in achieving lending targets and warding off competition from rival banks. With an efficient monitoring system, MSME loans can be quickly approved compared to relatively bigger sized loans. Banks need to stop shying away from promising new business plans.[4] If higher self-approval rights are given to banks and the wages of bank employees are linked with loan quality, banks will work harder to collect soft information in order to find high quality customers.[5] All violations to targets recommended by RBI must be monitored and intimation must be sent periodically to the violating banks. Though the MSME sector needs a financial boost to grow, it also does not warrant that all MSME borrowers will utilize the borrowed

---

[3]TransUnion CIBIL (December 2018). "MSME Pulse Report". TransUnion CIBIL & SIDBI.

[4]Singh, C. & Wasdani, K.P. (2016). "Finance for Micro, Small, and Medium-Sized Enterprises in India: Sources and Challenge". *IIM Bangalore Working Paper No. 525-Asian Development Bank Institute Working Paper Series*. https://www.iimb.ac.in/sites/default/files/2018-07/WP%20No.%20525.pdf. [Accessed May 18, 2019].

[5]Shen, Y., Shen, M., Xu, Z. & Bai, Y. (2009). "Bank Size and Small-and Medium-sized Enterprise (SME) Lending: Evidence from China". *World Development*, 37 (4), 800–811.

amount to successfully run the business and contribute to GDP. Also, there should be strict penalties for delays in payments and defaulters. This will discourage wilful defaulters from misusing the relaxations offered. It is important to ensure that credit flow is directed to deserving borrowers and not wilful defaulters.[6]

An innovative debt instrument in the form of quick loans online has been introduced in 2018 for the benefit of MSMEs. An online lending portal: www.psbloansin59minutes.com with majority ownership of 6 Public Sector Banks (PSBs)/Financial Institutions (FIs) along with their associated companies, has been launched which facilitates' in principle approval for loans to Micro Small and Medium Enterprises (MSMEs) up to Rs. 1 crore within 59 minutes from PSBs. Key features of the portal, inter-alia include enabling borrowers to connect with multiple banks without visiting the branch, financial technology (Fin Tech) based architecture with a high level of information security, analysis of data from various data points, loan products in line with scoring models and assessment methods within approved credit policies, prima facie eligibility checks for credit guarantee from CGTMSE (Credit Guarantee Fund Trust for Micro and Small Enterprises), etc. The applicant will get an 'in principle' approval from the website after uploading necessary documents and then needs to approach the assigned bank for further monitoring and disbursal of the loan. Among the criticisms about the portal being managed by a private firm based in Ahmedabad, many MSMEs have reportedly expressed unease over giving up private business information to a portal owned and managed by a private party. There is also a processing charge of 1000 INR in addition to GST charges. Without an efficient monitoring system in place, the scheme has the potential to become a failure.

[6] Singh & Wasdani. op. cit.

https://doi.org/10.1142/9789811212741_0008

Chapter 8

Surmounting the Resource Crunch

Gaurav Joshi and Bhawna Mehra

8.1 MSMEs: An Overview

After 72 years of independence, 50 years of bank nationalization, 27 years of liberalisation and globalisation, decades of priority sector lending norms and various government schemes for small scale sector and, most importantly, consistent efforts of successive governments, the MSME sector has emerged as one of the most vibrant and dynamic sectors in India.

Industrial undertakings which are set up with little investment in plant and machinery and generally use locally available raw material and human resources to produce goods of average complexity are collectively referred to as Small Sector Industries. Such industries are further categorised into Micro, Small & Medium Enterprises (MSMEs).

The International Finance Corporation, a World Bank arm, based on its experience of working with various developing and developed

Table 1: MSME categories

Size of the Enterprise	People Employed	Accumulated Assets	Annual Sales
Micro	< 10	≤ USD 100,00	≤ USD 100,00
Small	10–50	≤ USD 3 million	≤ USD 3 million
Medium	50–300	≤ USD 15 million	≤ USD 15 million

Source: International Finance Corporation, World Bank Group Report, November 2018.

Table 2: MSME categories in India

Enterprise Category	Manufacturing Sector (Machinery Investment Limit)	Service Sector (Equipment Investment Limit)
Micro	Less than Rs 25 lakh	Less than Rs 10 lakh
Small	Rs 25 lakh–5 Crore	Rs 10 lakh–2 Crore
Medium	Rs 5 Crore–10 Crore	Rs 2 Crore–5 Crore

Source: Micro, Small & Medium Enterprises Development Act, 2006.

countries, categorises MSMEs on the basis of workforce strength, asset value and annual sales.[1,2]

As per the IFC World Bank Group Report (November 2018), there are 55.8 million MSME firms in India.[3] Of this, 44.1 million are active in the service sector and the remaining 11.7 million are manufacturing MSMEs. Around 14 percent of these MSMEs are women-led. Close to 60 percent are based in rural areas. The MSME sector employs close to 124 million people. With a share of 45 percent in the total exports of the country, the MSME sector contributes 31 percent of India's GDP.[4]

In India, however, the categorisation into Micro, Small or Medium Scale Enterprises is done solely on the basis of the quantum of investment in plant and machinery, for which the limits are prescribed by the government from time to time.

MSMEs have been a focus area for Indian policymakers since independence. Even under Nehru, the first Prime Minister of the country and an avowed believer in the potential of large-scale enterprises, due attention was paid to stimulate the MSME sector. The Industrial Policy, 1956 outlined the ruling dispensation's intent to spur the MSME sector through subsidies and tax concessions, by restricting production volumes in large scale units and by reserving some items for exclusive production in the MSMEs sector. Thereafter successive governments have more or less followed the template

[1]Ministry of Micro, Small & Medium Enterprises (2017). "2016–17 Annual Report".
[2]KPMG-IMC Chamber of Commerce and Industry (June 2017). "Catalysing MSME Entrepreneurship In India: Capital, Technology & Public Policy".
[3]International Finance Corporation, World Bank Group (November 2018). "Financing India's MSMEs: Estimation of Debt Requirement of MSMEs in India".
[4]Resurgent India Limited (2015). "MSMEs: Towards a Sustainable Growth".

to accord prime status to the MSME sector and unveil policies and programmes to stimulate their growth, and the reasons are aplenty.

8.1.1 *Significance of MSMEs for the Indian Economy*

The MSME sector contributes 31 percent to the country's GDP. Almost 45 percent of the country's industrial output is generated in the sector. MSMEs are generally labour intensive by nature and so have the capacity to absorb the workforce on a large scale. MSMEs also contribute to India's exports and help earn valuable foreign exchange. MSMEs do not require large investments or big land parcels to come up on and hence are spread across the country. Thus, they also correct the regional imbalance in economic development which is a result of the uneven concentration of large-scale enterprises. Many SMEs rely on farm output as the feedstock. Thus, they also provide an avenue for the farming community to augment their income. Also, by providing employment to people near their native places, they also act as a bulwark against forced urban-to-rural migration. Thus, a thriving MSME sector is a precondition for the health of the Indian economy.

8.1.2 *Problems Faced by MSMEs*

However, Indian MSMEs are beset with various problems peculiar to this sector and which limit their potential. Among these, access to credit is the foremost. Banking networks in remote towns and villages, where a substantial proportion of MSMEs are located, is still patchy. Banks are wary of lending to them fearing defaults and when they do, they ask for collateral as an assurance against such borrower-defaults. The loan approval process and the paperwork are onerous and time consuming. Many a time, banks lend significantly smaller sums than actually demanded, according to their own assessment — sometimes arbitrary — of how much is appropriate for the applicant MSME. This forces them to look for informal sources of funding from relatives, friends, money lenders and informal institutions.

Lack of access to timely credit puts a spanner in their plans to expand to different geographies or add variety to their product mix. Investment in technology upgradation and quality assurance takes a backseat and whatever meagre resources can be arranged, are devoted to ensuring day to day survival. For the same reason, MSMEs also find it difficult to open their purse strings to attract talented manpower for important technical and managerial positions. All this ultimately impacts the quality of their offerings and viability of their operations, and they lose out in the race for customers and market share to larger firms with deep pockets.

In addition to these, MSMEs that sell their products to large-scale industries also have to bear with delayed payments for their supplies. In this uneven relationship between the two, the former has no bargaining power and has to settle for the terms and conditions proposed by the latter.

Owing to these constraints, the MSME sector in India, despite its admirable growth, pales in comparison to its counterparts in other parts of the globe. And so, arranging financial, technical, human and other environmental resources becomes an important concern for the MSMEs.

8.2 Raising Financial Resources

MSMEs in India have traditionally relied on debt to finance their operations. Almost 84 percent of such funds are arranged from informal sources like friends, family members and money lenders. Institutional sources — banks and financial institutions, both public and private — account for the remaining 16 percent. This is not to say that the access to credit comes easy for the MSMEs. On the contrary, the Credit Gap — the difference between credit demand by the MSMEs and actual credit supply to them — was estimated to be around Rs 18.4 trillion in a 2018 report commissioned by the International Finance Corporation.

This is the case when, in appreciation to the role played by them, lending to MSMEs, both manufacturing and service, has been designated as 'priority sector lending' in India. This makes it mandatory for commercial banks, regional rural banks (RRBs) as well as co-operative banks to earmark a certain percentage of their loan disbursals for this sector. MSMEs can leverage this facility to arrange resources for their operations.

The credit flow to the MSME sector has also benefitted from the setting up of the Small Industries Development Bank of India (SIDBI). It was carved out of the Industrial Development Bank of India (IDBI) in 1990 to cater specifically to financing requirements — which are quite different from those of the large-scale industries — of the firms in the MSME sector. Apart from direct lending to MSMEs, SIDBI also engages in refinancing — extending credit assistance to banks for purpose of onward lending to the various firms in the MSME sector. This refinancing facility is also extended to Non-Banking Financial Companies (NBFCs) so that they may ensure smooth flow of credit to MSMEs even in unbanked or under-banked regions. NBFCs are an important source of financing for MSMEs — not only do they plug the credit gap in areas with low bank penetration, but they also process the loan proposals/requests faster and without the borrower MSME having to undertake copious amount of paperwork.

The setting up of the Micro Units Development & Refinance Agency (MUDRA) Bank, in 2015, by the central government has also made it easier for non-farm small and micro enterprises to avail loans up to Rs 10 lakhs. MUDRA Bank is conceptualised as a financial institution providing loans at low rates to other financial institutions — commercial banks, RRBs, microfinance institutions & NBFCs — to stimulate onward lending by them to small enterprises.

Under the 'Stand Up India Scheme' launched in 2016, loans in the range of Rs 10 lakhs to Rs 1 crore are being provided to green field firms (start-ups), set up or majority (greater than 51 percent ownership) owned by SC/ST and women entrepreneurs. Every single bank branch is expected to disburse at least one such loan to borrowers from each of the two beneficiary categories — SC/ST and women entrepreneurs. Enterprises set up with this assistance would most likely have a small scale of operations to qualify as MSMEs and shall add to the vibrancy of the sector.

With the RBI, in 2015, having granted licenses for the setting up of Small Finance Banks — to cater primarily to small-ticket credit needs of MSMEs — the sector is now spoilt for choice. More players and an increase in competitive intensity in the credit space has also had the effect of driving down the overall cost of funds for MSMEs.

Let us now take a look at some other financing alternatives for MSMEs.

8.2.1 *Leveraging the Co-Operative Model*

Adopting the co-operative model has spelt success for many MSMEs in India. The Gujarat Co-operative Milk Marketing Federation (GCMMF) Limited, which is better known as the seller of the iconic Amul brand and the main force behind Operation Flood, which revolutionised milk production in India and catapulted it to a milk-surplus country, is a fitting example of the worth of the co-operative model for MSMEs in India. GCMMF has now outgrown its status as a small-scale industry to earn revenue of almost Rs 38000 crore in 2018–19. Its success has inspired similar experiments in different parts of the country.

In a co-operative set up, members pool their resources to set up or run a business unit. The co-operative also has greater bargaining power which enables it to extract better prices from its customers.

The co-operative structure also suits the Indian psyche. This is because human beings have been found to display greater risk-appetite when they are part of a group than in their individual capacities. The psychological makeup of Indians renders them generally risk-averse which limits their propensity to take the risk of setting up their own enterprise. But when they combine as a co-operative, owing to the reason stated earlier, they are more likely to assume the risk of setting up a business venture. This transformation from low to moderate risk-taking is also significant in light of the fact that moderate risk-taking correlates highly with entrepreneurial success.

Shri Mahila Griha Udyog Lijjat Papad, a women-led cooperative, has witnessed phenomenal success. It was founded in 1959, as a cottage industry (similar to a micro-enterprise), by seven women in Mumbai with a seed capital of only Rs 80. These women had an eye to spot the marketing opportunity presented to them by the peculiar Indian habit of having *Papad* (a thin crisp cake eaten fried or roasted) with their meals. *Papad* making involves multiple operations like grinding, dough-making, rolling and sun-drying and takes a number of days. Ready-to-eat packaged *papad* was, therefore, launched to target those housewives who had had enough of this tiring work and were looking for an easy alternative.

From a small-scale firm, Lijjat Papad has now grown to have an annual turnover of more than Rs 800 crore and a 43,000 strong workforce.

8.2.2 *Tapping the Share Market*

Lots of money is flowing into the Indian stock markets from both within and outside the country. To enable the MSMEs to benefit from this inflow of funds, the National Stock Exchange and Bombay Stock Exchange have unveiled NSE Emerge and BSE SME platforms respectively. MSMEs with a good track record, viable business model and in search of funds to expand further can explore opportunities in capital markets by listing their shares on these platforms.

One spin-off benefit is that MSMEs — just like the large-scale sector firms — can now also introduce Employee Stock Ownership Plans (ESOPs) to attract and retain talent. ESOPs give ownership interest — in the form of a percentage of company shares — to employees and are therefore an attractive component of their remuneration package.

8.2.3 *Attracting Venture Capital Funds & Angel Investments*

Venture Capital has also taken off as a significant funding source for the MSMEs in recent years. Venture Capital Funds (VCFs) are professionally managed investment entities looking for handsome returns on the significant amount of funds, collected from their subscribers and, available at their disposal. So, they invest in newly set up or early-stage ventures with a high potential for future growth by buying up a stake in them. MSMEs with unique business model and attractive marketing opportunities can tap this source of financing too. Often, VCFs also rope in professionals to provide consultancy and mentoring services to the investee firm as a free add-on service. This makes VCFs an even more attractive option for MSMEs which are otherwise short of such in-house professional manpower.

SIDBI Venture Capital Limited (SVCL) — SIDBI's venture capital unit — alone manages seven such VCFs and has funded around 80 MSMEs and start-ups to date. SIDBI, itself, has also contributed to the corpus of another 88 VCFs from which more than Rs 5000 crore of funds have already been dispersed to almost 500 MSMEs in different regions and diverse sectors of the Indian economy.

Angel Investors — wealthy individuals, investing their own money in promising business ventures in expectation of high returns — offer another financing option for MSMEs. All that the MSMEs need to do is to participate in the various events held from time to time and which provide them a platform to interact with and present their business-plans to the Angel Investors and obtain their funding assistance.

8.2.4 *Crowdfunding*

In the current internet era, crowdfunding offers another unique opportunity for MSMEs to obtain finance for their businesses. We have seen how MSMEs can raise large amount of funds from some Angel Investors or VCFs. Crowdfunding is at the other end of the spectrum — here, small amounts are raised from a large number of people, typically over the internet. In return, these investors get a commensurate share in the ownership as well as in the profits that the MSMEs earn.

8.2.5 *Receivable Finance*

We have seen that delayed payments by institutional and business customers is one of the issues plaguing the health of MSMEs in India. To tackle this issue, RBI has recently launched the Trade Receivables Discounting System (TReDS). Under this system, an MSME is given an advance against a bill due to it from its customers for the products already supplied or service already rendered. This helps the MSMEs meet their working capital requirements despite payment-delays by the customers.

8.3 Arranging Technical Resources

MSMEs also face challenges owing to their inability to arrange technical resources to run their operations. Lack of funding limits their access to the latest tools and technologies, which affects the quality of their offerings.

8.3.1 *Utilising Government Assistance*

The government has started working on a plan to set up 20 Tool Hubs and 100 Tool Centres across the country to address this aspect. This would allow MSMEs access to equipment available in these centres at a nominal charge. Not only this, these centres would also provide services like installation and repair to manufacturing MSMEs at affordable rates.

In addition to this, in the Union Budget (2019–20),[5] the government has unveiled its agenda of launching 80 Livelihood Business Incubators (LBIs) and 20 Technology Business Incubators (TBIs), to provide hand-holding and mentoring to entrepreneurs planning to set up agro-rural MSMEs.

To make up for the inability of MSMEs to arrange technical resources, extension centres have also been set up by the government across the country. These extension centres disseminate technological know-how among the MSMEs and encourage faster adoption by them, of cutting-edge manufacturing techniques which have been researched and developed in the laboratories.

8.3.2 *Organising into Clusters*

The Indian government has adopted a 'cluster' approach to stimulate growth of MSMEs. MSMEs in a particular line of business require similar infrastructure and facilities, use similar processes and technologies and often face same set of constraints. Their production processes have to satisfy similar quality standards and have similar effluent treatment protocols; their manpower requires a similar set of skills enhancement training. So, having MSMEs in the same line of business activity located contiguously — as a cluster — helps the government to provide them all these enablers in an efficient and cost-effective manner. This is the reason why the government — in the Union Budget[6] — has declared its intent to set up 100 new clusters during 2019–20 under the Scheme of Fund for Regeneration of Traditional Industries (SFURTI).

Setting up business in such designated clusters can indeed improve access by MSMEs to many crucial technical resources.

[5]Government of India (2019). *Economic Census*.

[6]Borpuzari, P. (2019). "Budget 2019: 15 Key Takeaways for the MSME Sector". *The Economic Times*. https://economictimes.indiatimes.com/small-biz/sme-sector/budget-2019-15-key-takeaways-for-the-msme-sector/articleshow/70089949.cms (Retrieved on July 07, 2019).

8.3.3 *Collaborative Sharing Networks*

Manufacturing sector MSMEs need machines for certain operations. These machines remain idle when such operations are not being performed. MSME firms can share such machinery, equipment and other resources — otherwise lying idle — with other firms in the same line of activity. This reduces their overall cost of ownership of such assets.

The power of the internet can be leveraged for such purposes. Websites like Core Logs provide a platform for MSMEs to interact, discuss their requirements, source supplies and share resources.

8.4 Securing Raw Material & Other Resources

MSMEs buy raw material, machinery and other supplies in much smaller quantities than large business units. As such, suppliers are not very enthusiastic about selling to them, offering them considerable discounts on their purchase or providing complimentary transportation, installation etc. services. This increases the overall costs of production for MSMEs.

8.4.1 *Buying Alliances*

MSMEs in the same area of operations have similar raw material or machinery requirements. Such MSMEs can form a Buying Alliance and club together for the purchases of all alliance members. This would also add to their ability to bargain for better terms while dealing with the suppliers.

CoreLogs — an online forum for MSMEs — provides a platform for MSMEs to form such mutually beneficial networks. Alternatively, MSMEs can place orders with web-aggregators like Power2SME. It aggregates orders from MSMEs, purchases in bulk — and therefore at a considerable discount — and passes on the savings to them.

8.4.2 *Prospering from Locally Available Raw-Materials*

It makes business sense for MSMEs to concentrate on that line of activity which utilises locally available resources. More so, if such resources are exclusively available in the region in which the MSME is located, lending it a competitive advantage over outsider firms from other regions. Such a business model also guarantees timely supply of raw materials at affordable rates to the MSMEs.

Fruitage India

Many MSMEs, especially in the food processing sector, have excelled by leveraging the wealth of locally available raw material and human resources. Fruitage India is one such small entrepreneurial venture that has grown into a well-known brand owing to this shrewd strategy. It was set up in 1994 in the Kumaun region of Uttarakhand state in North India.

At higher altitudes in Uttarakhand — a small hill state snuggled in the great Himalayas — rhododendron trees, having annual flowering season in early summers, are found in abundance. They bear flowers with medicinal properties. The hill state is also bestowed with a climate which suits the cultivation of fruits like apple, peach, pear etc. However, just like the rhododendron flowers, these seasonal fruits also have a limited shelf life.

In the 1990s, cold-storage facilities, wherein such perishable commodities could be stored, were non-existent in the region. The farming community was largely poor. So, selling their produce before it rotted and lost its worth used to be a greater concern for these farmers than trying to extract as high a price as possible in the market. The traders, in the business of procuring these products from the farmers, transporting it to and selling in the foothills and faraway plains would exploit this situation to their advantage and bargain for dirt-cheap prices. They would then sell to fruit-vendors in the plains where there was a substantial demand for such seasonal fruit at considerable profit.

Fruitage India sensed a business opportunity here. To work around the issue of perishability and lack of storage infrastructure, they decided to process the raw produce into offerings like juices, squash, pickle, and jam which have a considerably longer shelf life. Since, the locally grown fruit already had a loyal customer base in the foothills and the plains, this captive market were readymade customers for these value-added products.

However, at that time, the processed food space was dominated by multinationals with huge advertising budgets. To carve out a space for themselves as a strong regional player, they decided to sell under the 'Fruitage' brand name. Educating the customer about this brand and creating a perception of good quality called for some promotional expenditure in the beginning; however, with the passage of time, as the brand gained considerable customer recognition in the foothills and plains and started being equated with quality, the spurt in sales more than made up for the initial expenditure. To compete against the MNCs and wean away customers from them, Fruitage chose its price points carefully and sold its offerings at attractive prices.

Fruitage also chose its product mix judiciously with greater focus on those products which were processed from fruit and fruit-varieties unique to the region. These included juices extracted from rhododendron (*buransh*) flowers and blood orange (*Malta*). Their small-volumes made it unattractive and unviable — owing to less scope for achieving scale — for big MNCs to deal in products processed from them. Thus, Fruitage turned the locally available resources into a sustainable competitive advantage for themselves.

They also shared a greater proportion of their profits with the farmer-suppliers to lure the best of them into their fold. However, this went beyond just a transactional relationship. Fruitage, in addition, provided advisory services to these farmers. Good quality agricultural inputs were also made available at affordable prices. These initiatives guaranteed them sustained supply of the best quality produce in the region.

To keep the human resources cost in check, Fruitage zeroed in on those women from nearby villages who were looking to augment their family income, trained them and put them in employment. This proved to be a much less expensive option than getting workers from far off areas to work in the processing units, thus giving Fruitage the scope to earn handsome margins despite selling at a lower price than the other competitors in the market.

Fruitage also exemplifies how an MSME can work around its limitations. Not having deep pockets to fund investments that a countrywide expansion calls for, Fruitage India has taken to online retailing of their products on various e-commerce platforms now.

8.4.3 *Plug and Play Offices and Co-Working Spaces*

MSMEs in the service sector need office space to operate from which entails a significant rental cost for them, especially if they are based in urban centres. Additionally, they also have to bear the cost of furnishing the office space and buying office equipment like photocopiers, water coolers etc. Plug and Play Office Spaces (PPOS) provide them a hassle-free alternative. These are 'ready to move-in' office spaces with all the necessary infrastructure — meeting rooms, seating, air-conditioning, internet connectivity — already in place. Additionally, they provide many other complimentary services. The monthly rentals are indeed higher but the tenant MSME can save a lot on the upfront investments that furnishing a barebones office space demands.

In a similar fashion, Co-working Spaces can also be a viable solution for the resource crunched MSMEs both in manufacturing and services sectors. As the name suggests, infrastructure and facilities in a co-working office space are shared and used by all the tenant firms as per their requirements. A co-working space for manufacturing businesses may have a common quality-testing facility, packaging apparatus or product-testing laboratory to be utilised by the tenant firms on a rotational basis. Such co-working spaces allow MSMEs to locate closer to their clients or in prominent business hubs and have a multicity presence without incurring significant expenses. It also enables them to attract and retain workers who do not want to work in small towns.

Both Co-working Spaces and PPOS are major draw among MSMEs coming up in the Information Technology (IT) & IT Enabled Services (ITES) space.

8.5 Procuring Manpower

Arranging sufficiently skilled manpower for crucial technical and managerial functions is another main concern for MSMEs. Highly skilled white-collar professionals do not want to relocate to small towns and villages where the bulk of MSMEs are located. MSMEs also lack the financial wherewithal to offer attractive salary packages to attract such talent.

However, MSMEs can make up for this manpower shortage by obtaining assistance from the various Extension Centres set up by the government and having qualified staff to provide technical consultancy to them. Alternatively, MSMEs can target funding by Angel Investors and VCFs which also provide technical and managerial handholding to the firms that they provide funds to.

8.5.1 *Thinking Out-of-the-Box*

MSMEs also need to look for creative solutions to this issue. Retired professionals with relevant skills, and settled in their hometowns and ancestral villages, can be hired part-time. Industrial Training Institutes (ITIs) in small towns can also be good source of technical manpower. A few MSMEs can collaborate to jointly hire technical and managerial professionals and utilise their services. They may also seek volunteers from among those city-based professionals who are inclined towards social service and can devote a few hours every week to help MSMEs benefit from their expertise.[7]

Since service sector MSMEs rely primarily on their human resources — unlike the manufacturing MSMEs, which have substantial investment in materials and machineries as well — arranging skilled manpower is an even bigger concern for the former. However, the experience of DesiCrew Solutions Private Limited shows how this challenge can be converted into an opportunity.[8]

DesiCrew

In 2007, Saloni Malhotra, decided to venture into the BPO (Business Process Outsourcing) Sector, which was growing at a fast pace and therefore, presented, a lucrative business opportunity. Thus, DesiCrew was born. Considering the high real estate and manpower costs in urban

---

[7]Pareek, U. (1967). "A Motivational Paradigm of Development", *Indian Educational Review*, XXIV (2).

[8]Swain, S. (2010). *Applied Psychology: India Specific and Cross-Cultural Approaches*, 2nd Edition. New Vishal Publications, India.

centres, she decided to operate out of smaller towns and villages. An office was set up in Chennai to interface with the client and bring in the business and pass it on to the delivery centres in the rural areas. These delivery centres were meant to perform and deliver the work to the client's satisfaction. The work was to be done on computers and delivered over the internet. Rural youth, with an intermediate (Class XII) degree and basic knowledge of computers, were recruited to work in these delivery centres and provided with initial training.

DesiCrew focused on performing elementary kind of work — digitisation services (data entry), data editing, document formatting etc. — for their customers as it fitted in perfectly with the low skill levels of their employees. As the skill levels in the employees rose, they added services such as content creation and GIS based mapping to their repertoire. Once they gained a reputation for quality work, business started flowing in.

Their unique business model bestows several competitive advantages on DesiCrew. As the cost of living is lower in rural areas, DesiCrew pays substantially lower salaries than its city-based counterparts, which drives down their salary costs. Despite this, the rate of attrition, which is a major problem faced by most BPOs, is almost zero at DesiCrew.

DesiCrew currently has around 360 employees with the majority of them being women and has witnessed consistent growth. It has also brought about a sea-change in the standard of living of its predominantly rural employee-base, as well as in the mind-sets of the communities in the villages and small towns from which they are operating. They have also created a template for tackling the problem of rural outmigration by providing gainful employment to rural communities on their doorsteps.

8.5.2 *Technology*

MSMEs can also leverage technology to make up for the scarcity of manpower.

For instance, Chatbots-computer programmes having the ability to carry out conversations can be employed to answer regular customer queries and for outbound calls for the purposes of prospecting and lead generation. While the basic programmes follow a predetermined script, the more advanced versions of Chatbots have the capability to learn from experience of earlier conversations and gradually improvise. They can work round the clock and just require an initial one-time investment with almost no maintenance cost. MSMEs can buy standard Chatbot-packages from the market or get customised ones built by vendors.

In a similar fashion, MSMEs can make use of various freely available mobile software applications, to keep track of inventory, cash and sales, thus removing the need to employ costly manpower for such jobs.

8.6 Conclusion

Setting up and managing an MSME entails a multitude of challenge on various fronts, some of which have been discussed and how MSMEs can work around them. However, these remedies may not work in all scenarios and for all businesses. Ultimately, what separates a thriving enterprise from a failing one is the determination of the management/founders to emerge unscathed from every challenge that the environment poses and their ingenuity to arrange resources amidst scarcity. The concluding case study in Appendix 1 illustrates this succinctly.

Appendix 1: Entrepreneurial Adventures at 60: Bull's Eye Academy

In Indian society, 60 is the age of retirement. At this age, one gets rid of the hustle and bustle of working life and settles into a more relaxed routine. Retirees often spend time reading newspapers, watching TV and socializing. D P Joshi (DPJ), however, could not adjust to this transition. He retired in 2010 and it took him just six months to realise that this relaxed pace of life did not exactly suit him, having slogged hard in his government job in a career spanning three decades.

Born to a poor family struggling to make ends meet, he toiled hard and managed to land a teaching position with the Department of School Education in Uttarakhand around 1976. Over the next 30 years, he served in various positions, mostly in his hometown Pithoragarh (Uttarakhand) and retired as Principal of Government Inter College. In professional circles, he was famous for his integrity and diligence. His students remember him as the strict principal who would stand guard at the college gates to catch those trying to bunk classes and run away. After his retirement, DPJ realised that three decades of his working life moulded him into somebody who cannot remain idle. So, he decided to do something worthwhile. The only thing, which he could claim to be an expert in, was school administration. In fact, he had offers from some private schools in the town of Pithoragarh, but things never materialized into something concrete. Money was never an issue as he was getting a handsome monthly pension, rather he was seeking the satisfaction of doing something constructive for society, and the thought struck him — 'why don't I start a school of my own?' Thus, an entrepreneur was born at the ripe old age of 61.

This was how the Bull's Eye Academy (BEA) came to be founded in 2011. The school started functioning with just a handful of teachers, around 40 students enrolled from Nursery to Class 2 and modest infrastructure and facilities. By 2017, just eight years from inception, the school had expanded to Class VIII and student numbers risen by more than six times. The school now has a staff of 30 teachers, and two buses ply daily to fetch students from villages near and far. BEA is now a well-known brand in school education in Pithoragarh. However, this entrepreneurial journey was never a smooth ride.

The Funding Dilemma

The first issue faced by DPJ was that of funds, a common refrain among all aspiring entrepreneurs. DPJ already had 2 *naali* (a unit of measurement used locally, 1 *naali* = 2160 square feet) to his name, some ancestral land on the roadside in his native *Jajardeval* village, and five kilometres from the town. He had the option of pledging this land parcel as collateral to procure bank-loans and construct the school building. However, since he could not have predicted the future, he found it to be imprudent to mortgage his land for bank-loans and end up losing that too in the event of failure of his entrepreneurial venture. DPJ felt that a conservative investment would be a better alternative. He had received a lump-sum of 12 lakhs at the time of retirement and decided to use up half of that sum for the initial construction of a barebones school building, administrative office, four classrooms and toilets. This way his fledgling enterprise would not have to bear the burden of liabilities — monthly loan repayment obligations — right from the beginning. And if the venture turned out to be successful, the revenues thus generated could then be used to fund the expansion. If unfortunately, it failed, he had the option of renting out the building as commercial space. DPJ, thus displayed moderate risk-taking behaviour, which researchers have found correlates highly with entrepreneurial success. Entrepreneurs also need to have a Plan B, since the majority of enterprises do fail. DPJ was up to the task here also: he had thought through the alternatives available to him if his entrepreneurial plans did not work out.

The Branding Riddle

Often, enterprises, especially the small ones, fail due to a lack of marketing skills. Their offering may be of the best quality, but they are unable to convince the customers that it is so. This prevents them from obtaining initial trial by the target customers.

Purchase actions are also influenced by customer-perceptions: Savlon (ITC) could never challenge Dettol (R&B) despite having better attributes simply because customers perceived that a lack of burning sensation (which Savlon promoted as its USP!) was an indicator of its ineffectiveness. Patanjali has cornered a big chunk of the FMCG market owing to its carefully crafted promotional campaign, which has had the effect of customers perceiving its offerings as natural, though many of its products have chemical ingredients in significant amounts. New ventures generally lose out on this perception race against the entrenched market players, which have deep pockets and huge budgets for the promotional blitzkrieg.

DPJ had originally planned to name his school Shiv Jayanti Memorial School after his late parents. But eventually he decided against this. His interactions with the parents and guardians of the students over the years had taught him that today's parents perceive English education as indispensable for their children to have a reasonable chance of securing a decent job later in life. DPJ was also shrewd enough to sense that the inhabitants of the predominantly rural *Jajardeval* area were not discerning enough to understand that the name of the school had no relationship, whatsoever, to the level of English language proficiency that it could impart to its pupils. Hence, a proper English sounding name could very well determine the initial success of his school. 'Bulls Eye Academy' — Bull's Eye is a compound noun, used in Archery to designate the main target — perfectly fitted the bill: it sounded sufficiently English and also conveyed the school's result orientation and relentless focus on providing quality education.

Staffing Challenge

This branding strategy also required DPJ to take an important call on the staffing front. He needed qualified — with a bachelor's degree in education (B.Ed.) — teaching staff for his school. While scouring for such trained staff, he discovered that the candidates that suited his requirements expected a much more handsome remuneration than what his venture could viably afford to pay. He could not have matched the salaries paid to the teaching staff in the other schools; most of these schools had been operating for a long time and had a large number of students so they could indulge in requesting high compensation packages. To compound the problem, most of the candidates lived quite some distance away from *Jajardeval* in the main town area and sought a higher allowance to offset their travel expenses.

Entrepreneurs are known to be prone to out-of-the-box thinking to wriggle themselves out of such situations. DPJ showed the same entrepreneurial streak in finding a creative solution to this recruitment issue. He started recruiting bright young women with excellent educational attainments — those without a B.Ed. degree but aspiring to get one and therefore preparing for B.Ed. course entrance exams. He deliberately sourced such candidates from nearby villages only, mentored them for a few weeks while working until they matured into proficient teachers.

To maintain the pedagogical quality, he allowed his teachers considerable free time during their workhours so that they could work on expanding their knowledge base. This aligned perfectly with the personal goals of the newly recruited teachers, most of whom needed time to prepare for competitive exams. This also led to the word going around that BEA was an employee friendly entity: unlike the other schools, it did not exploit the teaching staff by burdening them with excruciating workloads. BEA also had a more satisfied workforce, despite the smaller paycheques, owing to the opportunity for personal growth, which no other employer in the area seemed to be providing.

However, this also meant that the school had to employee a greater number of faculty members and put up with a consequent increase in the salary outlays. But in the final analysis, this was a much better proposition than sourcing even more expensive teaching resources from the Pithoragarh town. Plus, now BEA had the opportunity to brag about its excellent teacher-pupil ratio, which was the best in the whole district and a handy marketing message too.

Inducing Customer Trial

However, the issue of obtaining initial customer trial — first few admissions to the school — still remained. Though untrained in marketing, DPJ leveraged his goodwill among the Opinion Leaders (OLs) to his advantage.

In markets — especially rural ones, the OLs have a disproportionate impact on inducing customer trials and purchase actions. Opinion leaders are considered trustworthy and people seek their advice. They, thus, exert considerable influence on fellow customers. So, once the marketer convinces the OL about the product quality, he can bank on their spreading a good word of mouth about his products, which increases the likelihood of customer trials and repeat purchases. The government agencies in India are known to have used the OLs — religious heads in village communities — to good effect to obtain consent from villagers to immunise their children against polio through periodic vaccination drives.

DPJ displayed astute understanding of this consumer-behaviour dynamics. He personally visited the *gram-pradhans* and other influential families — the OLs — in the nearby villages to promote his school among them. He had a long-standing reputation for being one of the first few villagers to have secured a well-paying and respected government job. It was, therefore, easy for him to convince these OLs. Once he managed to do this, the word quickly spread, and the admission requests started coming in soon after. The admission number in the first year itself stood at 40, which was indeed creditable, especially in view of the fact that DPJ hardly spent money on any other promotional gimmick.

Quality Orientation

Marketers acknowledge that customers can be drawn in by promotions, but they can only be retained by delivering quality consistently and at a level that matches or exceeds their expectations and, therefore, satisfies them.

DPJ, therefore, did not rest on his laurels. He knew very well that this initial success would amount to nothing if he failed to deliver on his promises of providing good quality education in his school. On the other hand, satisfying the customers would have guaranteed him a good reputation and a favourable word of mouth, which being much more effective than costly promotional campaigns, would have brought him many more admissions.

This made it incumbent on him to be ever vigilant about the pedagogical quality in his school, for which he devised an ingenious method. He would fill in for the teachers whenever they were absent — this gave him the opportunity to interact with the students, assess their learning levels and thus gauge the effectiveness of the respective teachers without appearing intrusive. On other occasions, he would inspect the students' notebooks randomly. Co-curricular activities were organised on a regular basis. DPJ also roped in some of his ex-colleagues, on an honorary basis, as members of an advisory board, which met once in a while to deliberate and provide guidance on future courses. He also made it a habit to interact with the parents and guardians on a regular basis to assess their satisfaction levels and benefit from their feedback.

Hitting the Bull's Eye

DPJ's relentlessness on the quality front did bear fruit and his venture witnessed steady growth. The BEA felt it necessary to buy a minibus in 2014 to collect students as enquiries started coming in from villages as far as *Bisa-Bajed*, six-seven kilometres (roughly a 15-minute drive) from *Jajardeval*. This was followed by purchase of another bus in 2017. BEA has expanded to Class VIII and student enrolment numbers have now grown to 300. The school building has added two more floors and some office space and a couple of laboratories have also come up. Quite a few faculty members have registered for the Diploma Course in Distance Education (correspondence mode) and are due to complete it in 2019. BEA's workforce has also grown to 38 now and gives DPJ an added satisfaction of being a provider of jobs to the needy and the deserving.

DPJ now plans to apply for recognition from the Uttarakhand Board of School Education so that the school may be expanded to Class X and eventually to Class XII. Money making was never his primary objective and he only aspired with his venture to generate enough revenue to sustain itself without any external support. All he wants is to leave behind a lasting legacy. He has shaped his venture as a social enterprise: an institution providing quality education at affordable rates to the children of the less privileged and those in remote inaccessible villages. He has also kick-started the process of converting the school into a trust so that his venture may continue to serve the after his demise.

https://doi.org/10.1142/9789811212741_0009

Chapter 9

MUDRA — A Resourceful Resolution Bank of India

T. Kadalarasane and Tripura Sundari C.U.

9.1 Introduction

India is the second highest populated economy with a large market. Both male and female entrepreneurs, are relatively rare here compared to other emerging economies (OECD, 2018).[1] Only 23.7 percent of eligible Indian women are part of the workforce compared 75 percent of men, also India ranks low in terms of economic participation of women. The Global Gender Report 2015 by the World Economic Forum ranked India at 139 out of 145 countries. The Micro, Small and Medium Enterprises (MSMEs) sector accounts for more than 90 percent of the total number of enterprises, and 90 percent of non-agriculture employment. The sector continues to grow regardless of issues, like non-availability of credit, limited market linkages, technology obsolescence, etc. It is one of the wildest growing sectors of the Indian economy which plays a significant role in driving economic growth. It produces more than 6,000 products and generates employment for more than 100 million people. According to the MSMEs report, "*the sector contributes around eight percent in India's GDP, 45 percent of the manufacturing output and 40 percent in exports*".[2]

---

[1]OECD Report (2018). "Financing and Women-Owned Small Businesses: The Role of Size, Age and Industry".

[2]Ministry of Micro, Small and Medium Enterprises (2013–14). http://dcmsme.gov.in/ANNUALREPORT-MSME-2013-14P.pdf [5 September, 2014].

"Indian GDP can be increased by raising women's labour force participation".[3] According to the World Bank *"In 2012, only 27 percent of adult Indian women had a job when compared to 79 percent of men and about 20 million women had dropped out of the workforce between 2005 and 2012"*.[4] According to the National Sample Survey Office (NSSO), *"India's unemployment rate during 2017–18 has reached the highest at 6.1 percent compared to 2012–13, which was 2.2 percent"*.[5] According to this report:

> *"Joblessness was higher in Urban than Rural, within that 18.7 percent belong to urban male and 27.2 percent of jobless youth are female. Significance for women empowerment and employment started early from second five year plan (1956–61) and continues till date, currently 32 schemes for women is been implemented by various Departments and Ministries and not much is effective and few have not reached the rural areas to benefit those women"*.[6]

The workers and entrepreneurs belonging to weaker sections were facing problems regarding collateral security and they were not getting due encouragement from banks.[7] Hence there is a need to explore the schemes of the government and its benefit to the economy.

Financial untouchability[8] creates a problem of social discrimination. The only solution for this is to promote financial inclusion, which can be achieved by ensuring access to financial services, affordability of services, and actual utilization of financial services. One of the mission mode

---

[3]OECD report. op. cit.

[4]Dixon, A. (2018). "Women in India's Economic Growth". *The Economic Times Women's Forum*, 16 March 2018. https://www.worldbank.org/en/news/speech/2018/03/17/women-indias-economic-growth.

[5]NSSO (2013–14). "Ministry of Statistics and Programme Implementation Annual Report of the Ministry of MSMEs". http://www.mospi.gov.in/sites/default/files/publication_reports/mospi_annual_report_2013–14.pdf [Accessed 30 January 2019].

[6]ibid.

[7]Government of India, Labour, Employment & Manpower (LEM) Division (2011). "Report of the Working Group on Employment, Planning & Policy for the Twelfth Five Year Plan (2012–2017)". http://planningcommission.gov.in/aboutus/committee/wrkgrp12/wg_emp_planing.pdf [10 July 2017].

[8]The Pioneer (2014). "War on Financial Untouchability". https://www.dailypioneer.com/2014/page1/war-on-financial-untouchability.html [29 August 2014].

projects of the Government of India is the MUDRA,[9] which acts as one of the tools to achieve financial inclusion. The main aim of this scheme is to empower small micro business enterprises. This was formed with an order to refinance and regulate microfinance institutions and to provide financial assistance to small units that are typically excluded from the majority banking system. Mudra loans are provided to income generating microenterprises engaged in manufacturing, trading and services up to 10 lakh. This is divided into three categories[10] which stimulates the growth, development and funding needs of the beneficiaries. Various studies are available on MSME such as Parashuramulu and Naik (2013),[11] Balasubramanian and Madhavan.[12] Whereas Shahid and Irshad,[13] Manish Agarwal and Dwivedi,[14] Talekar and Pimple[15] and Ashish Mahajan[16] have exclusively done their research papers on MUDRA.

Based on the above literature, the current paper focuses on the growth and development of overall MSMEs and specifically MUDRA i.e.,

[9]Micro Units Development and Refinance Agency Ltd, to deliver loans (up to 10 lakhs) through Banks/Non-Banking Finance Companies and Micro Finance Institutions.

[10]**Shishu:** Loans up to 50,000, **Kishore:** Loans from 50,001 to 5,00,000 **Tarun:** Loans from 5,00,001 to 10,00,000.

[11]Parashuramulu, B., & Naik, D.N. (2013). "Performance of regional rural banks in India". *SAARJ Journal on Banking & Insurance Research*, Vol. 2 No. 2, pp. 67–79.

[12]Balasubramanian, K. & Madhavan, S. (2017). "Sector-wise Analysis of MSME Contribution to Growth of Indian Industry". *International Journal of Management Studies*, Vol IV, Special Issue-1, September 2017. http://researchersworld.com/ijms/vol4/specialissue1/Paper_11.pdf [Vol-IV, Special Issue-1, September 2017].

[13]Shahid, M. & Irshad, M. (2016). "A Descriptive Study on Pradhan Manthri Mudra Yojana (PMMY)". *International Journal of Latest Trends in Engineering and Technology Special Issue*, December 2016. https://www.researchgate.net/publication/323829595_A_DESCRIPTIVE_STUDY_ON_PRADHAN_MANTHRI_MUDRA_YOJANA_PMMY [Accessed on 13th February 2020].

[14]Agarwal, M. & Dwivedi, R. (2017). "Pradhan Mantri Mudra Yojna: A Critical Review". *KIIT Journal of Management* (December 2017). https://ksom.ac.in/wp-content/uploads/2018/01/97-106-PRADHAN-MANTRI-MUDRA-YOJNA.pdf [Accessed on 13th February 2020].

[15]Talekar, S.D. & Pimple, B.N. (2017). "A Study of Performance Evaluation of Mudra Bank in India". *Online Interdisciplinary Research Journal*, Special Edition, July 2017. https://oiirj.org/oiirj/blog/2017/08/06/volume-07-july-2017-special-issue/ [Accessed on 13th February 2020].

[16]Mahajan, A. (2018). "An Analysis of Performance and Impact of MUDRA Yojana Under PMMY in the Year 2016". *Research Journal of Management Sciences*.

number of accounts and loan sanctioned under MUDRA and its sub-categories in India. Secondary data has been considered for the study from India's statistics, etc. and MUDRA websites. Simple ratio, growth rate, data visualization techniques are used to examine the above objective. Data visualization helps to understand the significance of data by placing it in a visual context. Patterns, trends and correlations that might go undetected in text-based data can be exposed and recognized much more easily.

The data from OECD regarding International trade and SMEs with a digital presence is provided in Table 1. India is in 10th place when compared to the few other world countries, regarding SMEs' exports and

Table 1: International trade and SMEs with a digital presence

SI. NO	Countries	SMEs Exporting	SMEs Trading Internationally
1	Korea	20.7177814	28.22185971
2	Portugal	17.23862729	25.29928172
3	Belgium	14.99202552	27.59170654
4	Czech Republic	13.57526882	23.38709677
5	Russian Federation	12.96023564	20.17673049
6	Turkey	12.87878788	16.96969697
7	Germany	12.64637002	17.72053084
8	Ireland	12.5748503	20.15968064
9	France	12.38317757	18.69158879
10	India	12.03007519	15.7059315
11	Netherlands	11.94029851	18.9316575
12	Poland	11.81229773	17.39482201
13	Italy	11.66666667	14.84848485
14	Sweden	11.41141141	24.92492492
15	Viet Nam	11.38147567	21.11459969
16	Hungary	11.09969168	19.21891059
17	Romania	11.03710752	24.07231208
18	United Kingdom	10.97276265	15.56420233
19	Ecuador	9.957924264	22.58064516
20	Australia	9.901738473	17.38473167

Table 1: (*Continued*)

SI. NO	Countries	SMEs Exporting	SMEs Trading Internationally
21	Spain	9.828741623	17.87043931
22	Greece	9.480122324	22.47706422
23	South Africa	9.381044487	16.6344294
24	Indonesia	9.040880503	13.67924528
24	Israel	8.776978417	15.68345324
25	Peru	7.648320229	18.08434596
26	Colombia	7.61614623	16.29855293
27	Canada	7.515822785	14.08227848
28	Mexico	7.142857143	14.95535714
28	United States	6.83127572	9.62962963
29	Chile	5.888125613	19.13640824
30	Japan	5.218068536	10.82554517
31	Argentina	3.711952487	6.978470676
32	Brazil	3.698113208	7.547169811

Source: Facebook — OECD-World Bank Future of Business Survey (database), June 2017.

international trade. SMEs contribute to eight percent of India's GDP and 40 percent to exports.[17]

According to the 2018 McKinsey Report,[18] women account for half of Asia Pacific's population but contribute only 36 percent of the USD$26 trillion to GDP (Graph 1). This is in line with the global figure of 36 percent. Traditional economic theory clearly reveals that GDP cannot capture unpaid care (looking after spouse, children and the elderly, shopping, cooking, cleaning) by women; if this could be captured, it could roughly result in 15 percent of the region's GDP. Economic prosperity depends on the huge and unrecognized contribution of women through unpaid care work.

[17]Ministry of Micro, Small and Medium Enterprises (2013–14). op. cit.

[18]McKinsey & Company (2018). "McKinsey Quarterly 2018 Number 1: Overview and Full Issue". March 2018. https://www.mckinsey.com/business-functions/strategy-and-corporate-finance/our-insights/mckinsey-quarterly-2018-number-1-overview-and-full-issue [McKinsey Quarterly 2018 Number 1].

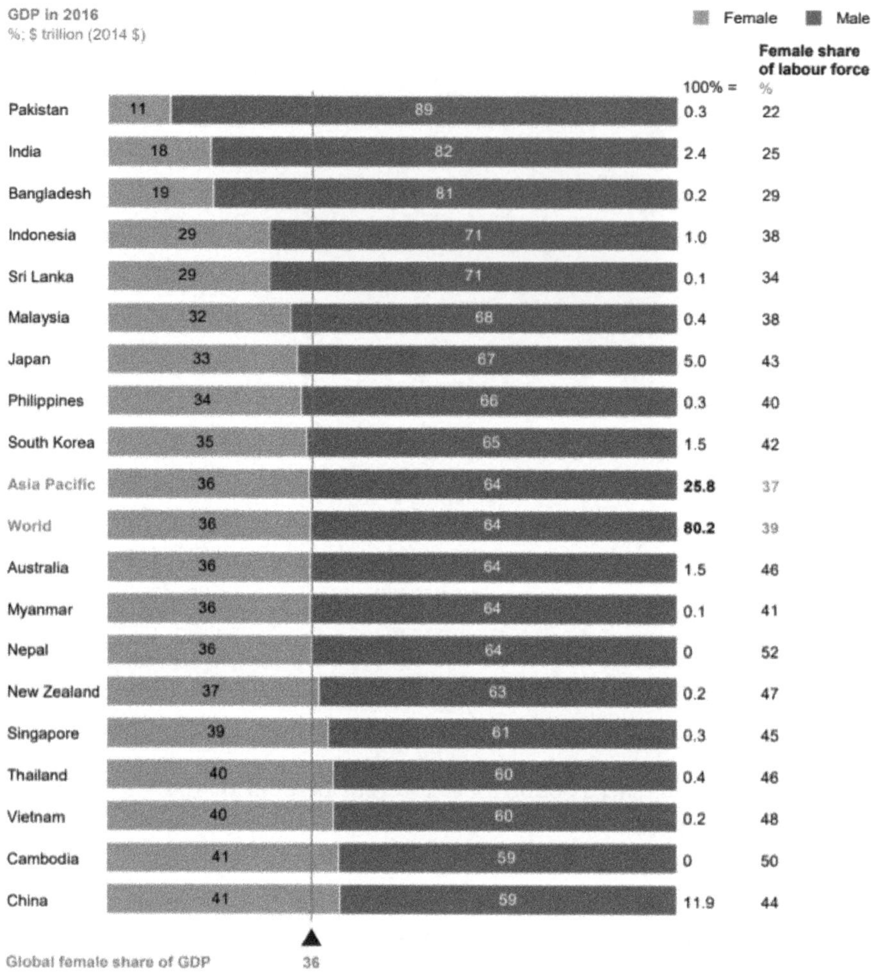

Graph 1: Global female share in GDP

Source: ILO; World Input-Output Database; IHS; national statistical agencies; Oxford Economics; McKinsey Global Growth Model; McKinsey Global Institute analysis.

9.1.1 *Household Savings*

India's Household savings[19] by women increased (Graph 2), which made the GDP rise but women's contribution to actual GDP is very low

[19]Trading Economics (2016). "India Household Savings". https://tradingeconomics.com/india/personal-savings [TRADING Economics].

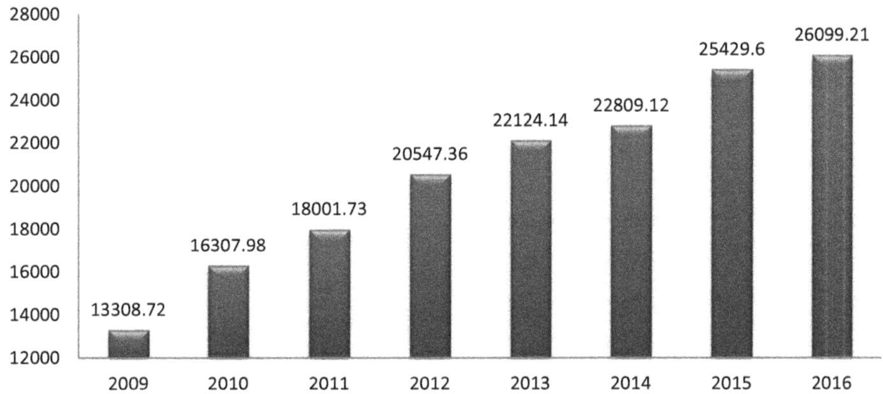

Graph 2: Household savings of India

Source: Tradingeconomics.com, Ministry of Statistics and Programme Implementation (MOSPI).

(Graph 1). Personal savings in India increased to 26099.21 INR Billion in 2016 from 25429.60 INR Billion in 2015, and overall, personal savings in India averaged 3811.44 INR Billion from 1951 until 2016, reaching an all-time high of 26099.21 INR Billion in 2016 and a record low of 6.34 INR Billion in 1952.

Region wise, ease of doing business, and India's ranking for 2019 is presented in Table 2, which clearly reveals that India ranks at 137 in terms of ease of doing business when compared to other countries with a score of 67.23.[20]

9.1.2 *Sectorial Breakdown of Male and Female Entrepreneurs*

The sectorial breakdown of male and female entrepreneurs with workers as per the OCED is presented in Table 3. The sectors which fall in the top ten are ranked along with percentage contributions and Graph 3 provides the same information in picture format. The graph reveals the broad activities and total number of persons (in percent) employed in establishments under women entrepreneurship by type of establishment. The

[20]The World Bank (2018). "Doing Business 2019 — Training for Reform". 31 October 2018. https://www.doingbusiness.org/en/reports/global-reports/doing-business-2019 [Accessed January 05, 2019].

Table 2: Ease of doing business rankings in India (2019)

Starting a Business	137
Dealing with Construction Permits	52
Getting Electricity	24
Registering Property	166
Getting Credit	22
Protecting Minority Investors	7
Paying Taxes	121
Trading across Borders	80
Enforcing Contracts	163
Resolving Insolvency	108

Source: Compiled from World's Bank Doing Business database.

manufacturing sector has the highest number where women are employed throughout India.

Graph 4 reveals the establishment (agricultural and non-agricultural activities, in percentage) engaged by male and female entrepreneurs. It is clear from the graph that female owners exceed male owners in agricultural activities and male owners dominate the non-agricultural activities. Overall the ownership in non-agricultural activities is much higher than agricultural activities and its breakdown (in percent) is clearly provided in Graph 5.

The percentage distribution of proprietary establishments by social group of the owner SC/ST, OBC, others in agricultural and non-agricultural activities is presented in Graph 6. It is clear from the graph that, the social group of owners are higher in non-agricultural activities than agricultural activities.

Graph 7 reveals the establishment by sector (rural and urban) in percent. It is again clear from the graph that establishment in non-agricultural activity is much more than in agricultural activity (as in Graphs 3, 4 and 5). About 79.4 percent of workers work in perennial (continuing) establishments, 50.28 percent work in seasonal establishments and 69.75

Table 3: Sectorial breakdown of male and female entrepreneurs

	Female Entrepreneurs		Male Entrepreneurs	
Rank	**Sector**	**%**	**Sector**	**%**
1	Retail trade, except of motor vehicles and motorcycles	17	Retail trade, except of motor vehicles and motorcycles	22
2	Manufacturers of wearing apparel	14	Wholesale trade, except of motor vehicles and motorcycles	7
3	Education	12	Food and beverage service activities	7
4	Other personal service activities	11	Land transport and transport via pipelines	7
5	Human health activities	9	Manufacturers of clothing/apparel	5
6	Manufacturers of textiles	6	Manufacturers of food products	5
7	Food and beverage service activities	6	Wholesale and retail trade and repair of motor vehicles and motorcycles	5
8	Manufacturers of food products	4	Manufacturers of textiles	4
9	Wholesale trade, except of motor vehicles and motorcycles	3	Manufacturers of fabricated metal products, except machinery and equipment	3
10	Manufacturers of wood and products of wood and cork, except furniture	2	Education	3

Source: OECD, (2015).[21]

percent work in casual establishments in the non-agricultural sector, whereas the remainder work in the agricultural sector. Also, it can be noted that the remaining 50 percent of seasonal workersperform agricultural activities (agricultural activity is seasonal) and 20 percent and 30 percent of the agricultural activity is done by permanent and casual workers respectively.

[21]Organisation for Economic Co-operation and Development (OECD). (2015). *Entrepreneurship at a Glance 2015*, OECD Publishing, Paris, https://doi.org/10.1787/entrepreneur_aag-2015-en.

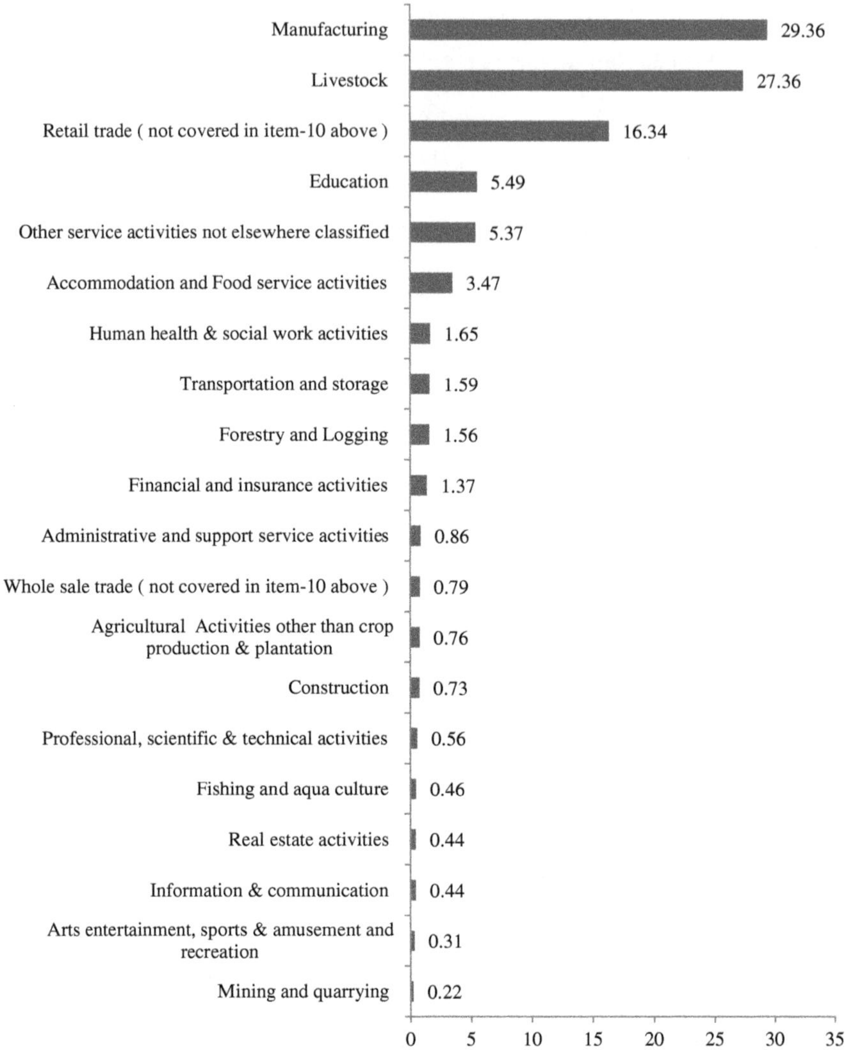

Graph 3: Broad activity wise total number of persons (%) employed in establishments under women entrepreneurship by type of establishment

Source: Calculated from the All India Sixth Economic Census Report, 2016.

Graph 8 reveals the percentage of establishments under women entrepreneurs by major source of finance such as loans, borrowing, self-finance etc. It is clear from the graph that almost 79 percent of the women establishments were self-financed, which reveals that the government should take

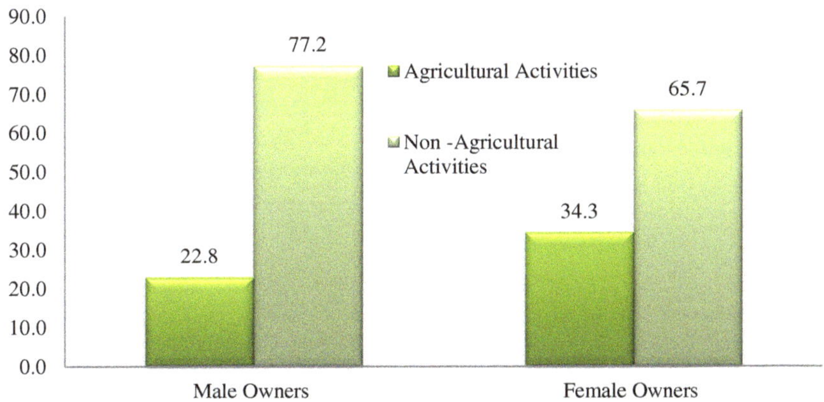

Graph 4: Establishments by gender (in percent)

Source: Calculated from the All India Sixth Economic Census Report, 2016.

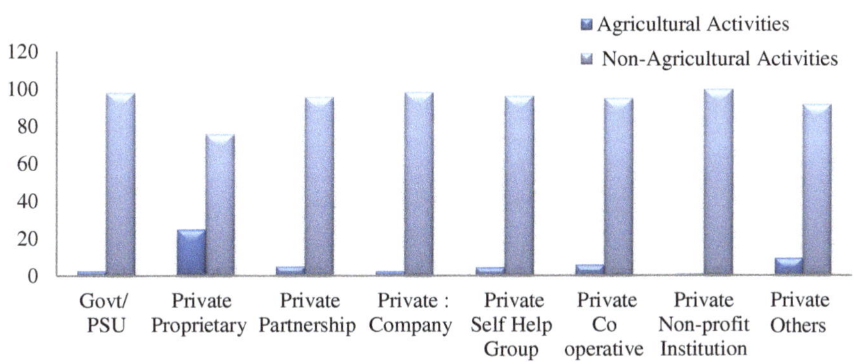

Graph 5: Total number of establishments by type of ownership

Source: Calculated from the All India Sixth Economic Census Report, 2016.

necessary steps to help entrepreneurs. The second important source at 14.5 percent is from donations or transfers from other agencies. The next important sources were assistance from government and borrowing from financial institutions which were 3.4 percent and 1.1 percent respectively.

The growth rate (%) of number of EM-II filed by the MSMEs at DICs under the various State/UT Commission rates/Directorates of Industries during 2007–08 to 2014–15 is provided in Table 4. The growth does not follow a constant trend because for many reasons some entrepreneurs

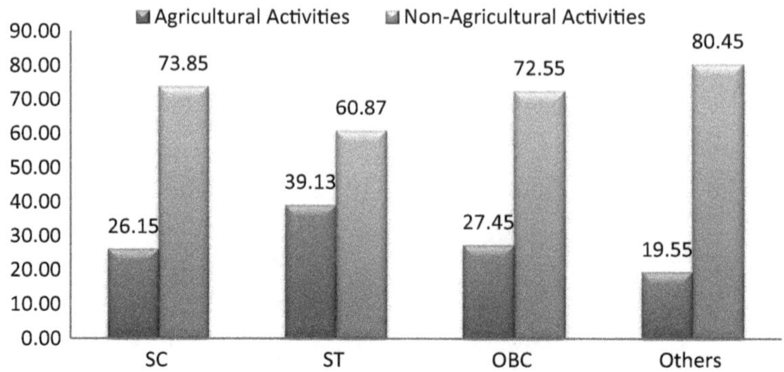

Graph 6: Percentage distribution of proprietary establishments by social group of the owner

Source: Calculated from the All India Sixth Economic Census Report, 2016.

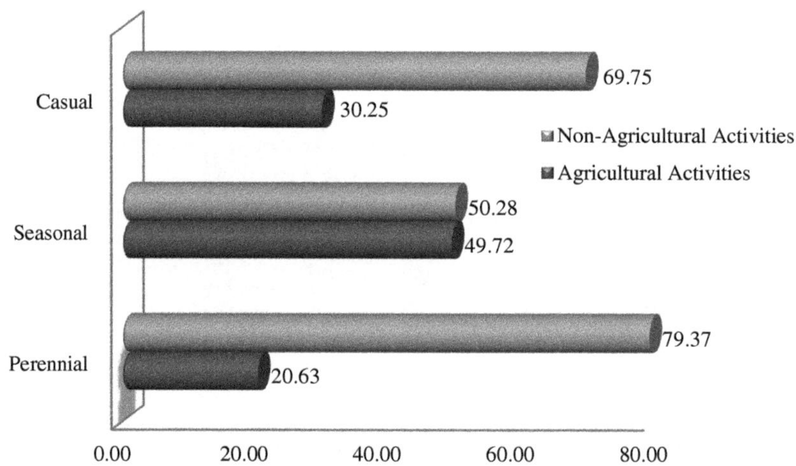

Graph 7: Establishments by rural and urban sector (in %)

Source: Calculated from All India Sixth Economic Census Report, 2016.

drop out. Hence there is a fall in growth rate. This created a need for the MUDRA bank in April 2015.

Under the MUDRA Yojana many businesses benefited, including small manufacturing units, shopkeeping, handicrafts, food processing (pickle), service sector enterprises, agriculture, hair salons, beauty parlours, auto operators, microentrepreneurs etc. It is available for both new units and expansion of existing units.

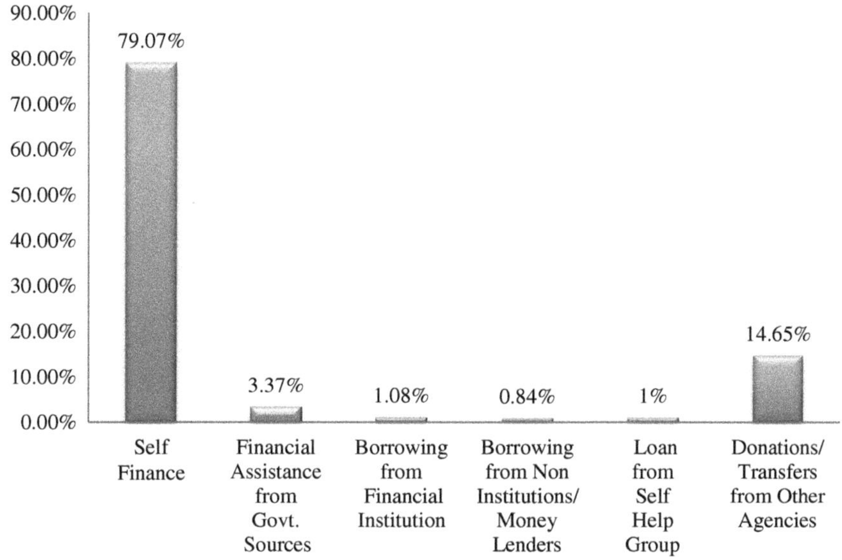

Graph 8: Percentage of establishments under women entrepreneurs by major source of finance

Source: Calculated from the All India Report on the 6th Economic Census, 2016.

Table 4: Growth rate (%) of number of EM-II filed by the MSMEs at DICs under the various State/UT commission rates/Directorates of industries during 2007–08 to 2014–15

Sl. No.	Year	Growth Rate (%)
1	2007–08 to 2008–09	11.77
2	2008–09 to 2009–10	10.45
3	2009–10 to 2010–11	11.83
4	2010–11 to 2011–12	18.45
5	2011–12 to 2012–13	14.3
6	2012–13 to 2013–14	12.44
7	2013–14 to 2014–15	17.18

Source: The State/UT Commissionerates/Directorates of Industries & MSME-Development Institutes, O/o DC (MSME), M/o MSME.

Table 5: Number of accounts, loan sanction and disbursement under Pradhan Mantri Mudra Yojana (PMMY)

2015–2016	No. of A/Cs	34880924
	Sanction Amount	137449.27
	Disbursed Amount	132954.73
2016–2017	No. of A/Cs	39701047
	Sanction Amount	180528.6
	Disbursed Amount	175312.2
2017–2018	No. of A/Cs	48130593
	Sanction Amount	253677.09
	Disbursed Amount	246437.41
2018–2019	No. of A/Cs	59870318
	Sanction Amount	321722.79
	Disbursed Amount	311811.36

Source: Compiled from MUDRA reports.

The number of accounts, loan sanctions and disbursements under Pradhan Mantri Mudra Yojana (PMMY) for the year 2015–16 to 2018–19 is provided in Table 5. The sanctions and disbursements made during 2018 stood at Rs. 3,21,722 crore and Rs. 3,11,811.36 crore respectively as against Rs. 2,53,677 crore and Rs. 2,46,437 crore respectively during the previous financial year. The comparative position of sanctions and disbursement in the last two financial years is lower. The Southern region has the highest share of both outreach and outstanding loans. Graph 9 provides the trend of the number of accounts since 2015. It is clear from the graph that from 3 crores in 2015, the number of accounts has increased to 5 crores in 2018. i.e. it has grown at a rate of 18 percent in the past four years.

It is clear from Graph 10 that the loan sanction and disbursement under Mudra has been increasing since 2015.

According to three years of Pradhan Mantri Mudra Yojana funding the unfunded,[22] there are 5.77 crore small business/micro units, mostly

[22]NSSO Survey. op. cit.

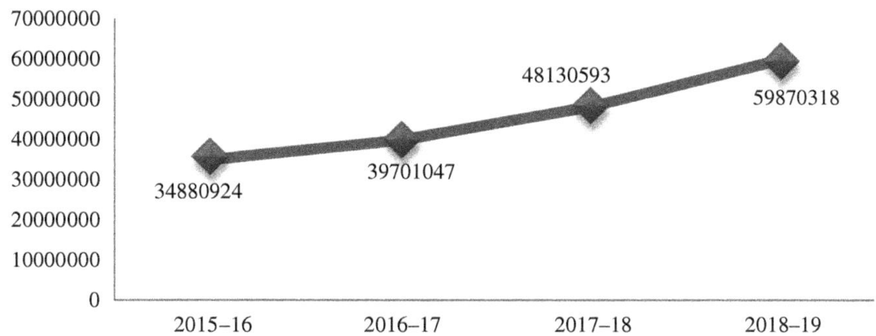

Graph 9: Number of accounts

Source: Compiled from MUDRA reports.

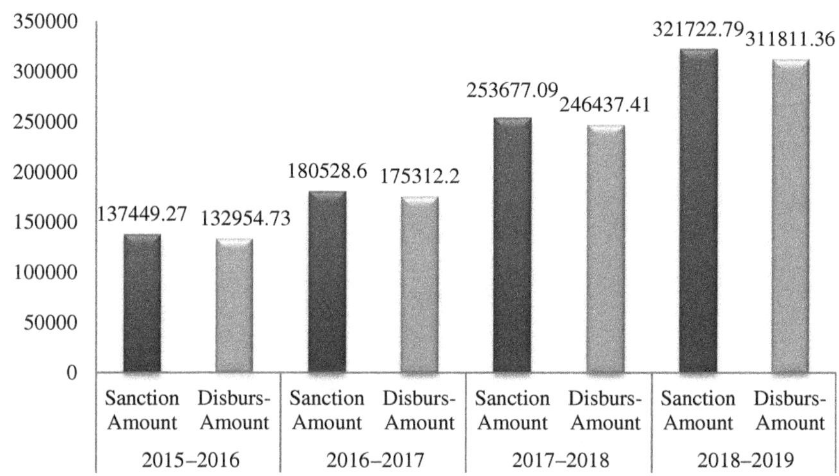

Graph 10: Loan sanction and disbursement under Pradhan Mantri Mudra Yojana (Rs in Crore)

Source: Compiled from MUDRA reports.

individual proprietorship or 'Own Account Enterprises' (OAE), and the majority of them are owned by people belonging to Scheduled Caste (SC), Scheduled Tribe (ST) or Other Backward Classes (OBCs). Graph 11 shows that the majority of the 53 percent of the loan is sanctioned to women and about 13 percent of the loan is sanctioned to the SC category, 22 percent to OBC and about four percent to the ST category.

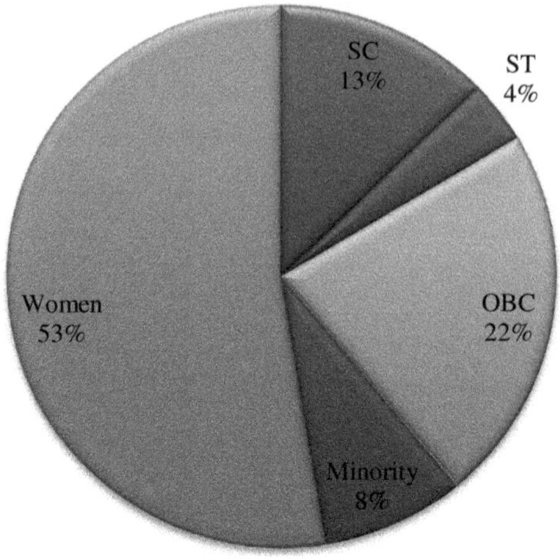

Graph 11: Number of loans sanctioned by social category under Pradhan Mantri Mudra Yojana (PMMY) in India (2015–18)

Source: Compiled from MUDRA reports.

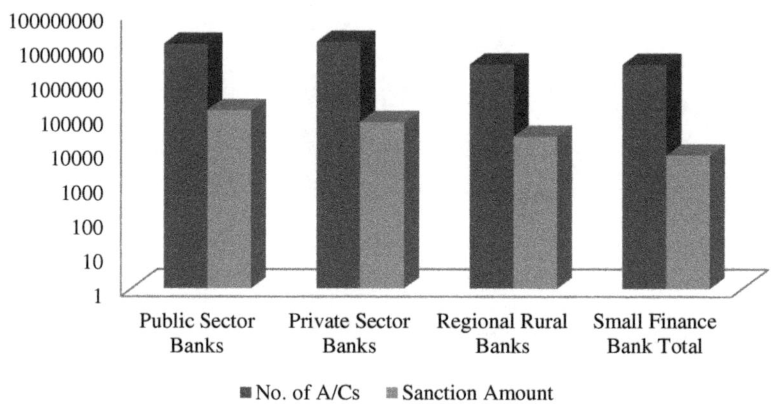

Graph 12: Number of accounts and loans sanctioned under Pradhan Mantri Mudra Yojana (PMMY) in India (2015–2018)

Source: Compiled from MUDRA reports.

Graphs 12 and 13 provide the details of the number of accounts and loans sanctioned under MUDRA from 2015–18. In order to provide vibrant data visualization, a normal scale and logarithmic scale is chosen for the same data set for comparative purposes.

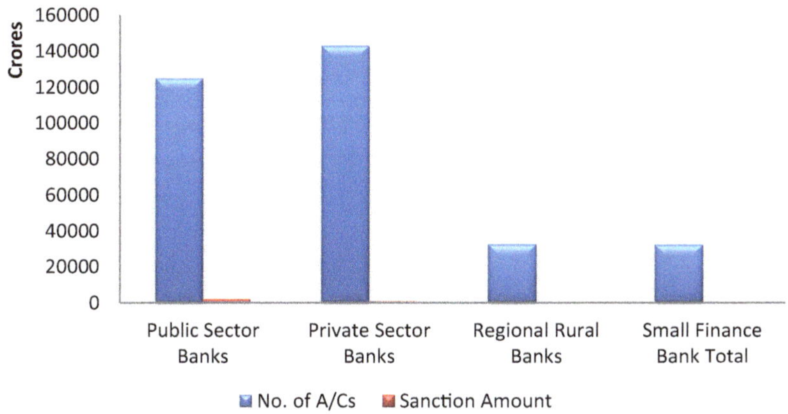

Graph 13: Number of accounts and loan sanctioned under Pradhan Mantri Mudra Yojana (PMMY) in India (2015–2018)

Source: Compiled from MUDRA reports.

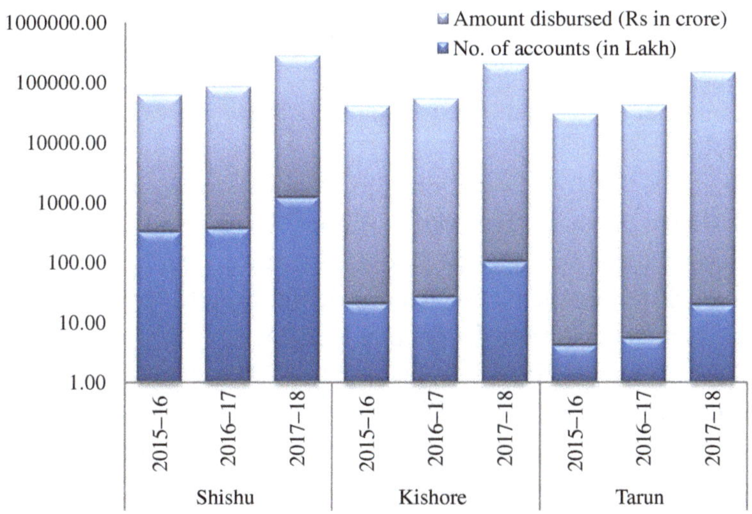

Graph 14: Category-wise Mudra loan beneficiaries

Source: Compiled from MUDRA reports.

MUDRA loan beneficiaries category-wise (Shishu, Kishore and Tarun) are presented in Graph 14 (a logarithmic scale is used to provide a clear view on the indicators). It is evident that the MUDRA Yojana has fulfilled the aspirations of many microentrepreneurs,

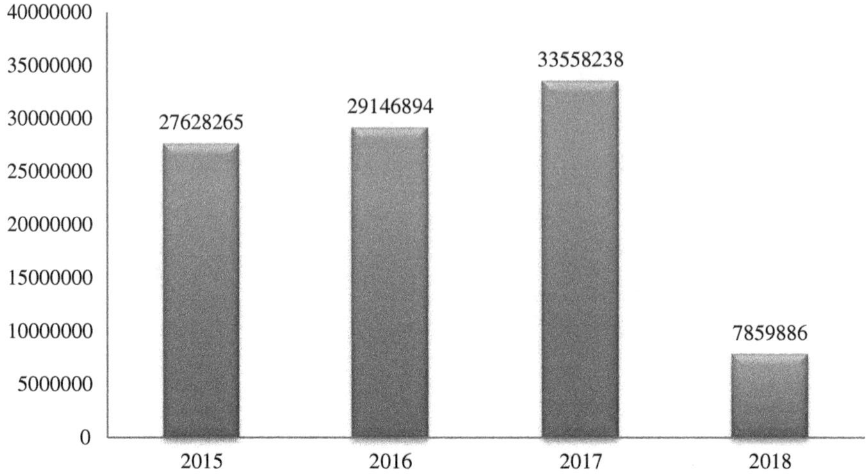

Graph 15: Number of loans sanctioned to women borrowers under Pradhan Mantri Mudra Yojana

Source: Compiled from MUDRA reports.

i.e. the number of accounts and amount disbursed has continued to rise since 2015.

The number of loans sanctioned to women borrowers under Pradhan Mantri Mudra Yojana is provided in Graph 15. It can be seen from the graph that the loans sanctioned to women borrowers has had an increasing trend since 2015 and then there is a drastic fall in 2018; demonetization in 2017 could be a reason for the decline in 2018.

Graph 16 shows MUDRA loans per 1000 women; it also clearly depicts that for 2015–16 and 2016–17, the loan sanction has increased from 36 percent to 39 percent and this reduced to 25 percent in 2017–18. The reason could be demonetization, which was a temporary disruption to economic and industrial activity.

9.2 Conclusion

Various schemes of the government have attempted to ensure access to various financial services such as availability of a basic savings bank account, access to need based credit, remittance facilities, insurance and

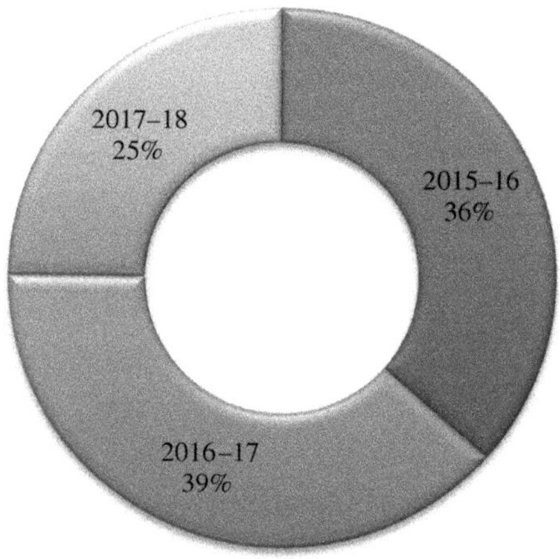

Graph 16: MUDRA loans per 1,000 women

Source: Compiled from MUDRA reports.

pensions to the excluded sections i.e. weaker sections and low-income groups. This deep penetration at an affordable cost is possible only with effective use of technology. The data visualization clearly reveals that, the participation of women, minority categories, and the weaker section of the economy has benefited through the MUDRA loan. The loan accounts of new and women entrepreneurs was slightly higher at 39 percent and 79 percent during FY2015–16. MUDRA Cards were issued to more than 1.84 lakh for an amount of 1,515.84 crore, during FY2016–17. MUDRA has recorded a total income of Rs. 535.08 crore, against a total expense of Rs. 362.75 crore, with profit after tax (PAT) at Rs. 107.84 crore in the FY2016–17. Based on these findings the following suggestions are provided:

1. more employment opportunities must be provided especially to those who should be employed in villages and trained in advance to promote more accounts.
2. more banks branches are needed within rural areas and more awareness must be created among rural people regarding banking services.
3. more training programs are needed to increase financial awareness among the people.

https://doi.org/10.1142/9789811212741_0010

Chapter 10

Leadership Styles to Aid Building Innovative, Agile, and Resilient Organizations

Kumar Shalender

10.1 Introduction

In the wake of rapidly changing technology, constant innovations, and a turbulent business environment, it is hard to find good examples of a typical control-and-command leadership style. It is equally interesting that nobody has come up with a credible alternative either. This might be because top executives in an organization are ambivalent about the correct idea of an organizational structure. While a centralized hierarchy is good for maintaining order, it often leads to stifling of the innovative spirit among employees. A flat structure, on the other hand, promotes new ideas and innovation though management becomes vulnerable of losing control. Now to understand this tension and suggest a possible way out, there are two examples of automobile organizations operating in two different segments of the Indian automobile industry — Maruti-Suzuki India Limited (MSIL) in the passenger vehicle (PV) category and Hero MotoCorp in the two-wheeler segment. Both organizations have been in the business for quite a long time now which means they have weathered many storms and have been able to survive despite accelerated pace of change and innovations.

A qualitative analysis technique which includes personal interviews and informal meetings with employees and management revealed some common characteristics underpinning these organizations — focus on inculcating a spirit of innovation, working in small-size multidisciplinary teams, and constant focus on fostering a culture of change. There are also three different kinds of leaders working at different levels in these two organizations they are uncannily similar in their working style and characteristics. Firstly, there are three different kinds of leaders:

1. Directional leadership at the highest corporate level;
2. empowering leadership at the middle business level, and;
3. entrepreneurial leadership at the base functional level.

Secondly, both Maruti-Suzuki and Hero MotoCorp have effectively imbibed these leadership styles into their culture, thereby making characteristics of these leaders' part and parcel of the organization's core values.

The three leadership styles coupled with cultural norms have done wonders for both organizations, especially in terms of anticipating and tapping new opportunities proactively. Employees have the freedom to choose their assignments and contrary to norms, new products are conceived from the base-functional level of the organization. The innovative ideas are rewarded, funded, and worked upon by multidisciplinary teams which effectively mean the organization is running like a collection of several start-ups. In effect, these processes help the organization to become nimble to adjust quickly in line with changing external conditions.

10.2 Types of Leaders

The three types of leaders and then suggest a conceptual framework which will help organizations to tap into opportunities by leveraging their strengths and working on their weaknesses.

10.2.1 *Entrepreneurial Leaders*

The frontline employees of both organizations exhibit entrepreneurial leadership style. They work in altogether different manners from what other employees do at the same level of hierarchy in other companies. The primary characteristics of these leaders are their ability to sense and seize opportunities, rallying the team towards a common goal, and pursuing the top management for allocation of resources. Some of the common characteristics of entrepreneur leaders include self-confidence, risk-taking ability, strategic vision, and team skills.

Entrepreneurial leaders are self-starters and they exhibit a higher level of self-confidence. They are highly motivated in their pursuit and even in the face of failure, they remain committed to their cause. Both organizations motivate frontline employees to pursue the risk associated with their entrepreneurial ideas. Even more important is the fact that these entrepreneurial leaders take full ownership of the project by leading from the front. Once the idea passes the exploratory stage, these leaders have the option to stay put in the commanding position or handover the project to a different team for further persuasion.

Along with a self-motivated attitude, entrepreneurial leaders are found to have a strategic vision which helps them align the objective of their specific project with organizational objectives. This alignment stems from the deep understanding that these leaders have about their organization, its vision, and long-term aspirations. Both Maruti-Suzuki and Hero MotoCorp have very clearly identified and communicated their core values throughout the organization. This has helped in the development of a clear understanding among frontline employees. For example, the dominant values in Maruti-Suzuki are novelty and innovation, while Hero MotoCorp focuses on value-creation and customer-orientation. Another important source from which entrepreneurial leaders benefit enormously is their deep connection with channel partners and customers' needs. Both aspects help entrepreneurial leaders to stay ahead of the learning curve and quickly sense future opportunities before they show up on the horizon.

Entrepreneurial leaders are not handed teams by the top management in both Maruti-Suzuki and Hero MotoCorp. Rather, these leaders create their own teams and attract others with their ideas. A true indication of an entrepreneurial leader is his/her ability to earn followers and then keep them together to work for a predetermined objective. Most of the new product development projects in both Maruti-Suzuki and Hero MotoCorp have not begun at the behest of top management; rather these initiatives have started from the lowest level of the hierarchy. This indicates that idea-mining is done by frontline employees who are motivated enough to pursue the projects. These initiators put the ideas across the top management and convince them to give the nod of approval while asking for resources. By this point, entrepreneurial leaders have also attracted some followers who will happily pool their efforts in the project. All this requires a great degree of persuasive skills, confidence, and people skills.

Teams formed by entrepreneurial leaders are significantly different from conventional teams owing primarily to two major factors:

1. the team has been constituted voluntarily with people joining out of their interest in the project rather than because of an official dictum, and;
2. team members have full liberty to openly express their viewpoints rather than blindly towing the line of a leader.

Any of the teammates can disagree and push back and in view of some genuine, evidence-based proof, entrepreneurial leaders do not hesitate to reflect on the project and make necessary modifications. This implies that entrepreneurial leaders not only have the confidence to attract people, but they are also receptive to constructive feedback and accordingly, make the required changes to the project.

10.2.2 *Empowering Leaders*

Empowering leaders operate one-level above the entrepreneurial leaders in the hierarchical structure and their key roles include helping frontline employees in project development, establishing connections, and staying updated with the largest strategic shifts happening in both organization and business environment. Empowering leaders possesses the following skills in Maruti-Suzuki and Hero MotoCorp:

- **Coaching and mentoring**: Empowering leaders are not like a typical boss who always talks in term of goal setting and achievements — they are more than that and act like a coach and mentor to entrepreneurial leaders. One of the key characteristics of empowering leaders is their ability to ask the right kind of questions rather than issuing directions to frontline employees. Often empowering leaders in these organizations belongs to a different discipline and that helps to bring a fresh perspective to the table rather than people trying to legitimise and redefine the established pattern time and again. These companies have deliberately assigned cross-functional mentors to the entrepreneurial leaders so that novel ideas and innovation continue to flow into the system. The working environment of these organizations is defined in a manner that nobody is hesitant, including mentors to admit their lack of knowledge of a problem/issue. Citing one incident, the production manager in Hero MotoCorp who had been assigned a mentor from the marketing team said that his mentor came and told him that he did not know about the problem but would get back to him soon. The very next day, his mentor came back and explained that he had come to grips with the issue and suggested an out of the box solution. Empowering leaders also help entrepreneurial leaders to successfully get through the product development process. More specifically, the role of mentors is to help frontline employees position opportunities effectively, prepare the presentation agenda, anticipate the tough questions, and galvanize the team behind the project. Providing quality and honest feedback is another important area where empowering mentors can make a world of difference.

- Owing to large field of vision, empowering leaders help project teams establish and maintain "*creative relationships*" much beyond their organization, segments and even industry. Empowering leaders have considerably large exposure and thanks to their ability to connect the dots, these people can help frontline employees to make larger impact with their company-specific projects. In some cases, mentors will enable project teams to have a better understanding of customers' needs while in other cases, their deep connections across industry lines will help entrepreneurial leaders to expand on the utility of their projects. For example, empowering leaders can easily tell project heads that one specific team in France or England is working along similar lines and connecting with these teams can help bring broader understanding and valuable inputs to the project. Additionally, empowering leaders also make sure that communication within the project team irrespective of the discipline must remain intact with each team member knowing exactly what the team has been up to.

- A great deal of importance is attached to communication today and empowering leaders really appreciate the importance of this facet in taking the organization forward. The simplest yet decisively difficult principle of communication is to make sure that all the project teams, as well as discipline in an organization, remain updated with latest happenings. Coaches and mentors do not restrict the information about emerging opportunities and their efforts remain focused on making sure that every organ of their organization must know exactly what is happening on other fronts. This is challenging especially in the context of large organizations such as Maruti-Suzuki and Hero MotoCorp where regional priorities must be aligned with global aspirations. In order to take both the aspects onboard, empowering leaders in these companies have had regular interactions with divisional heads. In the meetings, empowering leaders give detailed information about the upcoming projects of the company and explain how these projects are going to benefit them and the organization. Feedback is also sought from frontline employees who make this whole conversation more productive.
- Not just project teams, but empowering leaders also maintain a close interactive relationship with suppliers and channel partners of the company. These stakeholders are regularly consulted, and these organizations do not take singular decisions where only the interest of the firm is considered. Empowering leaders understand that without the cooperation of their suppliers and channel partners the delivery of quality products/services is not possible, and hence their interests also need to be considered while making an important strategic decision. The aspects of connection and communication are greatly enabled by advanced technology and seamless connectivity which both organizations have deployed throughout their divisions/departments. In addition, these organizations have clearly communicated their core values to employees and if anyone finds something unusual, he/she has an obligation to report it to higher management while taking a clear stand not to move ahead with proceedings.

10.2.3 *Directional Leaders*

At the top of the pyramid of the hierarchy are directional leaders who are primarily responsible for setting the vision and big picture for the organization. These leaders are responsible for driving important changes in the core values, culture, and organizational structure which ultimately help the firm to achieve its desired objective(s).

The role of directional leaders is the most difficult one simply because they must make decisions in a completely uncertain environment. The prominent factors that they need to take care are not only related to competition, economic environment, and market forces but also the ones connected with government policy changes, environmental issues, and legal aspects. This is especially relevant in the case of the automobile industry where more than market forces the effect of policy changes, environmental degradation, and legal challenges dominate.

Directional leaders must anticipate all these changes much in advance and the complete absence of any buffer zone makes things very difficult for them. Several crucial decisions have been taken recently by Maruti-Suzuki in the wake of changing political, environmental, and legal factors. The company decided to stop production of diesel vehicles from April 2020 as stringent BS-VI emission norms are coming into effect. Similarly, the decision to share models with Toyota which in return will share electric vehicle technology with Maruti has been taken in the interest of the company's future business stability.

A somewhat less discussed aspect of directional leaders' work is their contribution to keeping the organization together. For example, the push towards environmental sustainability that both Maruti-Suzuki and Hero MotoCorp are championing today might get amplified by the projects developed at the entrepreneurial level and mentored by the empowered leader. However, directional leaders have also played a key role by hiring employees and staff with specific competence in the field of environmental sustainability. These new recruits are contributing significantly to new projects and in a way mark the contribution of directional leaders in realizing goals at lower levels. Directional leaders in both organizations keep close tabs on the success/failure rate of new projects and continuously assess the feasibility of new ideas and pilot projects from a strategic as well as market perspective. For a project to reach the production stage, it is required that it meets specific objectives set by the directional leaders. There are instances when some tough decisions must be taken by the directional leaders and in such scenarios, the personal relationship and reputation that the top management enjoys with empowering and entrepreneurial leaders plays a key role. In sum, directional leaders work behind the scenes and their contribution can be realized in the form of synergy that is absolutely required for the successful culmination of new product development in a company.

10.3 Systemic Approach

The biggest merit of these three leadership levels along with their inherent characteristics is the creation of a systemic approach whereby the whole comes to be greater than the sum of individual parts. Both Maruti-Suzuki and Hero MotoCorp have benefitted tremendously from this systemic approach. One of the unique characteristics of the systemic approach is its flexibility which allows an organization to adapt itself according to the changes in business environment. Thanks to the freedom available to employees, talented entrepreneurial leaders are always busy exploring new possibilities and converting them into feasible market offerings. The empowering leaders, on their part, help frontline employees to push their projects while facilitating their engagement with the right kind of people. At the top level, directional leaders focus on the fluidity of these processes and make sure that the company's ethos and core values are reflected in its work philosophy. The following aspects of this systemic approach worth mentioning follow:

- **Shared leadership**: Unlike a typical organization, both Maruti-Suzuki and Hero MotoCorp take the practice of shared leadership strongly to heart. The employees — irrespective of their level — can take over the leadership role as and when situations warrant. As a result, both these companies have several employees ready to hold the leadership baton and more importantly, they quickly pass it on to another group as per the requirement. Another important characteristic is the way seamless communication happens between all three kinds of leaders that have already been mentioned in the study. This will help in the more holistic development of ideas with inputs/feedback coming from a wide variety of stakeholders. It is important to understand that power and influence in the case of a shared leadership stem from one's abilities rather than the position he/she holds in both these organisations.

- **Synergistic effect**: We have witnessed synergy playing an important role in fuelling the growth of both Maruti-Suzuki and Hero MotoCorp. The initiative taken at the entrepreneurial level is well-groomed by empowering leaders while directional leaders very subtly mould these projects to fit in the broader vision framework of their companies. This all translates into a synergistic effect whereby a system is created that channels the flow of energy in a single direction. Complementing this synergy is the constant interaction of employees with customers, aside from among themselves, which help the company to stay nimble and up to date with changes happening in the external and internal business environment.

10.4 Pulling It Together

It is indeed a difficult task to balance authority and responsibility in real-world conditions and while it might be easy to propagate in a theoretical form, it is very difficult to implement. This is especially true in view of the current prevailing tumultuous business environment. However, notwithstanding difficulties, companies like Maruti-Suzuki and Hero MotoCorp have demonstrated that such a system can be conceived and successfully run amidst all the turbulence and chaos. During the interactions with employees of these organizations, there is a contagious enthusiasm with employees constantly engaged in exploring, discussing, and deliberating new ideas to develop novel products. There is a feeling of freedom and these companies have provided enough space for new ideas to be born, mature, and have a fair chance of making it to the final product. This amazing sense of balance between authority and responsibility make both Maruti-Suzuki and Hero MotoCorp ideal organizations to be followed and take note of.

https://doi.org/10.1142/9789811212741_0011

Chapter 11

SMEs and Digital Marketing Design

Jugal Kishor and Swati Sharma

11.1 Introduction

The advent of the internet has directly increased the use of e-commerce on the commercial web. For instance, data or information can be managed, commercial orders can be placed online, with product delivery channels, and service execution.[1] Consequently, digital marketing creates new avenues for the millions of SMEs to enter into global markets by providing them a platform to communicate globally as good as any big organisation can.[2–5] Digital marketing has helped overcome the many obstacles to attempt to compete in a competitive market.

---

[1]Ching, H.L. & Ellis, P. (2004). "Marketing in Cyberspace: What Factors Drive e-Commerce Adoption?" *Journal of Marketing Management*, 20, 409–29.
[2]McCue, S. (1999). "Small Firms and the Internet: Force or Farce?" *International Trade Forum*, 1, 27–9.
[3]Hoffman, D.L. & Novak, T.P. (1996). "Marketing in Hypermedia Computer-mediated Environments: Conceptual Foundations". *Journal of Marketing*, 60, 50–68.
[4]Herbig, P. & Hale, B. (1997). "Internet: The Marketing Challenge of the Twentieth Century". *Internet Research*, 7(2), 95–100.
[5]Nguyen, T.D. & Barrett, N.J. (2006). "The Adoption of the Internet by Export Firms in Transitional Markets". *Asia Pacific Journal of Marketing & Logistics*, 18(1), 29–42.

Notwithstanding, corporate culture makes widespread use of the internet unlikely as SMEs showed varied usage.[6] It is observed that digital technology used in marketing practices can encourage huge economic benefits to enterprises. Conversely, the SMEs are not involved in digital marketing practices may confront perils in this competitive environment.[7] In the last few years, it has been observed that there has been a positive growth in the research work on internet applications used to benefit businesses.[8] Based on the study undertaken in 2000, the authors contended that the benefits drawn from digital marketing activities were observed to be dwindling as compared to the extensive use of it.

Furthermore, many scholars have estimated a positive impact of digital marketing in the future as direct business generated through digital marketing activities.[9] The aim of the study undertaken in 2004, was estimating the influence of digital marketing on SMEs. Subsequently, the explicit aim of the current work is to cultivate and gain a thought process of the key barriers and employment issues of digital marketing when it comes to adopting digital marketing practices by SMEs in a developing country like India. Moreover, examining the consequences of implementing digital marketing practices in SMEs businesses. In the selected region, this study was conducted to see the potential impact of digital marketing design to stimulate SMEs to comprehend a sympathetic understanding of digital marketing.

Furthermore, earlier studies reviewed here portray the dearth of significant facts that depict the contribution of digital marketing in SMEs' performance. However, there are numerous studies focused on the use of the internet, but it is evident that as a constraint there is not enough research on the issue. Similarly, contribution of the internet

---

[6] Sadowski, B.M., Maitland, C., & Van Douyer, J. (2002). "Strategic Use of the Internet by Small and Medium Sized Companies: An Exploratory Study." *Information Economics and Policy*, 14(1), 75–93.

[7] Egan, T., Clancy, S., & O'Toole, T. (2003). "The Integration of e-Commerce Tools Into the Business Processes of SMEs". *Irish Journal of Management*, 24(1), 139.

[8] Venkatesh, V. & Davis, F.D. (2000). "A Theoretical Extension of Technology Acceptance Model: Four Longitudinal Field Studies". *Management Science*, 46(2), 186–204.

[9] Gallagher, D. & Gilmore, A. (2004). "The Stages Theory of SME Internationalisation: A Northern Ireland Case Study". *International Journal of Management Cases*, 7(1), 13–23.

Table 1: Classification of MSMEs

Enterprise Category	Manufacturing Sector	Service Sector
Micro Enterprise	Does not exceed twenty-five lakh rupees	Does not exceed ten lakh rupees
Small Enterprise	More than twenty-five lakh rupees but does not exceed five crore rupees	More than ten lakh rupees but does not exceed two crore rupees
Medium Enterprise	More than five crore rupees but does not exceed ten crore rupees	More than two crore rupees but does not exceed five core rupees

Source: Ministry of MSMEs.

regarding enterprise marketing activities, and overall feasibility of digital marketing for SMEs. Additionally, the scenario thus predicts digital marketing as a sole indicator to explore the possible scenario of SMEs.[10–12]

11.2 Classification

With reference to the Micro, Small and Medium Enterprises Development (MSMED) Act 2006, MSMEs are classified in Table 1.

11.3 Role in Indian Economy

Over the last five years SMEs have emerged as vibrant and a futuristic sector in the Indian economy. Notwithstanding, SMEs are considered the next potential sector after agriculture that significantly contributes to the Indian economy and its society's development through generating entrepreneurship and employment at a comparatively lower cost. SMEs are

[10]Ching & Ellis. op. cit.

[11]McCue. op. cit.

[12]Avlonitis, G.J. & Karayanni, D.A. (2000). "The Impact of Internet Use on Business-to-Business Marketing: Examples from American and European Companies". *Industrial Marketing Management*, 29(5), 441–459.

Table 2: Contribution of MSMEs in country's economy at current price

(Figures in Rs. Crores adjusted for Financial Intermediation Services Indirectly Measured (FISIM) at current prices)

Year	MSME GVA	Growth %	Total GVA	Share of MSMEs in GVA (%)	Total GDP	Share of MSME in GDP (%)
2011–12	2583263	—	8106946	31.86	8736329	29.57
2012–13	2977623	15.27	9202692	32.36	9944013	29.94
2013–14	3343009	12.27	10363153	32.26	11233522	29.76
2014–15	3658196	9.43	11481794	31.86	12445128	29.39
2015–16	3936788	7.62	12458642	31.60	13682035	28.77

Source: Central Statistics Office (CSO), Ministry of Statistics & Programme Implementation.

broadening their sphere towards various sectors of the economy and manufacturing a numerous range of products and services to fulfil demand of the domestic as well as global market. SMEs have been playing a key role in expanding entrepreneurial endevour through new business opportunities. With reference to the data provided by the Central Statistics Office, Ministry of Statistics & Programme Implementation, the contribution of MSMEs in India's Gross Value Added (GVA) and Gross Domestic Product (GDP) are shown in Table 2.

The above data depicts the future employment and entrepreneurship opportunities in the country that can be optimized by SMEs. Consequently, digital marketing may contribute as a key technique for the expansion and development of SMEs.

11.4 Digital Marketing Actions

A firm's business executed using digital technologies, and information technology may be termed as E-commerce, that resembles E-business and E-marketing. Digital marketing adopts technology, particularly as a rational extension of marketing practices for creating, communicating, delivering, and exchanging values to society. Under the right circumstances, digital marketing assists in the facilitation of a particular transaction mandate by business marketing activities.

In the same context, internet marketing and digital marketing are frequently cast in the same vein and considered to have the same meaning.[13–16] The scenario thus accompanied the view that the internet is the virtual space where e-commerce occurs, it shares the information and data from World Wide Web (WWW), e-mail helps in providing the 'actual moment' conversation, and empowers the exchange of information. In contrast, digital marketing has numerous dimensions to enable SMEs competency. It encompasses potential technology that empowers organisations' resource optimisation, customer relationship management, and supply chain management. In contrast to this study, the author contends that digital marketing encompasses the different dimensions known as email and the WWW to assist in accomplishing marketing goals in integration with supplementary marketing techniques. Digital marketing attempts to providing new opportunities to SMEs to explore the market that otherwise may not be accessible to them.[17]

11.5 Digital Marketing Activities and SMEs

The content of marketing has been improved substantially with the advent of modern technology. Digitization of marketing activities attempts to make marketing activities rich and optimized. Numerous studies have been executed on internet adoption that deliver a platform to understand big enterprises. In recent times, the technological model may be referred to understand the individual's acceptance level of computer usage on the grounds of apparent expediency and practise intent in relation to social

[13]Coupey, E. (2001). *Marketing and the Internet: Conceptual Foundations*. Prentice-Hall, Englewood Cliffs, NJ.

[14]Strauss, J. & Frost, R.D. (2005). *E-Marketing*. Prentice-Hall, London.

[15]Chaffey, D. (2003). *Internet Marketing — Strategy, Implementation and Practice*, 2nd ed. Prentice-Hall, Harlow.

[16]O'Connor, J., Galvin, E., & Evans, M. (2004). *Electronic Marketing: Theory and Practice for the 21st Century*. Financial Times Prentice-Hall, Harlow.

[17]Palmer, A. & McCole, P. (2000). "The Role of Electronic Commerce in Creating a Virtual Tourism Destination Marketing Organisation". *International Journal of Contemporary Hospitality Management*, 12(3), 198–204.

paradigms.[18,19] However, prior research interprets further aspects termed as ‘learning approach’ and ‘marketing approach’ as a potential reason for digital technology adoption by SMEs.[20] Furthermore, due insufficient prior research on SMEs and the internet, there is no comparative model while exploring SMEs.[21–23]

Carson *et al.*[24] delve into the difference in marketing practices in a larger organisation and small firm. It deduces smaller firms to be more spontaneous, competent, networking based, and executing underneath time, financial and human constraints but with the ability to serve a unique market and build a long-lasting relationship with customers — always considered to be a specific strength of SMEs. In recent times, this practice the internet has been able to positively impact enterprises of any scale. The SMEs dominated markets are having to confront threats from larger regional, national, and international firms due to lower transaction costs incurred to enter in the market conquered by SMEs. The scenario thus urges SMEs to understand all implications of digital marketing and create a rationale to adopt digital marketing. The scenario thus tends to analyze the importance of digital marketing to sketch a competitive surrounding for SMEs.[25]

Prior research delves into the fact that insertion of digital marketing into the marketing mix design may be beneficial to SMEs. For instance, one of the forms of digital marketing via an online quote could be incorporated to communicate product and services, justifying the time saving and print costs of the catalogues and other printing materials. Digital marketing helps SMEs to create their presence in the market by providing an efficient website, which develops an enhanced and professional image

---

[18]Venkatesh & Davis. op. cit.

[19]Davis, F.D. (1989). “Perceived Usefulness, Perceived Ease of Use, and User Acceptance of Information Technology”. *MIS Quarterly*, 13(3), 319–40.

[20]Nguyen & Barrat. op. cit.

[21]Ching & Ellis. op. cit.

[22]McCue. op. cit.

[23]Avlonitis & Karavani. op. cit.

[24]Carson, D., Cromie, S., McGowan, P., & Hill, J. (1995). *Marketing and Entrepreneurship in SMEs: An Innovative Approach.* Prentice-Hall, Harlow.

[25]Herbig & Hale. op. cit.

of SMEs. SMEs may indulge the online chat, replying about product and other offerings using different dialects and attempt market research at global level.[26,27] Despite the benefits, digital marketing offers and commercial potential forecasted through incorporating it, Gallagher and Gilmore[28] interpreted that SMEs were found to be reluctant to adapt to the changes in marketing design required by the internet, and not optimizing the potential for digitization in entrepreneurship.

Previous studies have shown that SMEs were reluctant to incorporate digital marketing within the whole organisation as they considered it a discrete unit. Despite the potential opportunities in digital marketing, it was not considered for futuristic long-term marketing design. Instead, it was employed in an extempore way. From a marketing communication perspective, SMEs could grab the direct operational benefits of digital marketing and make it a competitive advantage as well. This phenomenon urges many researchers to postulate digital marketing as potential futuristic replacement of traditional marketing practices and to become the sole tool for such enterprises.[29–31]

11.6 SMEs and Digital Marketing Adoption

Several factors emerged as proactive and reactive variables based on the literature reviewed, which make way for SMEs to adopt digital marketing activities. Proactive factors deal with the probability to eradicate the competitive disadvantage of SMEs in the market. It also benefits SMEs to lower operational and marketing costs. Proactive factors also provide an opportunity to build the brand and uplift the marketing communication design in meeting the modern scenario. Performing market research,

---

[26]Kula, V. & Tatoglu, E. (2003). "An Exploratory Study of Internet Adoption by SMEs in an Emerging Economy". *European Business Review*, 15(5), 324–333.

[27]McCue. op. cit.

[28]Gallagher & Gilmore. op. cit.

[29]Windrum, P. & de Barranger, P. (2003). "The Adoption of e-Business Technology by SMEs". in Jones, O. & Tilley, F. (Eds). *Competitive Advantage in SMEs*, Wiley, Cheltenham.

[30]Egan *et al.* op. cit.

[31]Gallagher & Gilmore. op. cit.

management involvement, and probability to increase revenue were other factors responsible for the adoption of digital marketing amongst SMEs.[32–35]

Increased competition from local vendors and large enterprises were found to be reactive factors, they enable SMEs to adopt digital marketing activities to confront the local as well as larger firms. The local market contraction was also a reactive factor which urges SMEs to incorporate digital marketing activities.

11.7 Obstacles for Digital Marketing Adoption by SMEs

11.7.1 *Generic Obstacles*

A theme constructed around much of the literature is that most SMEs adopt digital marketing activities due to the generic characteristics.[36] The authors propounded that human workforce issues refer to increased work activities in the organisation.[37] Consequently, work gets prioritized, and subsequently, other work activities are considered more important than digital marketing.[38]

Furthermore, finance is one of the generic constraints which restrict SMEs to adopt digital marketing, the reason being, before they consider incorporating it, they expect instant and actual tangible benefits against the traditional marketing design. Chapman *et al.*[39] contend that lack of technical skills and how to execute marketing activities on the Web compounded the obstacles confronting SMEs. It can be argued further that the

---

[32]Downie, G. (2002). "Internet Marketing and SMEs". *Management Services*, 14(7), 8–20.

[33]Dann, S. and Dann, S. (2001). *Strategic Internet Marketing*. Wiley, Sydney.

[34]Jeffcoate, J., Chappell, C., & Feindt, S. (2002). "Best Practice in SME Adoption of e-Commerce". *Benchmarking*, 9(2), 122–130.

[35]Poon, S. & Swatman, P.M.C. (1997). "Small Business Use of the Internet: Findings from Australian Case Studies". *International Marketing Review*, 14(5), 385–402.

[36]Windrum & Berranger. op. cit.

[37]Winkholfer, H. & Houghton, K. (2004). "A Typology of Websites: An Investigation of Exporting SMEs". *Proceedings of the 33rd EMAC Conference*, Murcia, Spain.

[38]ibid.

[39]Chapman, P., Szczygiel, M., & Thompson, D. (2000). "Building Internet Capabilities in SMEs". *Logistic Information Management*, 13(6), 35–60.

contribution of computer-based technologies in digital marketing strategy depends on the nature of the employees in the enterprise.[40]

Numerous daily operational activities related to the implementation and preservation of digital marketing and concerned technologies develop possible obstacles in front of SMEs that may result in unwilling consequences.[41] It is further argued that web design and its maintenance are high costs to SMEs.[42] Moreover, cost and challenges incurred in web design, termed as dimensions of the website, update frequency of the website, and decisions on developing the website on its own or should they outsource to a vendor. Subsequently, due to the high costs incurred in dependency on the external service provider, many SMEs fail to keep long term business term with their vendors. Along the same lines, issues such as widening of human resources and lack of technical skills, SMEs are unable to keep digital technologies updated. Downie[43] and Herbig & Hale[44] added that irregular updates and poor maintenance, poor customer support, insufficient awareness and lack of trained employees will earn little incentive in terms of repeat customer visits of which ultimately cause a financial consequence.

During technical execution of digital technology many issues are confronted such as information overload, unsuitable web design, deprived effectiveness, and unrelated links and advertising banners that could harm the brand image.[45]

When it comes to the adoption of digital technologies, SMEs may enjoy the benefits of the internet's low-cost communication to become an international enterprise at the nascent stage. However, if the enterprise is not fully prepared to adopt digital platforms, it may cause potentially harmful effects to SMEs if opened to the global market.[46] Hence the

[40]Jeffcoate *et al.* op. cit.

[41]Merrick, B. (2003). "Internet Marketing Done Right". *Credit Union Magazine*, 69(10), 12.

[42]Hormozi, A. & Harding, W. (1998). "Is the Internet Feasible for Small Businesses". *SAM Advanced Management Journal*, 63(3), 20–30.

[43]Downie. op. cit.

[44]Herbig & Hale. op. cit.

[45]Downie. op. cit.

[46]Burns, S. (2003). "How Companies Use the Internet". *Far Eastern Economic Review*, 30 November.

potential of digital marketing may be questioned by SMEs.[47] Chapman *et al.*[48] contended that due to the size of SMEs and the close proximity of employees, they fail to optimize the advantages of digital marketing compared to big enterprises that grab it due to their size.

11.7.2 *Organisational Obstacles*

Cost effectiveness appears a genuine issue when it comes to adopting digital marketing by SMEs. Ching and Ellis[49] discovered that SMEs confronted low conversion rates of online enquiries, i.e. very few of the enquiries were turned into complete orders. Furthermore, partners, suppliers, and customers' ability to access digital technologies are some of the factors which restrict SMEs from optimising the benefits of digital marketing.

11.8 Objectives of the Study

This study was carried out in the Jaipur region incorporating all the preceding issues for discussion. The purpose of the research demonstrated here is to examine the impact of digital marketing on SMEs commercial activities. The specific objectives of the study are detailed as follows:

1. Explore the specific factors and execution issues during the adoption of digital marketing by SMEs.
2. Identify the impact of implementing digital marketing on SMEs.
3. To enable SMEs to acquire worth understanding of digital marketing and thus draw optimised benefits from it.

11.9 Research Methodology

Considering the research objectives of this assignment, a qualitative research approach was deemed to be an appropriate technique to provide an in-depth understanding of SMEs' perceptions towards digital

[47]Downie. op. cit.

[48]Chapman *et al.* op. cit.

[49]Ching & Ellis. op. cit.

marketing. The rationale behind attempting the qualitative research approach was to "elucidate instead of forecast phenomenon"[50] and "to comprehend factors instead of measure them",[51] and is likely to be more appropriate in understanding SMEs' activities.[52]

Marketing professionals or IT professionals of 25 enterprises who were engaged in introducing and implementing digital marketing activities within their respective enterprises were approached to participate in the one-to-one structured interviews. In-depth interviews had been decided the optimal way to elicit detailed information from managers or IT professional related to their perception and involvement in digital marketing for commercial activities. This technique also enables the interviewer to customize content and sequence of the data according to the interviewee's convenience.[53] Furthermore, in-depth interviews enabled the process for thorough conversation and emphasis to derive the rationale of execution problems, and the benefits of using digital marketing. Each discussion with respondents took 25–40 mins at the respective enterprise location. Each interview was recorded and transcribed to facilitate depth analysis. Enterprises which were engaged in using digital marketing for at least five years were selected for the interview so that the enterprise could share relevant information regarding a wide variety of issues related to digital marketing.

11.10 Research Findings

The findings of this research are based on the key theme of this study and envisaged from the literature. SMEs encountered many problems as described in the literature specifically related to limited time, expertise, and resource constraints.[54] All enterprises had the following major

[50]Leavy, B. (1994). "The Craft of Case-based Qualitative Research". *Irish Business and Administrative Research*, 15, 105–18.

[51]Gordon, W. & Langmaid, R. (1988). *Qualitative Market Research: A Practitioner's and Buyer's Guide*. Gower, Aldershot.

[52]Gilmore, A., Carson, D., & Grant, K. (2001). "SME Marketing in Practice". *Marketing Intelligence & Planning*, 19(1), 6–11.

[53]Carson, D., Gilmore, A., Perry, C., & Gronhaug, K. (2001). *Qualitative Marketing Research*. Sage, London.

[54]Windrum & Berranger. op. cit.

stumbling blocks to digital marketing in common: time scarcity, skilled human resources, and finance.[55]

For instance, most respondents reported that "*As a SMEs, we have a scarcity of finance: consequently, we don't spend an exorbitant amount of money or time on digital marketing and web designing.*"

23 out of 25 enterprises cited that skilled human resources constraints had a direct impact on the engagement of digital marketing activities. Many of these enterprises were involved in hiring professionals to create, implement, and maintain websites. A frustrating situation developed among the enterprises regarding decentralization of digital activities. For example, they did not have a designated employee to whom they could assign digital activities and maintenance of websites. Furthermore, it was observed during the interviews that managers of the enterprises were distracted due to spontaneous or imperative business matters.

However, some of the firms overcame technological constraints by sharing skills and involvement. For instance, a few of the enterprises had technically skilled personnel to promote their web presence; some had employed regular IT system professionals to maintain the computer software packaging for the enterprise, and some of the enterprises employed specialised people to maintain their digital presence.

This study brought up a disparity against the literature that depicts the cost of maintaining a virtual presence creating a potential obstacle to digital marketing activities. In this study, SMEs specified that economic cost is not insurmountable. However, it was observed that SMEs openness to learn, empowered the SMEs to implement digitization, perform, and incorporate digital marketing activities at some stage. These research outcomes propose that SMEs should create a digital presence. Subsequently, generating a Web presence is an essential phenomenon for the present and future.

11.11 Practical Implementation and Maintenance Issues

Website design and maintenance of the enterprise was one of the important issues to discuss in this study. 18 out of 25 enterprises shared their experience about inappropriate web design at some point in the process of digital

[55]Winkholfer & Houghton. op. cit.

marketing implementation. Consequently, the majority of the enterprises felt that their websites had to be majorly revamped. Some of the enterprises experienced their websites to be stationary, not attractive, interactive, incommunicative, uninteresting, and added no complimentary value to the enterprise. Enterprises confronted obstacles in getting customers to register on the website portal so that they could access information through the website. Subsequently, it was observed as a problem for a few customers.

SMEs also lacked providing multilingual websites. Many of the enterprises were engaged in international trade, but only 18 out of the 25 enterprises offered their website in different languages. Among these enterprises, only eight out of 25 conveyed that they were using websites and domains in foreign languages to expand their business in another market. However, a few of the entrepreneurs reported the high cost of employing translators to translate the content of the website to be completely multilingual.

18 of the 25 entrepreneurs mentioned that employees were provided access to the internet; it was observed that some of the departments such as marketing, and sales were engaged in greater use compared to others. Online marketing was mainly used for approaching customers, vendors, and exchanging data among themselves, specifically through email. 18 entrepreneurs reported that each employee was well versed in accessing the internet and required applications at work. Subsequently, every entrepreneur provided relevant staff with basic training related to internet usage at work.

However, this study's emphasis on the practical implementation and maintenance issues, as discussed in the literature review are related to SMEs in the present scenario. Consequently, the majority of the entrepreneurs are now involved in identifying the issues related to the websites and other forms of digital marketing and discovering solutions to resolve implementation and maintenance issues through better digital marketing education and staff training.

11.12 Organisational Obstacle

This study is centred around the practical implementation and maintenance issues however SMEs reported many other issues which were responsible for frustration and creating trouble for daily digital marketing activities. The most encountered issue was the gradual shift in spam emails. Entrepreneurs found it frustrating and annoying to see their inboxes filled with spam. They felt that email is having a negative effect on personalising customer relations by reducing people's talk-time either face-to-face or on the phone. These issues have a resemblance to those discussed in the literature.[56]

It is evident from discussions with the entrepreneurs that digital marketing is not being optimised to its potential benefits due to its implementation and maintenance issues. Ten of the entrepreneurs reported that digital marketing activities had been stalled due to the reluctant attitude or lack of knowledge of customers, supplier, or partners to deal with digital technologies. This finding resembles Dann and Dann's[57] research findings. It would put entrepreneurs in the fast lane of their customers, partners, and suppliers to conduct business using electronic methods.

Of all the entrepreneurs included in this study, none of them reported that they incorporated any system to measure the cost effectiveness of using digital marketing. Since having a website, most of the entrepreneurs experienced several enquiries and interest in their work, but none of them recognized any immediate transaction as a result of using digital marketing. With the current dearth of evidence and accurate measurement of digital marketing activities, it is difficult to indicate how it can be optimized in the future.

11.13 Implication and Conclusion

The outcomes of this assignment envisaged digital marketing operating in the nascent phase as far as SMEs in a regional economy are concerned and this highlights a significant potential use in future perspectives. Although the SMEs have been using digital marketing since 2000, its impact seems very low. SMEs considered digital marketing as a valuable tool to enhance enterprise reach, adopting communication strategies in various marketplaces at lesser cost via email usage, and lowering the cost of printing paper catalogues and brochures.

---

[56]Downie. op. cit.

[57]Dann & Dann. op. cit.

It seems that these entrepreneurs are not drawing the optimum benefits from digital marketing to build a brand image. The scenario thus compounds the ability to rationalise and interpret the impact of digital marketing on SMEs as forecasted earlier, as it has not happened due to the obstacles and execution issues initially discussed in the review of literature.[58,59] Notwithstanding, the dearth of financial resources, expertise, and time, quite often it appeared as SMEs having inappropriate websites which may not be interactive to their technophobic customers. The scenario thus indicates that entrepreneurs in this study had not drawn all the benefits from digital marketing in terms of information sharing, attaining new markets, developing competitive advantage, building corporate image, boosting trade, maintaining CRM, and lifting SMEs' performance, which are all potential opportunities of digital marketing.

The adoption of digital technologies by SMEs may result in offering benefits such as effective brand building and healthy customer relationships. Furthermore, a mechanism to measure generating revenue still remains to be seen. Some of the entrepreneurs felt that digital technologies and digital marketing would never surpass traditional marketing techniques. However, entrepreneurs have a strong belief that digital marketing is very much required in the present scenario and will be a competitive advantage in the future.

The implication of the findings of this study are that the full potential of digital marketing is not visible in SMEs in the peripheral region. The findings of this study brought up a few issues and solutions for SMEs operating in the peripheral area. These SMEs must recognise the importance of digital methods to generate returns on investment and gear up sales through digital marketing instead of merely providing a website and digital promotion of the SMEs to compete in vibrant markets. SMEs have to employ adequate time and specific resources for this to happen and to surpass the general phenomenon that is implied by the current scenario. Appropriate time management and other required resources will bring professionalism, proper design, and interactive websites which are required to be competitive.

---

[58] Winkholfer & Houghton. op. cit.

[59] Windrum & Berranger. op. cit.

Further, this can be accomplished by maintaining control on websites and appointing skilled personnel to look after their digital marketing activities. This may be further updated by supplementing staff with a training and development programme, and awareness dossiers regarding digital marketing and IT enabled technologies. The government must give greater attention to these areas and this must be reflected in local government policies and regulations. The government also has a responsibility to look after the requirements of internet related skills development platforms for regional SMEs in order to make the economy competitive in the developing digital commercial world.

11.14 Research Limitations and Further Research

The sample was one of the main limitations of this study because the sample size was small and selected from the peripheral location. However, the small number of SMEs enabled comprehensive, in-depth interviews to be conducted with all the entrepreneurs that may not have been possible had a larger sample been selected. This study explored the impact of the adoption of digital marketing activities and implementation issues and significance for SMEs in a peripheral location.

Future research may investigate a similar sample in another location and explore how their implementation and maintenance issue of the use of digital marketing has been rationalised. This scenario thus empowers social scientists to investigate how a number of case studies have developed and what other implications that are likely to occur.

https://doi.org/10.1142/9789811212741_0012

Chapter 12

Effective Corporate Social Responsibility in Small and Medium Enterprises

Gaurav Dawar, Seema Singh, Mihir Joshi and Prashant Kumar

12.1 Introduction

In the early 2000s there was extended discussion and writing about Corporate Social Responsibility (CSR) that became increasingly prominent within large companies and government.[1] Since then CSR has come a long way, with community involvement and sustainability becoming standard practice for most well-known corporate leaders. Large companies like Tata and Wipro have been praised for their contribution to society. But, giving something back ought not to be the responsibility of huge corporates, small and medium enterprises are equally responsible towards society. CSR is an important activity for SMEs and most of them are likely to remain informal and intuitive due to limited resources.[2] To value the significance of CSR to SMEs, first an investigation into the conflicting view of CSR and why

[1]Bryane, M. (2003). "Corporate Social Responsibility in International Development: An Overview and Critique". *Corporate Social Responsibility and Environmental Management*. 10(3): 115–128.

[2]Russo, A. & Tencati, A. (2009). "Formal vs. Informal CSR Strategies: Evidence from Italian Micro, Small, Medium-sized, and Large Firms". *Journal of Business Ethics*, 85(2):339–53.

organisations have regard for it was undertaken and then to what CSR means to SMEs given their qualities and how they vary from huge corporations.[3]

12.2 Conflicting Perspectives on CSR

The issue of social obligation brings out differing and frequently passionate reactions from both scholars and businesspeople. Within the discussion about CSR, on the basis of the development of the concept of CSR thoughts and practices, can be categorised (see Chart 1) as Classical (until 1970), Philanthropic (1971–1990) and Strategic or Inclusive (1990 onwards).

12.2.1 *Classical Thoughts*

The earlier thoughts on the practices of CSR before 1975 are considered as 'Classical' theory and the major contributors to this theory were Adam Smith and Milton Friedman.[4] The views of authors largely referred to the economic perspective of CSR as they argued for the direct form of capitalism and were against economic freedom. The economic model of CSR

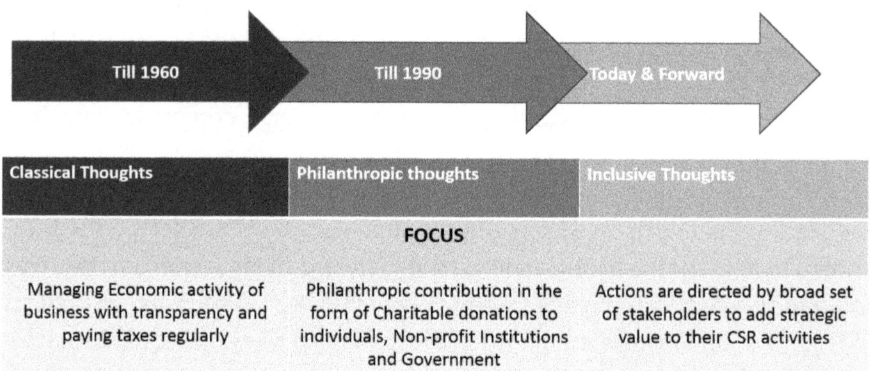

Chart 1: Development of CSR thoughts & practices

Source: Author's own representation.

---

[3]Howells, C. (2013). "When It Comes to CSR, Size Matters". *Forbes Magazine*. https://www.forbes.com/sites/insead/2013/08/14/when-it-comes-to-csr-size-matters/#49b4953a52a2 [Accessed 20 July 2019].

[4]The taxonomy adopted from Brummer (1991) (see Brummer, J.J. (1991). *Corporate Responsibility and Legitimacy: An Interdisciplinary Analysis*. Praeger) and contributors to classical theory, as discussed by Fernando, A.C. (2011). *Corporate Governance: Principles, Policies and Practices*, 2nd edition. Pearson Education India.

holds that organisations' sole responsibility is to fulfil the economic function of business and managers are responsible for profit generation and maximization; and organisations often ignore the activities that do not generate revenues like running charitable society. The development of society is largely a concern of Government and social institutions (NGOs) created by society.[5] The classical thoughts were criticised for being highly materialistic and promoting welfare of the masses as the sole responsibility of Government. Milton Friedman overlooked the aspect of change that businesses may go through at an explosive rate in future.[6]

12.2.2 *Philanthropic Thoughts*

In the 1970s, authors were revolutionising the meaning of CSR for business and society. Harold Jonson[7] in his book "*Business in contemporary society: Framework and Issues*", published in 1971, presented various models of CSR, critiqued and further analysed. Jonson presented an outline of socio-cultural system of conducting affairs of business.[8] The same year a landmark contribution to the concept of CSR was given by the Committee of Economic Development (CED) through their publication "*Social Responsibilities of Business*". CED highlighted that business has a broader responsibility towards society and have to contribute towards a better quality of life.[9] Though their thoughts have made businesses more introspective, what they are really seeking and inspired to do is contribute towards the community's social well-being instead of their own narcissistic existence. But the most influential thoughts on philanthropic CSR were given by Archie B. Carroll in 1979 in his publication "*A Three-Dimensional Conceptual Model of Corporate Performance*".[10] Carroll (1979)

---

[5]García-de-Madariaga, J. & Rodríguez-de-Rivera-Cremades, F. (2010). "Corporate Social Responsibility and the Classical Theory of the Firm: Are Both Theories Irreconcilable?" *Innovar*, 20(37):5–19.

[6]According to T.F. Bradshaw, past president of Atlantic Richfield Company cited by Fernando. op. cit.

[7]Jonson, H.L. (1971). *Business in Contemporary Society: Framework and Issues.* Wadsworth Publishing Company, University of Michigan.

[8]Adapted from the discussion of Carroll, A.B. (1999). "Corporate Social Responsibility: Evolution of a Definitional Construct". *Business & Society*, 38(3):268–295.

[9]ibid.

[10]Carroll, A.B. (1979). "A Three-Dimensional Conceptual Model of Corporate Performance". *Academic Management Review*, 4(4): 497–505.

highlighted the different dimensions of social responsibility i.e. ethical and discretionary or philanthropic along with economic responsibility.

Carroll's framework popularly known as the Pyramid of CSR was amended in 1991 to add the legal dimension. As indicated by this pyramidal system, a firm ought to grow its profit, comply with the law, be moral, and be a decent corporate citizen. The thoughts on the practice of CSR based on philanthropy recognised the importance of social responsibility beyond profit maximisation but were criticised as they failed to address the conflicting obligations and cultural manifestations.[11] The organisations used CSR discourse to hide the most vicious corporate activities and further use it as an argument to get the regulator not to impose stringent laws.

12.2.3 *Inclusive CSR*

In the decade post 2000, the relation between business and society has undergone a profound transformation as leaders from corporates, civic bodies and Government have made organisations look beyond economic value and make more meaningful social impact. The economic crisis in 2000s has drastically revolutionised CSR and has ushered organisations into a new era of responsibility applicable to global stakeholders. Organisations operating in volatile, uncertain, complex and ambiguous (VUCA) world focus on both local and global CSR, due to the absence of consensus definition, in order to achieve benefits. Thus, stakeholders are empowered by the current business environment that is collectively driven by globalisation, sustainability, affluence and communication; adding strategic value to CSR.[12] Effective inclusivity of CSR can reduce the risk,[13] add organisational capability[14] and focuses

[11] Crane, A. & Matten, D. (2004). *Business Ethics: A European Perspective: Managing Corporate Citizenship and Sustainability in the Age of Globalization.* Oxford: Oxford University Press.

[12] Chandler, D. (2016). *Strategic Corporate Social Responsibility: Sustainable Value Creation.* Sage Publications.

[13] Husted, B.W. (2005). "Risk Management, Real Options, Corporate Social Responsibility". *Journal of Business Ethics*, 60(2): 175–183.

[14] Sharma, S. & Vredenberg, H. (1998). "Proactive Corporate Environmental Strategy and the Development of Competitively Valuable Capabilities". *Strategic Management Journal*, 19(8): 729–753.

on gaining potential competitive advantages[15,16] while failure to do so may lead to serious economic consequences.[17] Thus, an inclusive framework is version two of CSR that targets CSR implementation as per stakeholder expectation[18] to make social impact more meaningful as the whole system is contributing rather than single-issue activities and programs.

12.3 Definition of CSR by Various Authors and Institutions

The literature in the field of social responsibility by a large number of scholars has attempted to define whether an organisation should pursue a dual objective of economic and social development.[19,20] Currently, corporates are facing the notion of behaving responsibly on a wide range of issues.[21] In both corporate and academic work there is no certainty regarding the definition of CSR as there is an abundance of literature.[22] The most influential in academic literature is Carroll's[23] after the first one given by Bowen[24] in

---

[15]Kanter, R.M. (1999). "From Spare Change to Real Change: The Social Sector as Beta Site for Business Innovation". *Harvard Business Review*. May–June 1999 Issue.

[16]Porter, M.E. & Kramer, M.R. (2006). "The Link Between Competitive Advantage and Corporate Social Responsibility". *Harvard Business Review*, 84(12):78–92.

[17]Barlett, C.A. & Ghoshal, S. (2002). *Managing Across Borders: The Transnational Solution*. Harvard Business Press.

[18]Visser, W. (2010). *The Age of Responsibility: CSR 2.0 and the New DNA of Business*. John Wiley & Sons.

[19]Friedman, M. (1970). "The Social Responsibility of Business to Increase its Profits". *The New York Times Magazine,* 13 September.

[20]Galbreath, J. (2010). "How Does Corporate Social Responsibility Benefit Firms? Evidence from Australia". *European Business Review*, 22(4): 411–413.

[21]Welford, R. & Frost, S. (2006). "Corporate Social Responsibility in Asian Supply Chains". *Corporate Social Responsibility and Environmental Management*, 13(3): 166–176

[22]van Marrewijk, M. (2003). "Concepts and Definitions of CSR and Corporate Sustainability: Between Agency & Communion". *Journal of Business Ethics*, 44(2–3): 95–105.

[23]Carroll (1999). op. cit.

[24]Bowen, H.R. (1953). *Social Responsibilities of the Businessman*. Harper, New York.

Dahlsrud.[25] Among, others Drucker[26] highlighted the idea of seeking public opinion in the organisational decision making process regardless of size or industry; Davis[27] highlighted the concept of "*Corporate Constitutionalism*" that organisations should look after the interests of the agents who are affected by their actions in order to gain their support; Walton[28] and Wallich *et al.*[29] highlighted that the essential quality of social responsibility is the degree of voluntariness, as these actions are not mandatory, but the decision to do it involves cost and risk that can affect the success or failure of a business, hence businesses must maintain balance between the economic and social interests of stakeholders.

The most referenced definition of CSR was given by Holme & Watts[30] through their paper "Corporate Social Responsibility: Making Good Business Sense" for the World Business Council for Sustainable Development (WBCSD). They defined CSR as "*…a continued commitment by business to behave ethically and contribute to economic development while improving the quality of life of the workforce and their families as well as local community and society at large*". The European Commission[31] defined a common CSR framework for entrepreneurs and managers in Europe as "*A concept whereby companies integrate social and environmental concerns in their business operations and in their interaction with their stakeholders on a voluntary basis*". These thoughts promote progressive concern by institutions to develop responsible

---

[25]Dahlsrud, A. (2006). "How Corporate Social Responsibility is Defined: An Analysis of 37 Definitions". *Corporate Social Responsibility and Environmental Management*, 15(1): 1–13.

[26]Drucker, P.F. (1954). *The Practice of Management.* New York: Harper & Row.

[27]Davis, K. (1960). "Can Business Afford to Ignore Social Responsibilities?" *California Management Review*, 2(3): 70–76.

[28]Walton, C.C. (1967). *Corporate Social Responsibilities*. Belmont, CA: Wadsworth Publishing Company.

[29]Wallich, H.C., McGowan, J.J., Likert, R., & Baumol, W.J. (1970). "A New Rationale for Corporate Social Policy". *Committee for Economic Development.* 1 December.

[30]Holme, R. & Watts, P. (2000). "Corporate Social Responsibility: Making Good Business Sense". *World Business Council for Sustainable Development*, Conches-Geneva, Switzerland.

[31]Commission of the European Communities (2001). "GREEN PAPER: Promoting a European Framework for Corporate Social Responsibility". *Brussels*, 18 July.

behaviour and include social responsibility as a part of organisational goals. In the last decade, organisations that were able to demonstrate their contribution towards the global sphere of operations were trusted more by their stakeholders.

12.3.1 *Indian Thoughts on CSR*

The conceptual perspectives of CSR though developed by Western thinkers also has a strong linkage with Indian history and its culture. Sharma and Talwar[32] and Muniapan and Das[33] have linked the evolution of CSR with Ancient Indian *Vedic-Literature* that is 5,000 years old. This way of thinking was not only suggested by religious philosophies but also by the leaders of pre- and post-independent India. One of the most popular Indian models of CSR is the "Ethical Model" also known as the "Theory of Trusteeship" as proposed by Mohandas Karamchand Gandhi. The trusteeship theory adopts realistic and descriptive perspectives in governing. It considers organisation as social institutions with a corporate personality that work to maximise stakeholder value. The philosophy of Trusteeship as defined by Mahatma Gandhi:

> *"Supposing I have come by a fair amount of wealth — either by way of legacy, or by means of trade and industry — I must know that all that wealth does not belong to me; what belongs to me is the right to an honourable livelihood, no better than that enjoyed by millions of others. The rest of my wealth belongs to the community and must be used for the welfare of the community."*

Gandhi advocated the application of trusteeship at multiple levels to attain equality in society. The theory emphasises the intelligent use of wealth, and believes in the strength of considering others equally and motivates people to respect everyone's rights, with a prioritisation of

---

[32] Sharma, A.K. & Talwar, B. (2005). "Corporate Social Responsibility vis-à-vis Vedic Approach". *Measuring Business Excellence*, 9(1):35–45.

[33] Muniapan, B. & Dass, M. (2009). "An Indian Leadership Perspective from Literature Works of Poet Kannadasan". *International Journal of Indian Culture and Business Management*, 2(4): 326–340.

commitment to principles of social reformation rather than policies, and that affluent people should distribute their wealth towards local schemes and plans. This theory is a feasible solution to the social issues prevalent at the beginning of the previous century and predictable future.[34]

Nehru in 1946 propounded the "Statist Model" that focuses on state ownership and legal requirements of CSR.[35] The model developed post-independence when the nation adopted a mixed economy framework with large public sector and state-owned enterprises. The responsibilities of state enterprises were clearly defined for society and elements related to community and workers' relationships were enshrined in labour laws and management practices.[36]

12.4 CSR Practices in SMEs

The large corporations in India are mostly engaged in Corporate Social Responsibility (CSR) so as to enhance their reputation with key stakeholders and are better resourced at it. However, for Small and Medium Enterprises (SMEs), engagement in CSR is based on reasons, expected benefits and the ways of practicing CSR.[37] The adoption of CSR activities for SMEs are exposed to barriers such as limited resources and the capabilities they possess.

SMEs are an important backbone of a healthy economy in India because they account for 60 percent of total manufacturing employment, 40 percent of National Income[38] and are closely linked to local community in developing countries. Yet they have received relatively little attention in

---

[34]Prasad, R.N. (2016). *Trusteeship, Corporate Social Responsibility and Peace*. LAP LAMBERT Academic Publishing.

[35]Shivastava, H. & Ventateswaran, S. (2001). *The Business of Social Responsibility — The Why, Where and How of Social Responsibility of India*, Bangalore: Books for Change.

[36]Kanji, R. & Agrawal, R. (2016). "Models of Corporate Social Responsibility: Comparison, Evolution and Convergence". *IIM Kozhikode Society & Management Review*, 5(2): 141–155.

[37]Smith N.C. (2013)."When It Comes to CSR, Size Matters". *Forbes.* https://www.forbes.com/sites/insead/2013/08/14/when-it-comes-to-csr-size-matters/2013 [Accessed 1 July].

[38]Beck T., Demirguc-Kunt, A., & Martinez Peria, M.S. (2008). "Bank Financing for SMEs Around the World: Drivers, Obstacles, Business Models, and Lending Practices". *The World Bank*, 4 December.

the broad research agenda pertaining to the role of SMEs in CSR in emerging nations.[39,40] SMEs follow an informal approach to CSR[41,42] due to high constraints of resources and capabilities. Though the relationship between financial performance and CSR[43] has been explored in developing nations, the area demands substantial attention. Hence, moving ahead with company level analysis, it is also important to affirm a grounded understanding of how CSR practices can be made effective considering institutional and contextual factors along with the pressure of global sustainability.

12.5 Examples of CSR Practices of SMEs

1. **Sports Goods Foundation of India (SGFI)** organises tuition centres for downtrodden children, campaigns for abolishing child labour in the sports goods industry and medical check-up campaigns for poor children.
2. **Agribusiness Corporation** based out of Hyderabad has established a CSR foundation **Green Universe Environmental Services Society (GUESS)** that endorses green initiatives and sustainable development in a rural context.
3. **Shashwat Foundation of Shashwat Systems** promotes Women's Wellbeing and Women's Enterprises in Ahemadabad and adjoint areas. It also helps in developing aspiring women entrepreneurs by guiding and teaching them.

[39] Harris, J.D., Sapienza, H.J., & Bowie, N.E. (2009). "Ethics and Entrepreneurship". *Journal of Business Venturing*, 24(5):407–418.

[40] Karam, C.M. & Jamali, D. (2017). "A Cross-Cultural and Feminist Perspective on CSR in Developing Countries: Uncovering Latent Power Dynamics". *Journal of Business Ethics*. 142(3):461–477.

[41] Jenkins, H. (2004). "A Critique of Conventional CSR Theory: An SME Perspective". *Journal of General Management*, 29(4):37–57.

[42] Baumann-Pauly, D., Wickert, C., Spence, L.J., & Scherer, A.G. (2013). "Organizing Corporate Social Responsibility in Small and Large Firms: Size Matters". *Journal of Business eEthics,* 115(4):693–705.

[43] Jain, P., Vyas, V., & Chalasani, D.P. (2016). "Corporate Social Responsibility and Financial Performance in SMEs: A Structural Equation Modelling Approach". *Global Business Review*, 17(3):630–53.

4. **HARF,** a charitable trust run by **Sohrab Enterprises** in Ludhiana, Punjab operates a widow stipend program, Orphan Girl Marriage Assistance and a primary healthcare centre. It is motivated towards maintaining communal harmony and service to mankind.
5. **MOTIF** is an organisation that provides a platform to new NGOs by providing financial assistance and also to encourage other NGOs by promoting the important work of existing NGOs.

12.6 Effective CSR Dimensions

This section explains the dimensions of effective and uniquely Indian CSR through Trusteeship theory. The Trusteeship theory proposed by Mahatma Gandhi defined the social responsibility of industries and focused on growth with equity to achieve an inclusive society. These views highlight the importance of shared values between firm and society, and also recognize that the CSR procedure may stay informal for most SMEs. The CSR outlook in India is unique because of a 'family-centred' style of management, and most of the firms are controlled by family groups.[44] The selections of social responsibility activities are influenced by cultural and social preferences of the family.[45]

Thus, India in the 21st century requires a holistic approach to CSR for SMEs that can bridge the gap between the different socio-economic sections of society, not always requiring State action, to achieve a sustainable future, thus the Trusteeship based framework is suitable for value creation. Gandhi believed that Trusteeship theory would lead to sustainable economic development,[46] because it blends technology, environment, people, economics and culture. The approach may also enhance the role of

[44] Sundar, P. (2000). *Beyond Business: From Merchant Charity to Corporate Citizenship.* Tata McGraw Hill.

[45] Kansal, M., Joshi, M., & Batra, G.S. (2014). "Determinants of Corporate Social Responsibility Disclosures: Evidence from India". *Advances in Accounting,* 30(1):217–229.

[46] Balakrishnan, J., Malhotra, A., & Falkenberg, L. (2017). "Multi-level Corporate Responsibility: A Comparison of Gandhi's Trusteeship with Stakeholder and Stewardship Frameworks". *Journal of Business Ethics*, 141(1):133–150.

affluent entrepreneurs in nation building.[47] The concepts of Trusteeship have been incorporated in CSR legislation building. The firms that come under the new act should form a CSR committee from existing board members, devise CSR policy, implement and monitor CSR activities. The CSR models derived from Trusteeship theory involve practicing social responsibility alone or in partnership with other organisations or in association with the community or a combination of all, but the essence of CSR can be maintained from the vision of the board, performance of responsible leaders, following environmental regulations, and creating social and economic value through every aspect of business.[48] The scenario at present is that in order to make CSR effective, it is required to be innovative concerning processes and new management thinking.

To meet the expectations and generate social value of CSR for stakeholders, the activities are categorised into internal CSR and external CSR. Internal CSR refers to care, help and support for primary stakeholders i.e. employees and suppliers, and External CSR is related to protection of the environment and the firm's engagement in the society.[49]

Internal CSR includes:

12.6.1 *Integration of CSR into Corporate Responsibility*

Integration of CSR into Corporate policy is related to developing a corporate code of conduct on ethics and incorporating the ethical codes into mission, vision, strategic issues and practices to develop the competitive advantage for the organisation. The Indian social responsibility theory of Trusteeship proposed by Mahatma Gandhi explains that managers in the businesses are responsible for the creation of a prosperous society.[50] The underlying idea is to prepare managers as public trustees, and to maintain balance between corporate resources and support of good causes. It can be

---

[47]Rolnick, P.J. (1962). "Charity, Trusteeship, and Social Change in India: A Study of a Political Ideology". *World Politics*, 14(3):439–460.

[48]Bajaj, R. (2016). "From Trusteeship Model to the New Vehicles of CSR". In *The Privilege of Responsibility: Perspectives from Corporate India.* CII.

[49]Murillo, D. & Lozano, J.M. (2006). "SMEs and CSR: An Approach to CSR in Their Own Words". *Journal of Business Ethics*, 67(3):227–240.

[50]Balakrishnan *et al.* op. cit.

achieved by integrating CSR into every activity of the business and making it a part of a policy at the business-level. SMEs can implement the critical tasks by increasing transparency through policy sharing with stakeholders (e.g. employees, suppliers etc.), developing organisational ethical principles, incorporating them in policies and conducting affairs responsibly to create sustainable value. The incorporation of a CSR approach in every aspect of the business may enable the organisation to gain competitive advantage but leaders of these companies are often the obstacle to gain notoriety for the enterprises.

12.6.2 *Priority of Board*

Priority of Board towards CSR is related to keeping track of wide-ranging social, environmental and ethical issues to ensure the right CSR priorities for the organisation. There are various reasons for heightened Board of Directors' attention towards CSR, i.e. moral obligations, sustainability, license to operate and reputation, and careful building on it leads to competitive advantage for the organisation.[51] As a result, the Boards of Directors and CEOs are devoting greater attention towards CSR and taking it up as a formal structure in the organisation.[52] Over the years CSR has gained a strategic advantage in the eyes of Boards, and it has resulted in the widespread engagement of corporations in various CSR activities including environmental friendly practices, supporting social causes, financing employees' education and encouragement of ethical training programs.[53] It can also be observed through the frequency of revision of CSR policy to cater to societal requirements, arranging social training programs for employees and encouraging a participative culture throughout the organisation in CSR activities. Overall, Trusteeship theory has revolutionary

[51]Porter & Kramer. op. cit.

[52]Crespin, R. (2012). "Where CSR Fits on the Board's Agenda". *Forbes*. https://www.forbes.com/sites/csr/2012/02/10/where-csr-fits-on-the-boards-agenda/#3a46fb4879c8, 10 February. [Accessed 18 July 2018].

[53]Maignan, I. & Ferrell, O.C. (2000). "Measuring Corporate Citizenship in Two Countries: The Case of the United States and France". *Journal of Business Ethics*, 23(3):283–97.

implications as it aims at developing a participative culture and promotes egalitarian values throughout the organisation.[54]

12.6.3 *Primary Stakeholder Involvement*

Primary Stakeholder involvement explains the perception of the organisation towards involving stakeholders in CSR practices to make them effective. It also elaborates on engaging different stakeholders (employees, suppliers, customers) in responsible practices that are mutually rewarded. The survival of the organisation is unfeasible without their support and hence, social responsibility activities should be customised to their involvement.[55] The Gandhian Trusteeship theory and stakeholder theory share synergies as both lay emphasis on working towards the community. Balakrishnan *et al.*[56] have highlighted that the Gandhian Trusteeship model integrates the role and responsibilities of various stakeholders towards economic value creation and building a prosperous society. His thoughts on an equitable system to manage societal resources have been endorsed by government committees.[57] The notion is all concerned stakeholders and actors must give serious thought to manage the societal and natural resources on trusteeship lines. SMEs can attempt to engage stakeholders by undertaking a customer education program, communicating with employees about organisations' CSR policies and developing criteria for supplier selection by environmental assessment. Higher primary stakeholder engagement in SMEs can create more work and complicate their exiting process, which manufacturing companies of small and medium scale businesses may not be able to support out of their existing capital. Thus, from a stakeholder perspective, business is about adding value to all stakeholders and creating good for everyone.[58]

---

[54]Ghosh, S. (1989). "Trusteeship in Industry: Gandhiji's Dream and Contemporary Reality". *Indian Journal of Industrial Relations*, 25(1):35–44.

[55]Freeman, R.E. & Velamuri, S.R. (2006). "A New Approach to CSR: Company Stakeholder Responsibility". In *Corporate Social Responsibility* (pp. 9–23). Palgrave Macmillan, London.

[56]Balakrishnan *et al.* op. cit.

[57]Joseph, T. & Joseph, S.K. (eds.). (2018). "Deliberative Democracy: Understanding the Indian Experience". *Routledge*; 29 March.

[58]Freeman & Velamuri. op. cit.

12.6.4 *Responsible Leadership*

Responsible leadership is related to the role and responsibilities of business leaders that centres attention on responsibility, accountability and moral decision making for those who are affected and have stakes in the business. Effective leadership has a key role in the integration of sustainability practices in the operations of the organisation as they are responsible for making meaningful transformations that can lead to the creation of socially responsible organisations.[59] Responsible leadership is a multilevel solution to emerging ethical, social and environmental challenges.[60] The Gandhian Trusteeship theory is closely linked to responsible leadership as it focuses on the moral and socially sustaining responsibility of trustees or leaders towards different stakeholders for economic and social issues. Thus, governance and leadership style are essential for the organisation to discharge their social responsibility effectively as they involve, recognise and motivate the employees in firms. SMEs engaged in manufacturing are implementing the agenda of responsible leadership through top management, considering stakeholders claims and involving them in decision making, achieving consensus among them and broadly working towards social participation. SMEs today are paying close attention to ethically oriented investors, and sustainability-focused think-tanks to maximise their value to the community.

External CSR includes:

12.6.5 *Environmental Regulations*

Environmental Regulations elaborates on concerns for environmental sustainability as a driver for effective CSR. Environmental protection and conservation are the important aspects of CSR policies of corporations. Gandhi had a deep sense of concern for the natural environment that accompanies industrialisation and modernity to maintain ecological

[59]Székely, F. & Knirsch, M. (2005). "Responsible Leadership and Corporate Social Responsibility: Metrics for Sustainable Performance". *European Management Journal*, 23(6):628–647.

[60]Pless, N.M. (2007). "Understanding Responsible Leadership: Role Identity and Motivational Drivers". *Journal of Business Ethics*, 74(4):437–456.

balance.[61] His thoughts and views are not intended towards a formal sustainable environmental structure but interlinking his ideas that can lead to a sustainable development model as he expected society and owners to be steward of natural environment.[62] The first significant relationship of supporting environmental regulations and effective CSR confirms the organisations' decision, influenced by free market value, to undertake related environmental practices. It indicates implementation of environmentally friendly practices within the organisation, consuming resources responsibly, and deliberate continuous and conscious evaluation of the environment. It also provides a suitable yardstick, important to measure if companies' pursuing environmental activities are a part of compliance or something beyond it.

12.6.6 *Partnering for CSR*

Partnering for CSR describes alliances organisation are building to address the societal problem through non-profit partnerships. Gordic Bader, President of Scott Bader Company in England, has defined Trusteeship theory as "*Fraternal partnership between all the factors of production, with the aim of achieving larger social benefit rather than working towards a narrow economic objective such as profit*". The Scott Bader Company established in the early 20th century, implemented the Trusteeship principles in 1951 and has become one of the successful examples of the theory in action.[63] But considering the concerns of contemporary economies today the Trusteeship institution can be practically implemented through partnership.[64] The model of an alliance between

---

[61] Kolge N. & Sreekumar, N. (2011). *Gandhi's Criticism of Industrialization and Modernity; An Environmental Perspective. Gandhi, Environment and Sustainable Future.* Wardha: Institute of Gandhian Studies.

[62] Daptardar, V. (2012). "Gandhian Relevance to Environmental Sustainability". In *Gandhi in the New Millennium — Issues and Challenges.* Khandwala Publishing House.

[63] Bader, G. (1995). "Ghandhi on Trusteeship: A Transforming Ethic". *World Business Academy Perspectives*, 9(4), 41–50.

[64] Kapoor, A. (2005). "Gandhi' Trusteeship". In Sankhdher, M. M. & Kaur, G. (2005). *Politics in India: Ancient India, Politics of Change, Modern India* (pp. 252–268). Delhi: Deep & Deep Publications.

business organisations with non-profit organisations (NPOs) was intended for the creation of knowledge and development of a voluntary code of conduct for contributions to sustainable development.[65] Large and medium organisations over the years have accepted the relevance of non-profit partnerships, and it has become a key driver for NPOs in fulfilling their overall mission.[66] Non-profit partnerships with peers are an established strategy followed by the significant number of business organisations as a part of their broader CSR Program.[67] It is one of the key factors for SMEs in discharging their responsibility effectively as it can help them in tackling social challenges through the expertise of public, private and non-profit partners. Finding a right partner is critical for the success of organisations' CSR strategies as it is expected to create value for both the organisation and society. SMEs are implementing social responsibility partnerships by encouraging employees to take-up voluntary activities, giving donations to NGOs and creating associations with the non-profit partner for societal activities.

12.7 Conclusion

CSR has become a byword for the socially conscious corporate world. Only microenterprises remain untouched by the ever-increasing importance of CSR. The corporations that were earlier driven by profit have now realised the importance of being responsible by giving back to society in order to justify their existence and future growth. This appreciation has also prompted many of them to integrate their CSR activities into business practices. Thus, CSR is no longer philanthropy but rather a part of business strategy.

---

[65]Arya, B. & Salk, J.E. (2006). "Cross-Sector Alliance Learning and Effectiveness of Voluntary Codes of Corporate Social Responsibility". *Business Ethics Quarterly*, 16(2):211–234.

[66]Álvarez-González, L.I., García-Rodríguez, N., Rey-García, M., & Sanzo-Perez, M.J. (2017). "Business-non-profit Partnerships as a Driver of Internal Marketing in Non-profit Organizations. Consequences for Non-profit Performance and Moderators". *BRQ Business Research Quarterly*, 20(2):112–123.

[67]Mutch, N. & Aitken, R. (2009). "Being Fair and Being Seen to Be Fair: Corporate Reputation and CSR Partnerships". *Australasian Marketing Journal*, 17(2):92–98.

https://doi.org/10.1142/9789811212741_0013

Chapter 13

Performance Improvement Using Value Stream Mapping and Simulation — A Case Study

Jagdeep Singh, Léo-Paul Dana, Harwinder Singh and Jagmeet Singh

13.1 Introduction

Lean manufacturing (LM) is a well-recognised approach to improve the competitiveness of the manufacturing system by eliminating waste and non-value adding activities. Waste can be in the form of over production, defects, excess inventory, inadequate processing, excessive transportation, waiting and unnecessary motion.[1] The paradigm is shifting around the manufacturing world and lean manufacturing is used as an approach all across industries to improve overall performance of the manufacturing. LM is identified as a key to survive and maintain continuous growth for the organisations in India.[2] Manufacturing operations are continually striving to increase productivity and output of their operations. Their goal is to satisfy the customer with the exact product, quality, quantity, and

[1]Womack, J.P., Jones, D.T., & Roos, D. (1990). *The Machine that Changed the World.* Harper Perennial, New York.

[2]Sharma, V., Dixit, A.R., Qadri, M.A., & Kumar, S. (2015). "An Interpretive Hierarchical Model for Lean Implementation in Machine Tool Sector". *International Journal of Productivity and Quality Management*, 15(3), 381–406.

price in the shortest amount of time. LM is more than a cost reduction program or a problem-solving approach. The main idea is that an efficient production can be achieved by a comprehensive approach to minimise waste. This means eliminating excess production and inventory, redundant movement of material, waiting and delays, over processing, excess worker motion, and the need for rework and corrections.[3]

Value Stream Mapping (VSM) allows firms to visualise their waste that help them propose enhancements in process flows. In accordance with Rother and Shook,[4] organisations must think about the flow, instead of implementing prudent manufacturing systems or isolated improvement processes. The VSM methodology has proved itself efficient by focusing its attention flow. VSM is a set of methods to visually display the flow of materials and information through the manufacturing process. VSM is the most recognised tool of LM implementation. This can be described as a structured process of visually displaying the flow of information and materials through the manufacturing process. The objective of VSM is to identify value-added activities and non-value-added activities. VSM demonstrates each element of the manufacturing process so that opportunities for improvement can be identified.[5] In this study, VSM has been developed for an auto parts manufacturing company of India. Creating VSM allows the company to document current production lead time, inventory levels, and cycle times in order to determine the ratio of value-added to total lead time of the product family being analysed, creating a vision of an ideal value flow. Then, the future state map is presented and suggestions to reduce the cycle time, change over time, and non-value-added activities, as well as, improving the communication of the information flow issues have been presented. The data collection before and after

---

[3]Singh, J., Singh, H., & Gandhi, S.K. (2019). "Assessing Lean Thinking Using Value Stream Mapping in a Manufacturing Unit — A Case Study", *International Journal of Business Excellence*, 17(3), 306–335.

[4]Rother, M. & Shook, J. (2003). *Learning to See — Mapping the Value Stream in Order to Earn Value and Eliminate the Waste.* Lean Institute Brazil.

[5]Silva, S.K.P.N. (2012). "Applicability of Value Stream Mapping (Value Stream Mapping) in the Apparel Industry in Sri Lanka". *International Journal of Lean Thinking*, 3(1), 36–41.

preparing the future state map and simulation have been analysed and results are presented.

13.2 Literature Review

This section includes a detailed description of the concept of VSM and case studies performed by different researchers in this field.

13.2.1 *Literature Related to Concept of VSM*

A value stream is a collection of all actions (value-added as well as non-value-added) that are required to bring a product (or a group of products that use the same resources) through the main flows, starting with raw materials and ending with the customer. These actions consider the flow of both information and materials within the overall supply chain. The ultimate goal of VSM is to identify all types of waste in the value stream and to take steps to try and eliminate these.[6]

Originally developed by Toyota, VSM has been widely used by many types of manufacturing companies, both large and small firms, as the preferred way to support and implement the lean approach.[7] For instance, Grewal[8] describes the implementation of VSM in a small manufacturing firm as a LM improvement initiative; this initiative involved mapping the activities of the firm, identifying opportunities for improvement, and then undertaking a quality improvement programme with the firm and achieving, in that specific case, a reduction in lead time, cycle time, and inventory levels. Figure 1 shows the process of information flow in VSM.

VSM is explained as a process of displaying the flow of information and material on a map in the form of current state with present status of

---

[6]Rother, M. & Shook, J. (1999). *Learning to See: Value Stream Mapping to Add Value and Eliminate Muda*. The Lean Enterprise Institute, Inc., Brookline, MA.

[7]Bevilacqua, M., Ciarapica, F.E., & Paciarotti, C. (2012). "Supply Chain Integration in an Italian Automotive Company: The Case of a Kitting System Implementation". *International Journal of Productivity and Quality Management*, 10(4), 428–446.

[8]Grewal, C. (2008). "An Initiative to Implement Lean Manufacturing Using Value Stream Mapping in a Small Company". *International Journal of Manufacturing Technology and Management*, 15(3–4), 404–417.

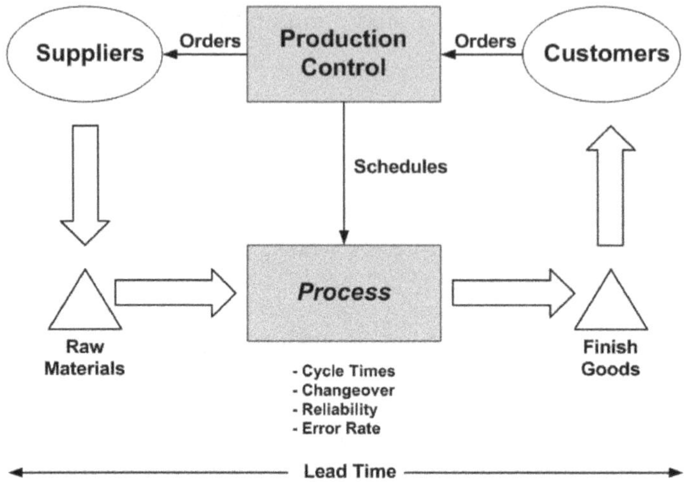

Figure 1: Information flow in value stream mapping

Source: Martins, G. H. & Cleto, M.G. (2013). "Value Stream Mapping and Earned Value Analysis: A Case Study in the Paper Packaging Industry in Brazil". *22nd International Conference on Production Research, Brazil*, pp. 1–9 (2013).

work in process (WIP) inventory, process cycle times, deployment of manpower and flow of information through the manufacturing process. Form and source of inbuilt process waste is identified with the help of drawing a current value stream map.[9] VSM is simply transferring information about the value stream to a 'map' which represents either current or future state of the manufacturing system. As the term implies, a current state map shows how materials and information flow through processes in the current production system. The value stream consists of all the materials and information required in the manufacturing of a particular product and how they flow through the manufacturing system.[10]

---

[9]Tortorella, G.L., Fogliatto, F.S., Anzanello, M., Marodin, G.A, Garci, M., & Esteves, R. (2016). "Making the Value Flow: Application of Value Stream Mapping in a Brazilian Public Healthcare Organisation". *Total Quality Management & Business Excellence*, 28(13–14), 1–15.

[10]Chen, J.C., Li, Y., & Shady, B.D. (2010). "From Value Stream Mapping Toward a Lean/Sigma Continuous Improvement Process: An Industrial Case Study". *International Journal of Production Research*, 48(4), 1069–1086.

13.2.2 *Literature Related to Case Studies*

Serrano *et al.*[11] utilised multiple case study methodologies in six industrial companies which display the results of a project whose main purpose was to evaluate the real applicability of VSM to redesign disconnected flow lines based on manufacturing environments with a diversity of logistical problems. Vinodh *et al.*[12] applied VSM for enabling LM implementation in an Indian camshaft manufacturing industry to reduce the lead time and total cycle time and to improve the delivery time. The application of VSM with 5S, stage inspection, automatic storage and retrieval system and IT enabled logistics system has provided sufficient reduction of idle time, cycle time and defects. Cookson *et al.*[13] have reported a case study on applying VSM for improving the quality of emergency care in a hospital, where they have eliminated the waiting time of patients to get the service of staff members and the waiting time of staff members for getting the results from testing centres. Goriwondo *et al.*[14] used a VSM tool to reduce waste in bread production. The results showed how the VSM tool helped to identify and reduce defects by 20 percent, unnecessary inventory by 18 percent and motion by 37 percent. Esfandyari *et al.*[15] investigated improvement of the production lead time using VSM as a technique in a Malaysian supplier, with a job shop production system. The main contribution of this research was reducing

---

[11] Serrano, I., Ochoa, C., & Castro, R.D. (2008). "Evaluation of Value Stream Mapping in Manufacturing System Redesign". *International Journal of Production Research*, 46(16), 4409–4430.

[12] Vinodh, S., Arvind, K.R., & Somanaathan, M. (2010). "Application of Value Stream Mapping in an Indian Camshaft Manufacturing Organisation". *Journal of Manufacturing Technology Management*, 21(7), 888–900.

[13] Cookson, D., Read, C., Mukherjee, P., & Cooke, M. (2011). "Improving the Quality of Emergency Department Care by Removing Waste Using Lean Value Stream Mapping". *The International Journal of Clinical Leadership*, 17(1), 25–30.

[14] Goriwondo, W.M. (2011). "Use of the Value Stream Mapping tool for Waste Reduction in Manufacturing. Case Study for Bread Manufacturing in Zimbabwe". *Conference Paper: International Conference on Industrial Engineering and Operations Management.* Kuala Lumpur, Malaysia.

[15] Esfandyari, A., Osman, M.R., Ismail, N., & Tahriri, F. (2011). "Application of Value Stream Mapping Using Simulation to Decrease Production Lead Time: A Malaysian Manufacturing Case". *International Journal of Industrial and Systems Engineering*, 8(2), 230–250.

production lead time when the TAKT Time is much higher than the highest station's cycle time and reducing unplanned released orders. The study evaluates the present routing events using current state map and the future state is created answering the eight standard questions. Then, a detailed simulation model was developed to verify the result from future state map and answering the questions that are unable to be addressed by VSM. Parihar *et al.*[16] developed a VSM for the assembly process of tractor parts with the goal of identifying and eliminating waste, which is any activity that does not add value to the final product in the assembly process. Bhamu *et al.*[17] demonstrated the effect of VSM implementation on the cost of poor quality, in–process rejections, percentage value addition, lead time, work-in-process inventory, the distance travelled by components, and the percentage of scrap through a case study of VSM implementation in the Indian automotive industry. Singh and Sharma[18] explained how VSM is useful to lean implementation, to develop the roadmap for minimising the lead time, WIP inventory and reduction in manpower in a crank shaft gear manufacturing unit.

13.3 Research Methodology and Objectives

In this study, mapping method using VSM is presented. The current state map has been prepared through directly observing the shop floor and analysing the collected data. Departments including research and development (R&D), production, purchasing and store departments were investigated to get detailed information of the current state and preparing a desired future state map. The following methodology has been adopted for this case study:

1. selection of critical product family
2. preparation of current state map
    a. documentation of customer information

[16]Parihar, S., Jain, S., & Bajpai, L. (2012). "Value Stream Mapping: A Case Study of Assembly Process". *International Journal of Engineering Research & Technology*, 1(8), 1–7.
[17]Bhamu, J. Kumar, J.V.S., & Sangwan, K.S. (2012). "Productivity and Quality Improvement Through Value Stream Mapping: A Case Study of Indian Automotive Industry". *International Journal of Productivity and Quality Management*, 10(3), 288–306.
[18]Singh, B. & Sharma, S. (2009). "Value Stream Mapping as a Versatile Tool for Lean Implementation: An Indian Case Study of a Manufacturing Firm". *Measuring Business Excellence*, 13(3), 58–68.

   b. establish process flow
   c. data collection (production lead time, non-value-added activities etc.)
   d. establish information flow
   e. quantify production lead time and processing time
3. analysis of current state map
4. incorporating changes in the current state map
5. preparation of future state map and simulation
   a. implementation of few new processes
   b. calculate TAKT Time
6. comparison of current state and future state map and simulation run of operations
7. assessing the potential benefits obtained after proposed change
8. results and conclusions

The objectives of the study are as follows:

- To reduce the cycle time and TAKT Time.
- To reduce production lead time and value-added activities.
- To reduce work in process and changeover time.

13.4 Case Study Setting and Discussion of Findings

13.4.1 *Current State VSM of Spring Pin Section*

Spring pins are used in the automotive suspension system for the mounting of a leaf spring and axle in vehicles. There area huge variety of spring pin manufacturers. Spring pins are available in different sizes including different lengths and diameters. Length and shape of spring pins are adapted as per customer drawings and requirements. All manufacturing processes available are involved in the manufacturing of spring pins, and for this case study the SPDT 283 code spring pin supplied to TATA motors has been selected. Customer demand for these three codes are 28,000 per month. The cycle time (C/T), WIP, changeover (C/O) and number of operators were observed to be recorded manually. The recorded data of C/T and C/O time is in the form of average time and the remaining information necessary for the current state map has been collected from the section in charge, foreman and operator.

The spring pin manufacturing section remains at work for 25 days in a month and there are two shifts of 11 hours each. The total available time for production is eight hours and four hours overtime. There is a 30-minute lunch break and three tea breaks of 15 minutes each. The breakdown is as follows:

- Total available time for work per shift of spring pin manufacturing = time per shift – total time of tea breaks and lunch.
- Total available time for work per shift of spring pin manufacturing = (12 hours × 60-minutes × 60 seconds) – ((30 + 15 + 15 + 15) minutes × 60 second).
- Total available time for work per shift of spring pin manufacturing = 39,600 seconds.
- For the spring pin manufacturing section, available time for production is 39,600 seconds per shift.
- TAKT time is 864 seconds. TAKT time is 79.5 seconds.
- TAKT time = Available time for work/Customer demand.
- Available time for work per shift = 39,600 seconds per day.
- Daily customer requirement = 28,000/25 = 1,120.

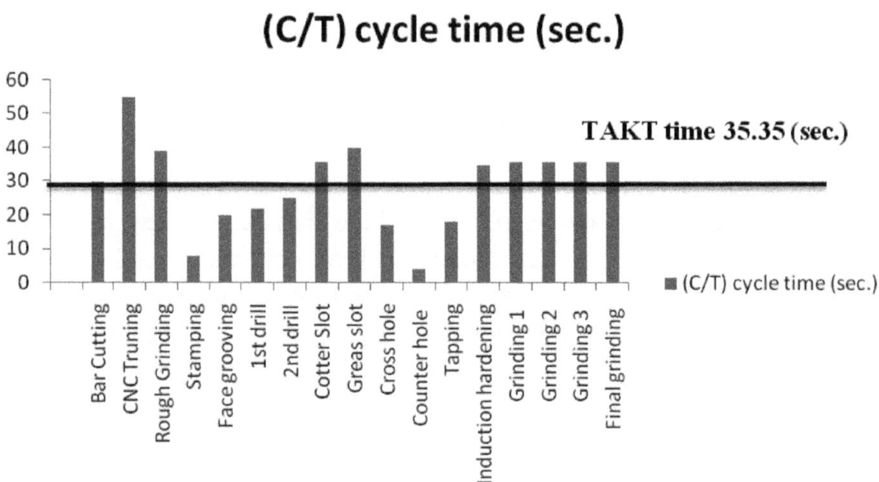

Figure 2: Comparison C/T and TAKT time

Source: Collected by Authors.

- TAKT time = Available time for work/Customer demand = 39,600/1,120 = 35.35 seconds. Figure 2 shows the comparison C/T and TAKT time.

Demand comes at the end of the month through suppliers to the marketing department, then they release the order to the production unit email the purchasing department and production planning and control (PPC) department. The purchase department releases orders for raw materials then at the same time the PPC department generates their daily planning sheet. As per their planning sheet they generate a batch card for raw materials. Then raw materials move from the raw materials yard to the bandsaw cutting operation. From the bandsaw cutting operation, they move toward other operations like turning, grinding, drilling, and milling etc. The monthly requirment of spring pins for TATA motors is 28,000 for a particular code that is SPDT 283, which is the same category that is run on this manufacturing section. From that data, the C/T is 493 seconds. Figure 3 shows the current state VSM of the critical product.

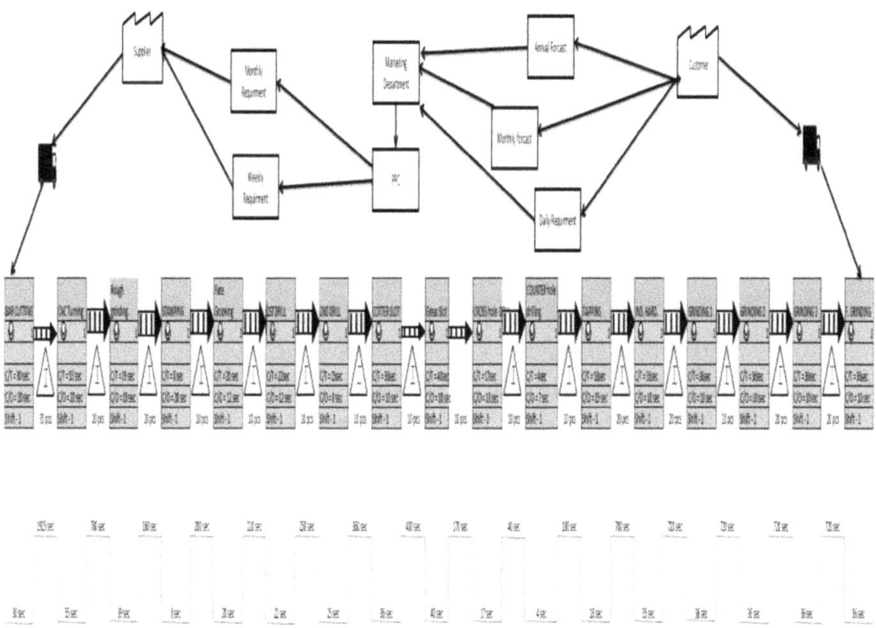

Figure 3: Current state of VSM of spring pin section

Source: Collected by Authors.

The maximum in process inventory is on CNC turning at 20 pieces while inventory in line is 260 pieces. Lead time of the product is 8,450 seconds. The whole product range is supplied to original equipment manufacturers (OEMs) as they directly assemble spring pins in their vehicles. The quality requirements of the product are very high and that is the main reason for high in-process inventory as well as high C/T.

13.5 Analysis of Current State of VSM of Spring Pin Section

From the current state of the VSM of the spring pin manufacturing section, the detailed analysis of process steps and sources required in manufacturing of spring pins has been done. This also helps to establish bottlenecks in the operation and their root causes. VSM provides a current scenario of the manufacturing process which helps to find out the gaps for improvement. It shows how things would work when some changes are adopted in the manufacturing process and with that a future state VSM of the spring pin manufacturing process can be prepared. In the current state VSM there are many gaps identified, which further helps as a roadmap for improvements.

The following gaps were observed from the current state VSM of the spring pin manufacturing process:

- Variation in C/T of manufacturing operations is high; that causes high WIP inventory from one stage to another of the manufacturing operation. C/T on a CNC turning machine is 55 seconds (high) due to a different set-up for each piece in terms of rough grinding operations and final grinding operations when compared to each other.
- WIP inventory inbetween different manufacturing processes is also very high. Table 1 shows the WIP inventory for each stage of operations.
- C/O time is high on different machines. At some stages of operations, C/O is very high on rough grinding operations and final grinding operations. There is a need to control the different parameters for grinding of different diameters. Also, there is a need for dressing on grinding wheels after 100 repetitions and this takes more time, which is also a main reason for WIP inventory.

Table 1: Summary of all attributes of current state of VSM of spring pin in each process stage

Operations	(C/T) Cycle Time (sec.)	(C/O) Change Over Time (sec.)	Value-added (sec.)	Non-value Added (sec.)	Available Time (sec.)	Uptime (%)	No. of Operators	(WIP) In Process Inventory
Bar cutting	30	1200	30	0	36900	96.75	1	35
CNC turning	55	1200	55	1925	36900	96.75	1	20
Rough grinding	39	1500	39	780	36900	95.93	1	20
Stamping	8	1200	8	160	36900	96.75	1	10
Face grooving	20	720	20	200	36900	98.05	1	15
1st drill	22	600	22	220	36900	98.37	1	10
2nd drill	25	480	25	250	36900	98.70	1	6
Cotter slot	36	600	36	360	36900	98.37	1	10
Grease slot	40	600	40	400	36900	98.37	1	10
Cross hole	17	780	17	170	36900	97.89	1	10
Counter hole	4	420	4	40	36900	98.86	1	10
Tapping	18	420	18	180	36900	98.86	1	10
Induction hardening	35	900	35	700	36900	97.56	1	10
Grinding 1	36	1500	36	720	36900	95.93	1	20
Grinding 2	36	1500	36	720	36900	95.93	1	20
Grinding 3	36	1500	36	720	36900	95.93	1	20
Final grinding	36	1500	36	720	36900	95.93	1	20

Source: Collected by Authors.

- Low uptime at rough grinding operation and final grinding passes, because of high C/O time.
- Production lead time is high — Production lead time is also high at 8,750 seconds.
- The difference between value added (VA) and non-value added (NVA) activities — there are some NVA activities which the product does not require but the process requires. Due to this, NVA activities are 16 times that of VA activities — there is potential to reduce these NVA activities.

- Low VA activities ration — in the current state map VA activities ratio is very low. The processing time of the spring pin manufacturing section is 493 seconds so the VA activities ratio for the spring pin manufacturing process is 5.9 percent.
- Rework is very high — there is rework required at the grinding machine stage which is very high so time there is more than one plunge cut on a grinding machine, causing the high C/T at the grinding machine stage. Refer Figure 4 for more details.

Refer to Table 2, Figures 5 and 6 to get more details.

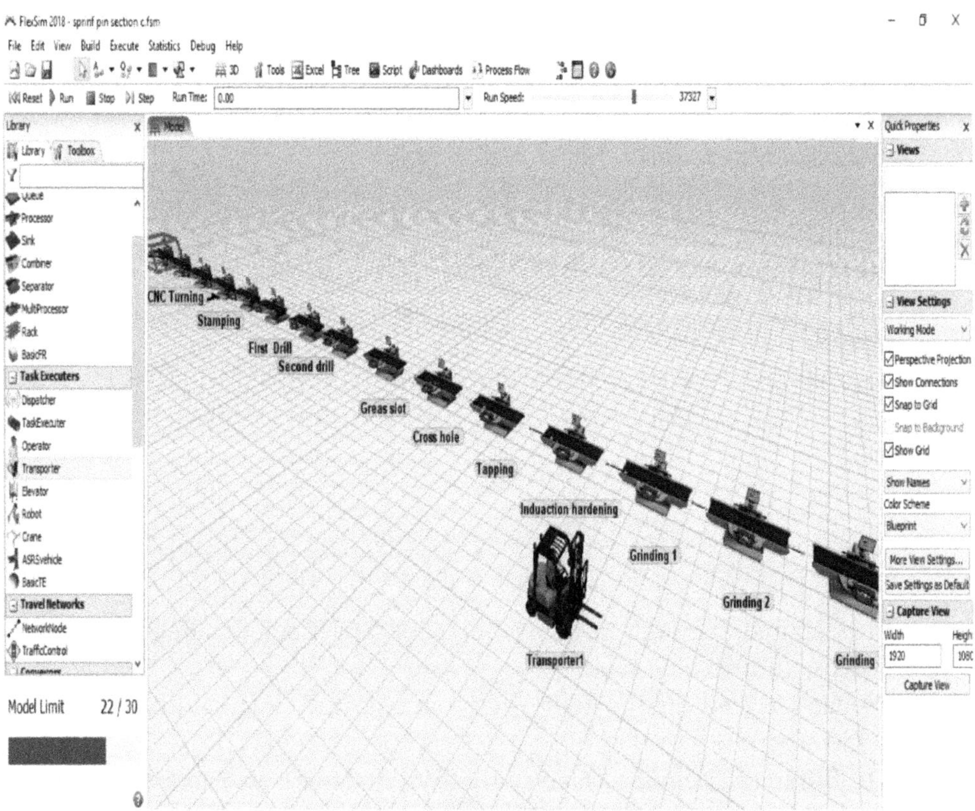

Figure 4: Simulation model of running current state VSM model of spring pin section

Source: Collected by Authors.

Table 2: Comparison of all attributes and manually noted with flexsim simulation software of spring pins section

	Cycle Time (in Seconds)		In Process Inventory (Numbers)		Change Over Time (C/O) (in Seconds)		Non-value Added (in Seconds)		Production Lead Time (in Seconds)		Uptime (in %)	
Processes	**Manually**	**Analysis**	**Manually**	**Analysis**	**Manually**	**Analysis**	**Manually**	**Analysis**	**Manually**	**Analysis**	**Manually**	**Analysis**
Bar cutting	35	36.6	65	67.9	1200	1193	0	0	35	36.6	96.75	96.9
CNC turning	35	36.6	55	57.2	1200	1193	1925	1922.5	1960	1959.1	96.75	96.9
Rough grinding	39	39.5	45	49	1500	1480	780	777	819	816.5	95.93	96.2
Stamping	8	7.5	10	11	1200	1107	160	154.3	168	161.8	96.75	97
Face grooving	20	19	22	23.5	720	664	200	212.3	220	231.3	98.05	98.3
1St drill	22	20.5	25	27	600	594	220	218.9	242	239.4	98.37	98.5
2Nd drill	25	26.3	30	31.2	480	478	250	245.6	275	271.9	98.70	98.8
Cotter slot	36	35.6	42	43.6	600	594	360	369	396	404.6	98.37	98.5
Grease slot	40	39.9	47	47.5	600	594	400	396	440	435.9	98.37	98.5
Cross hole	17	18.9	20	22.3	780	776	170	165.8	187	184.7	97.89	98.1
Counter hole	4	5	5	5	420	412	40	34.3	44	39.3	98.86	99
Tapping	18	19.6	20	22	420	412	180	178.6	198	198.2	98.86	99
Induction hardening	35	34.2	42	43.4	900	881	700	689.4	735	723.6	97.56	97.8
Grinding 1	36	35.8	45	46	1500	1465	720	716.5	756	752.3	95.93	96.3
Grinding 2	36	35.8	45	46	1500	1465	720	716.5	756	752.3	95.93	96.3
Grinding 3	36	35.8	45	46	1500	1465	720	716.5	756	752.3	95.93	96.3
Final grinding	36	35.8	45	46	1500	1465	720	716.5	756	752.3	95.93	96.3

Source: Collected by Authors.

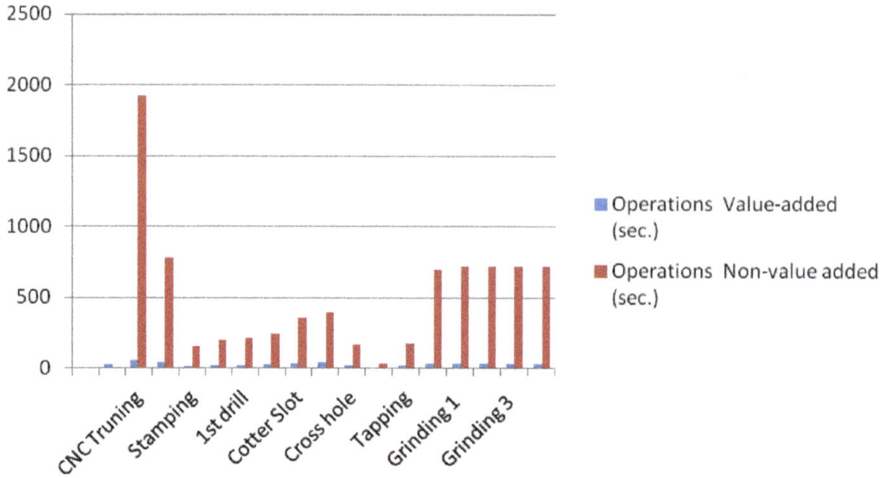

Figure 5: Comparison of VA and NVA time of spring pin section

Source: Collected by Authors.

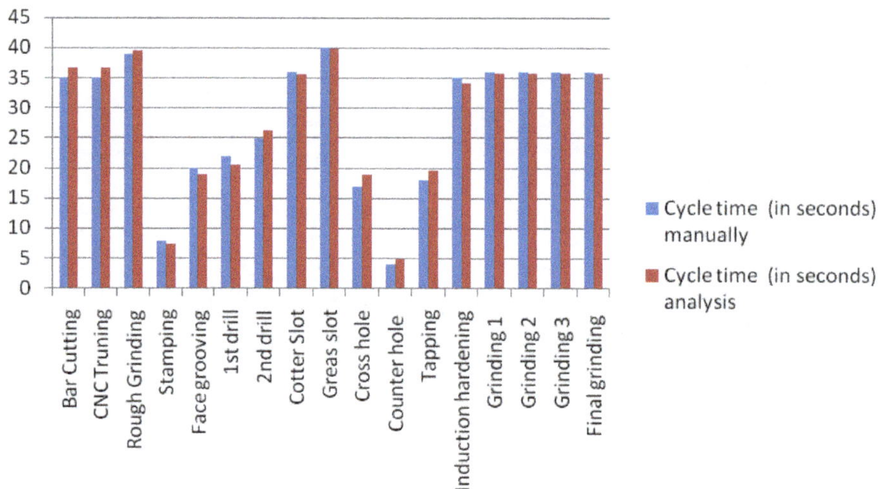

Figure 6: Comparison of all simulated and manually noted C/T of current state map of spring pin

Source: Collected by Authors.

13.6 Improvements and Suggestions for Spring Pin Section

From the current state VSM, it has been found that there is high WIP inventory and NVA processes are also there leading towards low VA ratio. From the VSM, bottleneck areas are easily identified and their root causes. Brainstorming helps to identify improvement areas and helps preparing the future state map. Table 3 shows the problems in the existing operations, suggested improvements and benefits.

Table 3: Improvement strategy to reduce waste of spring pin section

Operations	Problem Identification	Suggested Improvements	Recommendation/ Savings
Bar cutting	• WIP inventory is high • Change over time was high • Due to continuous running, need to change blade of saw so uptime was low	• Need to design simple structure for facing • With this C/T is low and uptime is high • Need to merge cutting operation on CNC turning machine	• Change over time is reduced • Manpower is saved • Operation cost is also reduced
CNC turning	• C/O time is very high • Taper is also not controlled on this setup	• For circularity control need to increase number of cuts which is also the cause of high C/T • Bar puller required so no line mark inbetween piece also work piece is cuton same setup	• Bar cutting operation is eliminated • No line mark in centre of workpiece
Rough grinding	• C/O time is very high • C/T is very high • Setting time very high	• Need to simplify this operation • If we use bar turning setup on CNC turning this operation is easily eliminated	• Decrease in rework • Decrease in WIP

(Continued)

Table 3: (*Continued*)

Operations	Problem Identification	Suggested Improvements	Recommendation/ Savings
Stamping	• Need to simplify this operation • Need to automate this operation	• Automation of this operation saves as manpower is eliminated from this operation	• Manpower is saved • Decrease in WIP
Face grooving	• Need an extra machine for this operation • Skilled workers are required	• Easily merge this operation with horizontal drilling machine which is used for 1st drill operation without increase in C/T	• Decrease in rework • Operation cost is eliminated
First drill	• C/T is high • Setting time on horizontal drilling machine is high	• Standard fixture saves setting time • Continuous flow of material is needed in this operation	• Decrease in operation cost • Decrease in change over time
Second drill	• C/T is high • Setting time is very high	• Face grooving operation is merged on this operation • Standard fixture saves setting time	• Decrease in operation cost • Decrease in change over time
Cotter slot	• Loading/unloading of work pieces takes more time • Shortage of trolleys	• Design of proper fixture setup reduces change over time • Trained worker increases uptime of process	• Reduction in change over time • Decreases in WIP inventory
Grease slot	• Material handling was not done properly • Variation is operated parameter in this setup	• Need to simplify material movement • Need standardisation in insert changing process	• Uptime increases on this operation • Change over time decreases
Cross hole	• VA ratio is lower than any other process • Variation in parameter is there	• Proper jig is required • Simple material handling should be there	• Increase in value added ratio • Decreases in delay • Decrease in cycle time

Table 3: (*Continued*)

Operations	Problem Identification	Suggested Improvements	Recommendation/ Savings
Counter hole	• C/O time is high • Loading/unloading of work piece take more time	• Standardisation of work required • Need to merge with cross hole operation	• Reduction in operational cost • Manpower eliminated from this operation
Tapping	• Shortage of trolleys for material movement • High waiting time	• Simple jig fixtures save changeover time of operation • Quality inspection is required on this operation	• Increase in uptime on this operation • Increase in value added ratio
Induction hardening	• Need skilled worker on this operation • Transportation form this operation to next consumes a lot of time	• Need to simplify this operation • Ejector attachment reduces loading/ unloading time	• Decrease in WIP • Operation parameters are controlled • Decrease in rejection rates
Grinding 1	• Operation cost is very high • Rework is high	• Need to simplify this operation • Using bar turning setup on CNC turning will easily eliminate this operation	• Decrease in rework • Decrease in WIP • Manpower eliminated from this operation
Grinding 2	• Operation cost is very high • Rework is high • Required helper for loading and unloading of material	• Need to simplify this operation • If we use bar turning, setup on CNC turning this operation can be easily eliminated	• Decrease in rework • Manpower eliminated from this operation
Grinding 3	• Operation cost is very high • Need for redressing grinding wheels after 150 pieces to achieve desired results so VA ration is low	• If we use bar turning setup on CNC turning than this operation is easily eliminated • Standardisation of operation saved turning machine this process is easily eliminated	• Reduction in operational cost • Decrease in rework • Manpower eliminated from this operation

(*Continued*)

Table 3: (*Continued*)

Operations	Problem Identification	Suggested Improvements	Recommendation/ Savings
Final grinding	• Operation cost is very high • Required helper for loading and unloading of material • Need to redress grinding wheels after 150 pieces to achieve desire results	• Need to simplify this operation • Standardisation of operations saved turning machine — this process is easily eliminated	• Decrease in rework • Decrease in WIP • Manpower eliminated from this operation

13.7 Future State VSM of Spring Pin Section

The current state map of the spring pin section is used as guideline for the future state map and helps identify problems. From the current state map of the spring pin section it is clear that there is high level of WIP inventory, lead time, change over time (C/T) and rejection rates.

Table 4 shows the future state VSM's C/T and TAKT time of the spring pin manufacturing operation. There are some operations that need to be eliminated or merged with other operations like bar cutting, face grooving and counter hole drilling operation. C/T of the CNC turning operation has been reduced by proposed changes but still it is higher than TAKT time. Also, C/T of operations like cotter slot, grease slot has been reduced in the future state VSM.

In this future state map, C/T is reduced at CNC turning operation and NVA processes like bar cutting, face grooving are also eliminated. For, counter drilling and grinding operations taper and desired surface roughness can be achieved (Ra) at CNC turning with a single cut, resulting in WIP inventory and lead time being reduced. Other aspects of the future state map can be seen in Figures 7–8 and include:

- Parting operation is combined with turning operation on the CNC turning machine.

Table 4: Summary of all simulated attributes of future state VSM in each process stage of spring pin section

Operations	(C/T) Cycle Time (sec.)	(C/O) Change Over Time (sec.)	Value-added (sec.)	Non-value Added (sec.)	Available Time (sec.)	UP Time (%)	No. of Operators	(WIP) Work in Process Inventory
Bar cutting	0	0	0	0	0	0	0	0
CNC turning	39.9	1512	35	0	36900	95.8	1	0
Rough grinding	0	0	0	0	0	0	0	0
Stamping	7	573	7	80	36900	98	1	11.3
Face grooving	0	0	0	0	0	0	0	0
1st drill	21.2	579.3	21.2	220	36900	97.9	1	36
2nd drill	22.6	474	22.6	250	36900	98.3	1	48
Cotter slot	21.2	474	21.2	132	36900	98.4	1	47.46
Grease slot	22.36	474	22.36	250	36900	98.3	1	53.61
Cross hole	16.4	442	16.4	170	36900	98.5	1	53.61
Counter hole	0	0	0	0	0	0	0	0
Tapping	17.3	442	17.3	180	36900	98.5	1	36.9
Induction hardening	33.6	579.3	33.6	350	36900	97.9	1	39.55
Grinding 1	0	0	0	0	0	0	0	0
Grinding 2	0	0	0	0	0	0	0	0
Grinding 3	35	579.3	35	360	36900	98	1	32
Final grinding	35	579.3	35	360	36900	97.9	1	32

Source: Collected by Authors.

- Bar cutting operation is eliminated and a bar is mounted on the CNC turning operation.
- There is no line mark in the centre of the piece, so no rough grinding operation is required.
- Rough grinding operation is now eliminated, and desired Ra is achieved on the CNC turning machine.
- Face grooving operation is merged with first drilling operation on horizontal drilling machine.

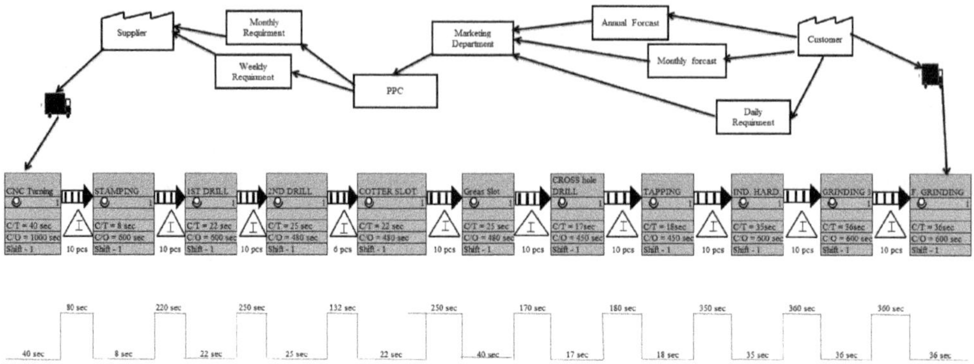

Figure 7: Future state VSM of spring pin section

Source: Collected by Authors.

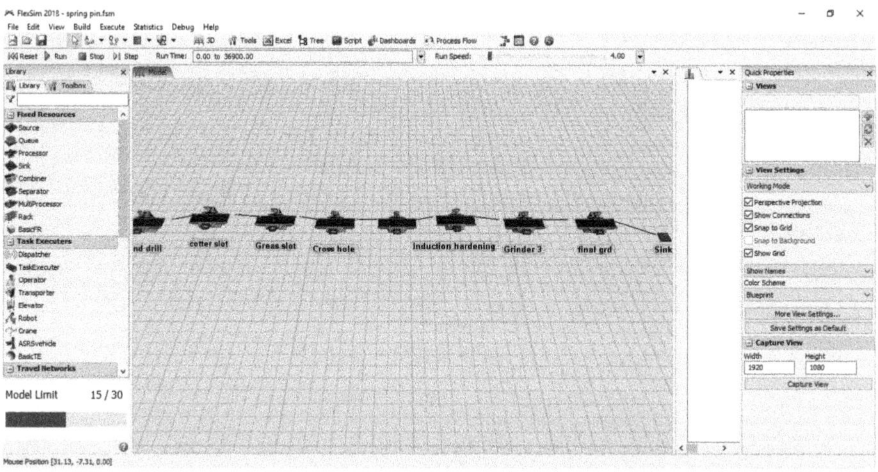

Figure 8: A screenshot of running future state VSM model of spring pin section

Source: Collected by Authors.

- Counter hole operation is merged with cross hole drilling machine and use of chamfer which is made from carbide has been started so there is no increase in C/T.
- Earlier there were four grinding passes due to single set turning but on same setup two grinding passes are eliminated.

13.8 Improvement Activities in Spring Pin Section

13.8.1 *CNC Turning Machine*

In manufacturing of spring pins, the raw material is available in the form of bars. From bars, work pieces are cut with the help of a bandsaw then put on a CNC turning machine for further machining process. While this work piece is machined on a CNC turning machine some portions of the work piece are under clamping on the CNC turning machine's three chuck jaws which remain unmachined during the turning operation. During this operation, a line mark appears at the centre of the work piece where both turning operations are joined. This line mark is caused due to an uncleaned work piece surface which further effects clamping operations of other machining processes. For removal of this line mark, a rough grinding operation is performed with the help of a centreless grinding machine.

On this turning operation, a bar feeder is attached on the CNC turning machine. In this bar feeder a 1.5-metre-long bar is directly loaded in a magazine and the work piece is machined with a single cut in a single setup. Moreover, Ra (average roughness) value which is obtained from this machining process is also affected on final grinding passes. Earlier there were four grinding passes out of which two are eliminated. Thus, it helps in eliminating in process inventory and the time-consuming machining processes, decreasing cycle time of the manufactured product.

13.8.2 *Bar Turning Machine*

On the bar turning machine it is necessary to control important parameters because the turned portion is used further as a pre-roll diameter and that threaded portion plays a major role in the application of another product. In another product, there is threading on both ends of the rod for tightening of the nut. Thread size is different for different types of product but for OEM these sizes are under 6 g thread category. In threading it is machined by a thread rolling operation. For a thread rolling operation the basic requirement is its roll diameter. For achieving 6 g thread the roll diameter needs to be maintained within 30 μm for its taper and circularity, on exiting setup. However, it is not possible to achieve this result and setup is also complicated, so C/O time is also very high due to these NVA processes added in the manufacturing line.

Figure 9: Modified face grooving tool

13.8.3 *Face Grooving Operation*

There is a groove on the face of the spring pin for machining and on this groove on phase an extra turning machine setup is required now this operation is easily performed on a horizontal drilling machine which is used for a second drill operation for this cup type tool holder designed and fitted on the drill chuck as shown in Figure 9. With the help of this, manpower and an extra operation are easily eliminated.

13.8.4 *Counter Drilling Operation*

In the cross-hole machine, there is an extra operation that is introduced in the manufacturing line for removal of blunt edges. For removal of this NVA process, a step drill is used for the counter mark which is an adjustable drill and the size can easily be adjusted as per requirements.

13.8.5 *Comparison of TAKT Time and Cycle Time After Improvements*

Figure 10 shows the comparison of TAKT time and cycle time (C/T) of the spring pin manufacturing process after improvements. The

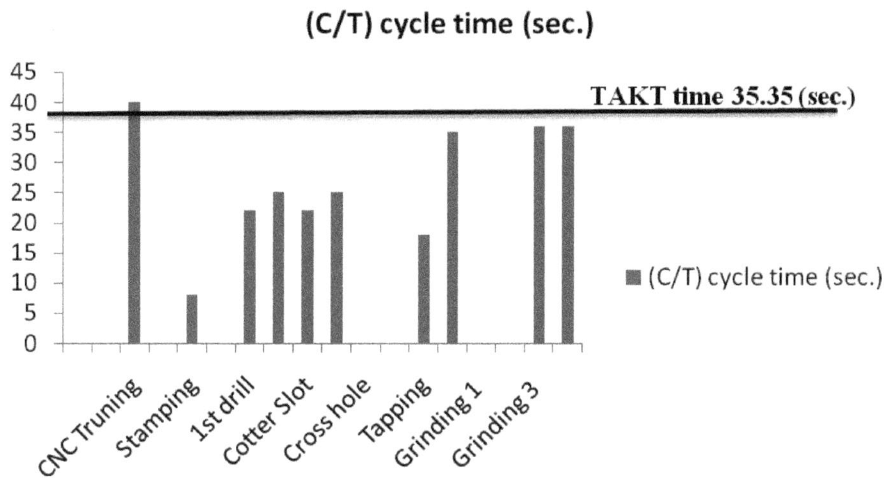

Figure 10: C/T and TAKT time comparison of future state spring pin section

Source: Collected by Authors.

Table 5: Future state map's attributes in each stage of spring pin section

Operations	(C/T) Cycle Time (sec.)	(C/O) Change Over Time (sec.)	Value-added (sec.)	Non-value Added (sec.)	Available Time (sec.)	UP Time (%)	No. of Operators	(WIP) Work in Process Inventory
Bar cutting	0	0	0	0	0	0	—	0
CNC turning	40	1200	40	0	36900	96.75	1	0
Rough grinding	0	0	0	0	0	0	—	10
Stamping	8	600	8	80	36900	98.37	1	0
Face grooving	0	0	0	0	0	0	—	10
1St drill	22	600	22	220	36900	98.37	1	10
2Nd drill	25	480	25	250	36900	98.70	1	6
Cotter slot	22	480	22	132	36900	98.70	1	10
Grease slot	25	480	40	250	36900	98.70	1	10
Cross hole	—	450	17	170	36900	98.78	1	10
Counter hole	0	0	0	0	0	0	—	10
Tapping	18	450	18	180	36900	98.78	1	10

(Continued)

Table 5: (*Continued*)

Operations	(C/T) Cycle Time (sec.)	(C/O) Change Over Time (sec.)	Value-added (sec.)	Non-value Added (sec.)	Available Time (sec.)	UP Time (%)	No. of Operators	(WIP) Work in Process Inventory
Induction hardening	35	600	35	350	36900	98.37	1	10
Grinding 1	0	0	0	0	0	0	—	0
Grinding 2	0	0	0	0	0	0	—	0
Grinding 3	36	600	36	360	36900	98.37	1	10
Final grinding	36	600	36	360	36900	98.37	1	10

Source: Collected by Authors.

C/T time of CNC turning is more than TAKT time, so these areas need to be further assessed. Table 5 shows the future state map's attributes in each stage of spring pin section.

13.9 Discussion of Findings

13.9.1 *Comparison of C/T*

Figure 11 shows a comparison of C/T of current state and future state of spring pin manufacturing processes, the CNC turning machine's cycle time is reduced from 55 sec. to 40 sec. and 6 non-value-added processes are eliminated.

13.9.2 *Comparison of Production Lead Time*

In the spring pin manufacturing process cycle time has been reduced by 209 sec. approximately which leads towards 42.39 percent reduction in production lead time of manufacturing process. NVA processes are eliminated which results in reduction in overall lead time which results in time delivery of production the customer. This production lead time for different processes is compared in Figure 12.

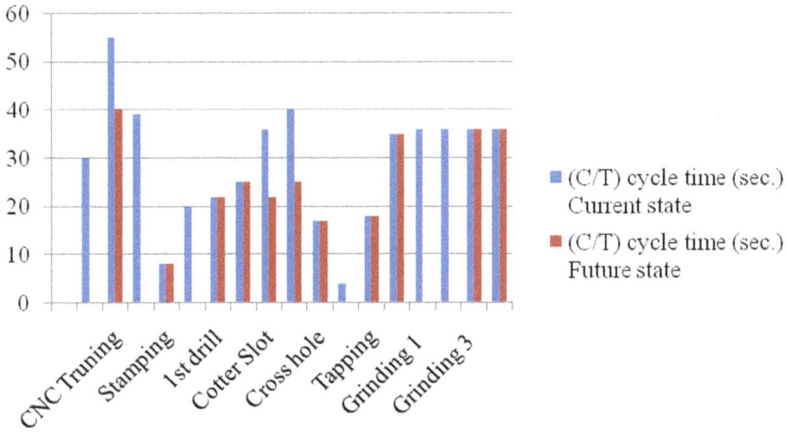

Figure 11: C/T comparison of current state and future state of spring pin section

Source: Collected by Authors.

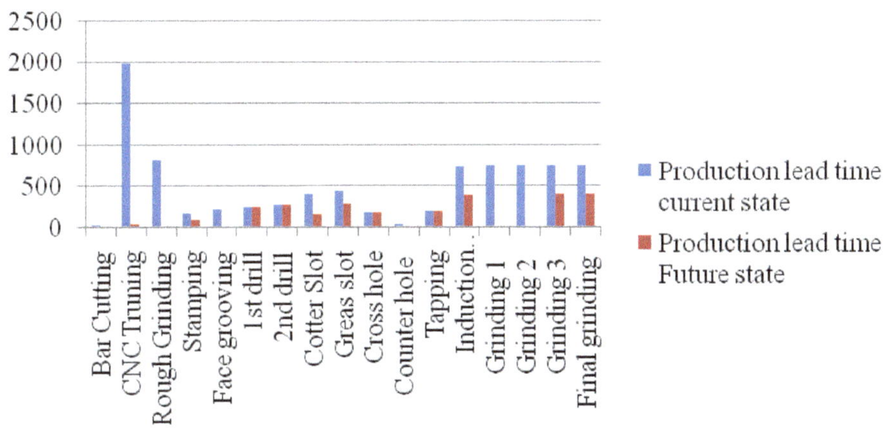

Figure 12: C/T comparison of current state and future state of spring pin section

Source: Collected by Authors.

13.9.3 *Comparison of WIP*

The existing system of spring pin manufacturing has huge WIP in between manufacturing processes which is major cause of chances of mistakes because inventory covers major areas of shop floor. WIP has been reduced from 256 to 116 which is approximately 54.68 percent. The comparison of WIP is shown in Figure 13.

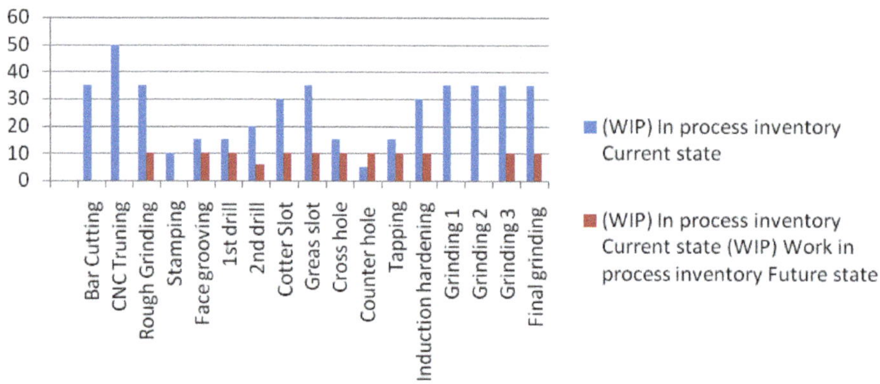

Figure 13: WIP comparison of current state and future state of spring pin section

Source: Collected by Authors.

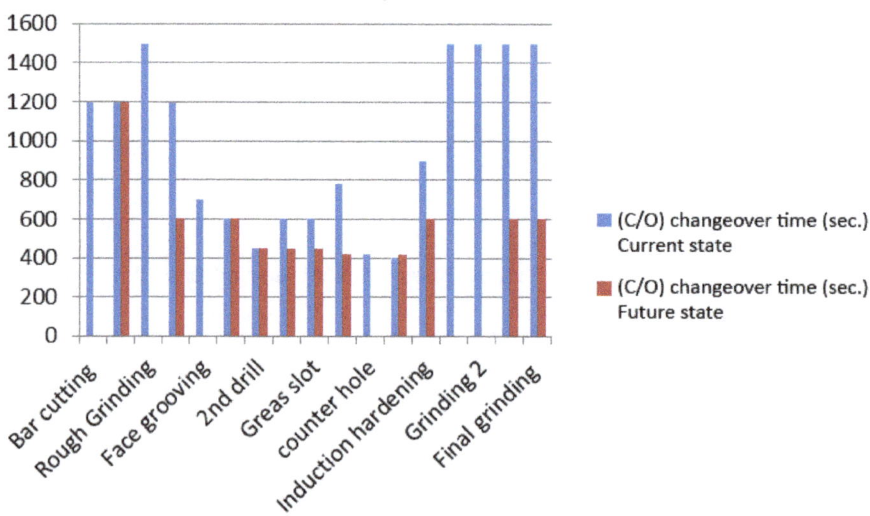

Figure 14: C/O time comparison of current state and future state of spring pin section

Source: Collected by Authors.

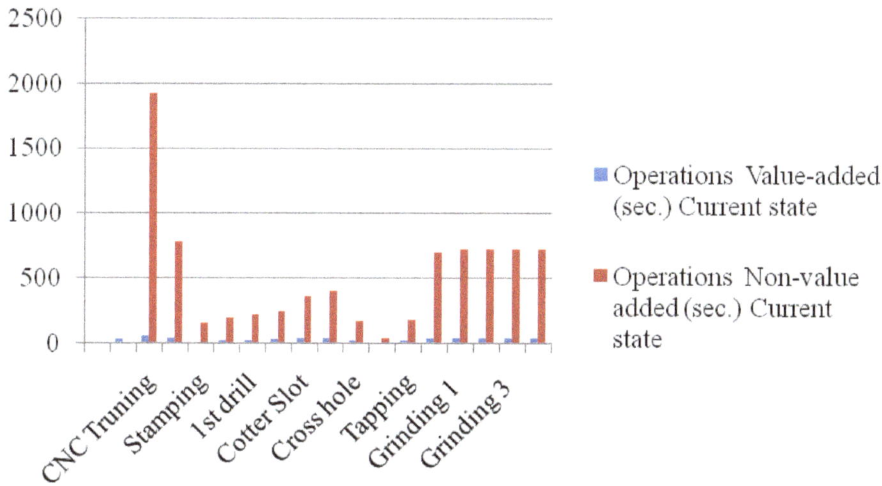

Figure 15: VA and NVA comparison of current state of spring pin section

Source: Collected by Authors.

13.9.4 *Comparison of C/O Time*

As seen in Figure 14, there is a huge reduction in changeover time at stamping machine from 1,200 seconds to 600 seconds, cotter slot machine from 600 seconds to 480 seconds, grease slot machine from 600 seconds to 480 seconds, cross hole machine from 780 seconds to 450 seconds and at grinding machine stage from 1,500 seconds to 600 seconds with and overall reduction in changeover time from 16,620 seconds to 6,540 seconds which is approximately 60.64 percent.

13.9.5 *Comparison of Total Lead Time, VA and NVA Time*

In the current state value stream map, the difference between value added and non-value activity is very high (Figure 15). This is due to re-working of components or helping hands of other manufacturing operations.

Figure 16 shows the comparison of future state VA and NVA activities where NVA activities on the cotter slot operation reduces from 360 seconds to 132 seconds. On the stamping operation it reduces from 160 seconds to 80 seconds; on the grease slot operation it reduces from 400 seconds to

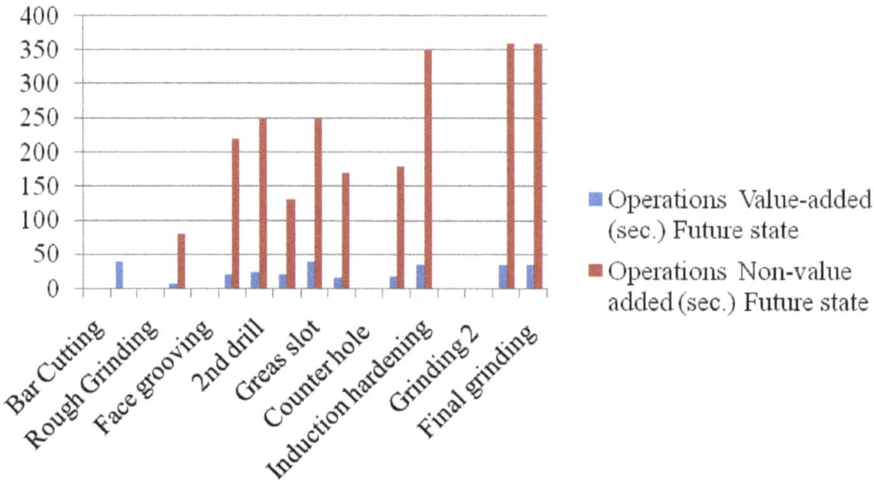

Figure 16: VA and NVA comparison of future state of spring pin section

Source: Collected by Authors.

250 seconds; on the induction hardening operation it reduces from 700 seconds to 350 seconds and on both grinding operations, the reduction in NVA activities is from 720 seconds to 360 seconds.

13.10 Conclusions and Limitations

Value Stream Mapping (VSM) is a valuable planning tool and can be used for developing and implementing lean improvement activities in the manufacturing system processes. The process of mapping the value stream and its simulation helps to implement lean techniques and reveals opportunities to reduce waste. The following are the benefits achieved after successful implementation of VSM and simulation in the company case study:

- C/T has been reduced from 493 seconds to 284 seconds which leads in reduction of 42.39 percent.
- WIP has been reduced from 256 units to 116 units.
- Production lead time has been reduced from 8,758 seconds to 2,651 seconds which results in reduction of 69.73 percent.

- VA ratio has been increased from 4.80 percent to 14.24 percent which shows an improvement of 66.08 percent.
- NVA has been reduced from 8,265 seconds to 2,352 seconds which results in a reduction of 71.54 percent.
- Number of operators has been reduced to 11.
- C/O has been reduced from 16,620 seconds to 6,540 seconds which results in a reduction of 60.64 percent.

The case study is limited to one product. However, it can be extended to other similar products. Moreover, the selection of the manufacturing industry has been done so as a convenient sampling technique.

https://doi.org/10.1142/9789811212741_bmatter

Index

Lightning Source UK Ltd.
Milton Keynes UK
UKHW020347231220
375701UK00001B/40

9 789811 212734